DOING BUSINESS IN THE
COUNTRYSIDE

DOING BUSINESS IN THE
COUNTRYSIDE

THE COMPLETE GUIDE TO RURAL COMMERCE

CONSULTANT EDITOR: JONATHAN REUVID

COUNTRYSIDE
ALLIANCE®

Published in association with Countryside Alliance

KOGAN
PAGE

First published in Great Britain in 2005

Chapter 12 originally appeared in Chapter 1.2 of *A Guide to Working for Yourself*, 22nd edition, Godfrey Golzen and Jonathan Reuvid, 2004, published by Kogan Page
Chapter 16 originally appeared as Chapter 5.3 of *Managing Business Risk: A practical guide to protecting your business*, 2nd edition, Jonathan Reuvid, 2005, published by Kogan Page
Appendix 2 originally appeared as Appendix II of *A Guide to Rural Business: Opportunities and ideas for developing your country enterprise*, Jonathan Reuvid, 2003, published by Kogan Page

Kogan Page Limited
120 Pentonville Road
London N1 9JN
United Kingdom
www.kogan-page.co.uk

© Kogan Page and individual contributors, 2005

British Library Cataloguing in Publication Data

A CIP record for this book is available from the British Library.

ISBN 0 7494 4389 8

Typeset by Saxon Graphics Ltd, Derby
Printed and bound in Great Britain by Thanet Press Ltd, Margate

Contents

Contents

Contents _____

Contents

Contents _____

Farm Diversification Opportunities

Conversion of Trees into Useable Sawn Timber

With an increasing need to generate farm revenues, and move into profitable and sustainable new businesses, farmers are hungry for real solutions.

When introduced to the UK eighteen years ago, the Wood-Mizer mobile saw was a revolution in timber processing, allowing local farm-based conversion of trees into valuable and useable timber.

Most users find that they have a need for sawn lumber on the farm for fencing, cattle housing and building repairs. Increasingly farmers are turning to the construction and conversion of farm buildings, and find that they can achieve significant savings by producing their own building materials from local timber, using local labour for most of the milling and building work.

Thanks to the support of various area and farm support grant schemes the farming community have been quick to seize the chance to move into new business activities. In Wales over half the sawmills sold benefit from such help, and similar programmes are soon to be rolled out in Scotland.

In England there are various streams of funding available delivered by a plethora of groups charged with revitalising local rural communities.

One notable example is in Hever, Kent where a range of buildings have provided the basis for diversification businesses. Initially Wood-Mizer sawmills were deployed in the development of a sawmilling, timber drying and finishing business, cutting locally grown oak. This has grown into a £550,000 turnover business servicing the needs of local builders, joiners and cabinet makers, whilst also manufacturing bespoke flooring for retail customers.

Elsewhere in the country a number of farmers have been busy using the ability to convert local timber on site to build units for both industrial and holiday lettings. This

work inevitably seems to lead on to new opportunities satisfying the

same needs for neighbours and other farms in the region. Add to that the local market of builders, joiners and furniture makers and business soon blossoms.

The use of Wood-Mizer sawmills allows farming families to keep the next generation gainfully employed, staying on the farm, and diversifying into a new and profitable business which is not subject to the vagaries of the farm produce markets. Certain area grants are aimed specifically at keeping the youngsters on the farm, developing diversification activity through successful new business. Furthermore, sales of sawn timber from your own woodland is exempt from taxation.

With the Wood-Mizer motto of "From Forest to Final Form" the company offers a full range of mobile and static sawmills, kilns, moulders and customer support/advice based upon 22 years of activity supporting 35,000 customers worldwide.

Since 1987 over 500 mills have been deployed in the UK, with about a third going to farmers. Several have since volunteered that literally, **"The Wood-Mizer saved the farm"**.

The UK branch office, based at the Woodland Centre in Kent, has agents in Wales and Scotland. Branch personnel are capable operators themselves, many with over 15 years of experience with which to underpin your new venture.

Wood-Mizer

01342 850 999

info@wmuk.net   www.woodmizer-europe.com

Foreword

I am pleased that the Alliance has had the opportunity to support this much-needed book. The key to safeguarding our countryside is to ensure that rural Britain can pay its way in our fast-changing modern economy. A countryside that is economically beholden to the urban majority – and to government paymasters – will always be a vulnerable one. A countryside that adds economic value has a chance of holding its own – and thus of preserving its own social and cultural integrity.

A thriving rural economy is also essential to the aesthetic and ecological well-being of the landscape itself. Our countryside has always been a place of production, enterprise, innovation and endeavour. Those who worry that more employment in rural areas will perforce erode the countryside are misguided. Local rural communities literally make our landscape – and maintain it. It is axiomatic that for these communities to be viable there must be local jobs.

But these jobs need to be of the right *type*. Supporting rural jobs of any kind, at any environmental or social cost, would be a risky mantra to follow. Our planners and politicians need to help rural areas steer a wise middle course in developing their economies, encouraging and supporting the right type and scale of businesses. Though many forms of business and commerce can benefit the countryside, others can harm it. Our rural areas could benefit from job-intensive light industry and administrative operations (such as call centres) but not, say, from manufacturing plants. The large-scale industrial developments that the RDAs tend to prioritize may suit the development needs of their regional conurbations but are no use for rural locations since they simply over-power the existing rural infrastructure and create in their wake an extensive new residential and commercial hinterland. Although a lack of jobs can undoubtedly degrade a rural area through depopulation and rural dereliction, industrializing our landscape would simply destroy large parts of it for good. Our countryside certainly needs to embrace change, to adapt and modernize, but the sustainable use of the land itself must underpin any change, not fall victim to it.

It follows that there are primarily two forms of businesses that can reconcile the twin imperatives of rural employment and rural conservation. The first type is those businesses that sustainably exploit or husband the land. To offset the projected decline in intensive farming we need to find replacement ways to maximize the amount of land productively worked. The first priority is to ensure that the mixed and small farming sector can thrive and expand (with or without diversifying); we can also develop the country sports industry, which already offers valuable primary or secondary land use opportunities, gener-ating domestic and foreign revenues; and we should extend the productive capacity of land well beyond traditional food farming into other crops and land uses such as biomass and environmental products.

The second type of business is non-land-based small- and medium-sized enterprises (SMEs), which can increase the commercial and social vitality of the countryside's towns and villages but which have a low environmental impact. A whole range of SMEs could be accommodated by, and prosper in, rural localities – ranging from traditional craft industries (which are enjoying a marked revival) right through to new high-technology and other contemporary sunrise industries, and in size from 'kitchen table' sole traders through to companies employing hundreds of staff.

Doing Business in the Countryside provides advice and ideas that will assist both land-based and other kinds of rural SME. I commend it to all those running, or thinking of starting, a business in the countryside.

John Jackson
Chairman, Countryside Alliance
Chairman, The Rural Regeneration Unit

Carter Jonas has been doing business in the countryside for over 150 years.

From a small land agency established by John Carter Jonas in Cambridgeshire in 1855, Carter Jonas has grown into a national multidisciplinary property company that currently manages about 750,000 acres on behalf of institutional and private clients. We offer professional advice to farmers and agri-businesses on all estate management issues and our Farm Agency Division handles every aspect of the sale and purchase of farms and estates through a national network of offices.

Such a long-established history of rural asset management means that Carter Jonas has a wealth of experience and professional knowledge to draw upon.

The firm also offers professional services in planning and development, building design consultancy, minerals and waste management and commercial property. In addition, a substantial residential business deals with the sale of farms and estates, as well as homes in London and in the countryside.

For more information about the services our Rural Division can offer, please contact:

Cambridge 01223 368771
Harrogate 01423 523423
Huddersfield 01484 842105
Kendal 01539 722592
London Country Agency 020 7493 0676
Marlborough 01672 514545
North Wales 01248 362536
Oxford 01865 511444
Peterborough 01733 588688
Shrewsbury 01939 210440
York 01904 558230

Contributors' Notes

Rupert Clark is the head of Smiths Gore's Rural Practice Department which is responsible for the management of over 2 million acres of land in the UK. Rupert's team provides advice on property management and planning and development matters to over 500 clients nationally.

Julia Colegrave and her family are the working owners of Wykham Park Farm. Julia planned and developed the farm shop diversification which she manages.

Philip Coysh is National Sales Manager of Farming & Agricultural Finance (FAF). A banker by training, he has specialized in agricultural and rural finance for almost 22 years.

Dixon Wilson is based in London and is one of the leading private client accountancy firms in the UK. The firm offers a partner-led, personal service to its clients.

Farming & Agricultural Finance (FAF) is part of NatWest and provides rural mortgages to those who live and work in the countryside.

Geoffrey Fitchew has been buying land and farm buildings for development since the late 1990s after a previous career running a successful conference and exhibition company. He indulges his passion for salmon and trout fishing when the opportunity arises and runs a non-commercial shoot in the Buckinghamshire countryside. Geoffrey is active in both local council and field sport organizations.

Peter R Fitzgerald is a consultant at Wilsons, the Salisbury law firm.

Gareth Gaunt is a farmer and qualified veterinary surgeon who diversified into biomass feedstock production. He is a founder member and Chairman of the Renewable Energy Growers Ltd.

Allison Grant is a Partner in the Employment and Human Resources Group of KSB Law. Her considerable experience covers unfair dismissal, redundancy, disciplinary issues, equal pay, TUPE, breach of contract and discrimination law, and she is a regular advocate at employment tribunals.

haysmacintyre is the largest single-office accountancy practice in the UK. As one of the top 30 firms it provides a full compliance and advisory service covering business and personal taxation, corporate finance and financial services, as well as high-quality audit and assurance work.

Rachel Hebditch is a leading UK alpaca breeder with her own business in Devon, Classical MileEnd Alpacas. She is also a director of UK Alpaca, a private company that manufactures yarns from the fleeces of alpacas bred in Britain.

Matt Howard is a partner and licensed insolvency practitioner at accountancy firm Larking Gowen. Based in Norwich, he is head of the business recovery department, which specializes in all aspects of personal and corporate insolvency. Matt joined the firm in 1996, having graduated from the University of East Anglia with a degree in accountancy.

James Kidgell is a partner in Dixon Wilson. His clients include rural businesses operating throughout the UK, and held in a variety of different ownership structures. He has advised on a number of diversification projects, including extensive property conversions.

KSB Law is a proactive medium-sized law firm, established for over 150 years in London and Hertfordshire. It is a member of Consulegis, an international association of law firms and was listed as one of 'The Rising 50' law firms to watch in *The Lawyer*, November 2004.

Larking Gowen is a Norwich-based firm of Chartered Accountants.

Myra Mortlock is the editor of *Natural Fibre News*.

NFU Mutual Insurance Limited is a national company offering a personal insurance service. With almost a century of experience, rural insurer NFU Mutual has earned a reputation for good competitive premiums and excellent local service with a personal touch. Through a network of over 300 offices across the UK, NFU Mutual provides a team that understands local requirements, giving a friendly service to meet individual needs.

Tim Price has been writing about farming and rural business for more than 20 years as a journalist on leading agricultural and business publications, and is now a member of the communications team at rural insurer NFU Mutual.

Andrew Pym is a Fellow of the Royal Institute of Chartered Surveyors. He trained as a land agent, worked for a national firm for 14 years and then joined the CLA in London as the Rural Surveyor before setting up his own rural property consultancy in 1996.

Jonathan Reuvid is an economist and was formerly engaged in investment banking, general management of a Fortune 500 multinational and business development in China. In 1989 he started a second career in publishing and is Consultant Editor and an author to Kogan Page for a number of its corporate and small business titles.

The Rural Regeneration Unit (RRU) is an independent organization dedicated to finding practical, progressive solutions to the problems and challenges facing rural communities. The RRU works to ensure a sustainable future for local rural communities – especially those that are disadvantaged – through devising, setting up and implementing social and economic initiatives which benefit the communities involved.

Phil Salmon is a senior manager with accountants haysmacintyre. He has specialized in VAT for over 15 years. He is a chartered tax adviser who commenced his career with HM Customs & Excise before moving into practice.

Duncan Sigournay is a solicitor at the Bath office of Thring Townsend specializing in agricultural property matters and subsidies. Prior to joining Thring Townsend, Duncan was Senior Legal Adviser at the CLA. He currently sits on the Agricultural Law Association's Tenancy Committee.

John Skinner has worked in public practice in Banbury since 1989 for Whitley Stimpson. Almost 16 years of experience has given him a broad range of knowledge about income and capital taxes, as well as audit requirements.

Smiths Gore is a multi-disciplined firm of property consultants with offices throughout the UK. Building on over 150 years' experience of property management, looking after some of the country's most important landed estates, the firm has a range of professional specialists offering a complete service for property of all types.

David Steel is the head of Smiths Gore's Field Sports Department which advises individuals, public bodies and institutions on the management of their sporting assets. His team of field sports specialists provide comprehensive and wide-ranging advice in all regions of the UK.

James Stephenson is senior partner of Stephenson & Son, York, established in 1871, with an earlier record of an ancestor's valuation activities going back to the post-1645 Civil War period. The Stephenson Group now runs two livestock markets, a professional rural practice and a Yorkshire network of 10 agency offices. The 19th-century business was formed by Jacob Stephenson, working first through Tadcaster market and then on to York. Under Reg Stephenson, James's father, the firm's professional rural activities were expanded into estate agency. Edward Stephenson is the sixth generation of the family to be a partner.

Richard Stephenson founded A Day in the Country in the 1980s with his wife Diane while senior partner in a local Oxfordshire medical practice. Since his retirement they have continued to expand and run the business with their son Jerry.

Thring Townsend is one of central southern England's leading law firms, providing a focused range of commercial and private client services. The firm has offices in Bath and Swindon.

Mal Treharne was a founder member of the RRU where he played a leading role in its early development. Mal has a long management experience in large international companies and small- to medium-sized enterprises and has served as a county council leader and member of the Council of Europe. He has a keen interest in preserving the sustainability of rural communities and remains a member of the government's Rural Affairs Forum.

Philip D Whitcomb is a solicitor at Wilsons, the Salisbury law firm.

Whitley Stimpson is a medium-sized independent firm of business advisers and chartered accountants in Banbury that has been in practice for over 70 years. The firm is also a member of Moores Rowland International, a global association of 170 accountancy firms. Its diversified client base stretches from the rural economy of North Oxfordshire to Scotland and into the West Country.

Wilsons is a Salisbury law firm offering a comprehensive range of legal and advisory services to private, agricultural and country-based clients in Wiltshire and further afield.

Michael Xenakis was educated in Greece and England. He worked in London for 25 years as a board member of one of the world's largest privately owned international shipping companies. During the 1990s Michael worked from inception to full deployment on the most renowned premium cruise vessels. The elegant style and pioneering design of the ships is now recognized as the most significant change ever made to passenger shipping.

Introduction

ALTERNATIVE BUSINESSES IN THE COUNTRYSIDE

This book is written for all those living and working in the countryside and involved either in the start-up or management of a business. Many of them will be farmers who find that they can no longer generate a sufficient income from traditional farming activities and need to diversify. Today, thanks to the complexities of the planning process and the law, even those who undertake development of their own land and buildings without starting up a business operation are involved in an activity that involves the attention to detail and decision making common to any form of business. This book is very much for them too.

This kind of multi-authored book which seeks to inform is only as good as the quality of the editorial contributions and I am particularly grateful on this occasion to my collaborators, all busy people, who have given so generously of their time to write authoritatively on the subjects in which they are expert. John Jackson, Chairman of the Countryside Alliance and the Rural Regeneration Unit (RRU), in his Foreword and Mal Treharne of the RRU, in his opening chapter, write with passion about the need to foster a thriving rural community, the interface between town and countryside and the need to find better ways to work with national and local government to that end. My further thanks are due to the RRU for sourcing the three trading business case histories in Cumbria from the many local business that they have counselled.

These opening statements provide the backdrop for the body of the book. In Part Two, which focuses on the development of land and local buildings, Andrew Pym leads readers through the maze of the British planning regime, including compulsory purchase and compensation, with a clarity that is uncommon among planning experts. Duncan Sigournay of Thring Townsend's Bath practice explains the legal complexities of agricultural tenancies and diversification in practical terms, while John Skinner of Whitley Stimpson addresses the capital gains tax and inheritance tax issues that may arise from any form of asset development and disposal. Rupert Clark of Smiths Gore takes us step by step through the business process of converting farm buildings, just as his colleague David Steel identifies the anatomy of sporting estates management in Part One. Finally, in Part Two, Phil Salmon of haysmacintyre explains the complexities of VAT on listed buildings and other residential conversions.

Part Three moves on to the key issues of which those who are starting a business operation need to develop a clear understanding. Duncan Sigournay explains the finer legal points of business tenancies, John Skinner outlines taxation issues, audit requirements and recommended accountancy practices, while James Kidgell of Dixon Wilson focuses on maximizing tax allowances in the rural environment. Allison Grant of KSB Law identifies the essentials in employment law and Tim Price of NFU Mutual categorizes the various types of insurable business risk and describes how they may be covered. Additional chapters are included on business licenses and regulations relating to change of use, limited company formation and maintenance and marketing and sales promotion.

Part Four provides advice for entrepreneurs in areas of financial management. Philip Coysh of Farming & Agricultural Finance Limited writes on finance and funding for rural projects and I have provided outlines of the basic equity alternatives. Matthew Howard of Larking Gowen has completed this section with a dissertation on the management and mitigation of insolvency, essential reading for those whose rural businesses are on the rocks.

In Part Five the experiences of 11 business owners engaged in widely differing business activities are reported individually as case histories in which readers may find inspiration for their own diversification plans. The first three range from Geoffrey Fitchew's wry account of the practical difficulties of farmhouse renovation and barn conversion in Cumbria (in counterpoint to Chapter 8) to Myra Mortlock's story of how she has created a thriving business in farm wool and Rachel Hebditch's account of the development of her commercial Alpaca UK business. They are followed by Gareth Gaunt's story of diversification into renewable energy from traditional farming and sketches of two complementary links in the food chain in Cumbria: Tim Copsey's long-established family market gardening business at Seaton and the retailing venture of Steve Hamilton and Jackie Johnston at Cockermouth.

The next two stories are of diversification ventures from traditional livestock farming in very different environments. Marie Stockdale tells how she and partner Alan Barrow in Cumbria diversified first into broiler production, then into meat retailing and finally into a more successful venture in portable pressure washing services for broiler producers. In contrast, Julia Colegrave recounts how she diversified her family farm in Oxfordshire progressively, first into asparagus production and sales, then into meat retailing at farmers' markets and finally into a flourishing farm shop.

The last three case histories are of more established but still growing businesses. James Stephenson, senior partner of his family firm of York-based auctioneers, reflects on the changes in livestock markets, the impact on his business and the wide variety of diversification projects that he and his partners have introduced at the York Auction Centre. Michael Xenakis describes how he brought his luxury cruise liner restaurant experience to bear on the restoration and conversion of a Grade II listed barn in Essex into a highly successful brasserie. Finally, Richard Stephenson recounts the continuing evolution from farming at Aynho Grounds in Oxfordshire into a broad-based leisure activity, catering and conference facility.

There are also lessons for government in our book. Two recurring themes throughout the book, to which many of our contributors refer, are the likely impact of the new farm Single Payment scheme which starts to be phased in from 2005 over eight years, and the expenditure of time and money involved in applying for funds from DEFRA.

Writing and coordinating *Doing Business in the Countryside* has been an enjoyable and informative experience for all of us who have been involved and I would like to thank Mal Treharne of the RRU and Nigel Henson of the CA for their personal support and encouragement throughout the gestation process. I hope that you will also find the book enjoyable and useful.

Jonathan Reuvid
Wroxton, Oxfordshire

Alpacas Completing the circle

Classical MileEnd Alpacas

We offer friendly courses where you can benefit from our experience over the last decade: plus sales of quality livestock, stud services and full after sales support and advice to new entrants.

www.alpaca-uk.co.uk

Alpaca World Magazine

We publish the only independent, full colour magazine for the international alpaca industry. Entertaining and informative, it's all you need to keep your finger on the alpaca pulse.

www.alpacaworldmagazine.com

UK Alpaca

Our aim is to assist UK alpaca fibre producers to market this highly prized fibre. We purchase UK alpaca fibre and manufacture specialist, high quality worsted yarns for knitting and textiles.

www.ukalpaca.com

Discover more about creating income from the beautiful and easy to care for alpaca: telephone Rachel Hebditch on 01884 243579 or Chas Brooke on 01884 243514 or visit any or all of our websites listed above.

Part One:

Rural Enterprise and the Community

COUNTRYMAN MAGAZINE

Embracing all that's important in the British countryside for more than 75 years. We are a lively and independent voice debating the future of rural Britain.

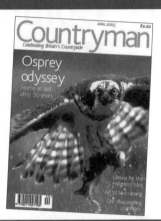

LATEST ISSUE AVAILABLE AT YOUR NEWSAGENT

1 Catalysts for the Community – Working with Local Government Agencies

Mal Treharne, The Rural Regeneration Unit

GOVERNMENT STRATEGY

Government evidence (see DEFRA Rural Strategy 2004) identifies rural areas and a dynamic rural society rapidly changing in ways that are reshaping communities and blurring urban–rural distinctions.

If this is true, then it places an enormous burden on those individuals and organizations that catalyse rural economies, engage communities and generate positive action for good in the countryside, which in turn provides prosperity, health, and a state of well-being for all. As a corollary, it follows that there is also an enormous responsibility on the government to understand and provide well-targeted delivery.

Let us examine some of the evidence displayed vividly in the government's own rural strategy for 2004, which reveals the following features between 1991 and 2002.

☐ There was a net migration of 60,000 people per year into wholly or predominantly rural districts.
☐ The number of people aged 65 and over living in rural districts increased by 161,000 (12 per cent) while the number aged 16–29 decreased by 237,000 (18 per cent).
☐ Prosperity in rural areas was relatively higher than the national average but with a disadvantaged minority amidst this prevailing affluence.

☐ Economic weaknesses with associated social deprivation persisted in a minority of lagging areas, characteristically in those areas adjusting to decline in mining, agriculture and fishing.

☐ There was convergence between urban and rural communities. Agriculture was still at the core of the rural economy and society, but employment in agriculture decreased by 30 per cent (151,000) in the last 20 years; employees in rural businesses were now more likely to be in manufacturing (25 per cent), tourism (9 per cent) or retailing (7 per cent) than in agriculture (6 per cent).

☐ Increased mobility through car ownership brought benefits for many but reduced the customer base for public transport; hence the difficulty for those without access to a car (14 per cent of rural households). In addition, there were also many households with a car unavailable to the family because it was used for travel to work.

☐ Pressures, in particular through demand for housing and transport, were impacting the countryside. Rural areas were a rich resource, valued by residents and visitors for fine landscapes, biodiversity and open space, and contributed to enjoyment and general well-being as well as to education and health. Sustainable development should ensure that the enhancement of this resource is for the benefit of all.

The strategy postulated that many of these features are part of trends dating back to and, perhaps, even before 1945. There have been extraordinary advances in technological development and restructuring in the global and national economy that are resulting in dynamic social, environmental and cultural changes. If these trends continue can we look forward to further urban rural convergence but with the vulnerable minority still lagging behind?

THE CHALLENGES FOR ENTERPRISE IN RURAL BRITAIN

The social and economic challenges that face the government and the public sector are formidable. They include:

☐ a continuing population growth of mostly wealthier people in the countryside (and the expectation that they will live longer);
☐ greater demands on public and community services that support the elderly;
☐ the need to maintain facilities and education for the young;
☐ the increased need for rural housing;
☐ pressure on shops and other local outlets;
☐ increasing isolation for those without cars;
☐ pressure on natural resources (such as water) and the need to preserve and improve them.

Further changes are inevitable as farmers respond to the reduction of farming's contribution to the economy and the reform of the Common Agricultural Policy.

There is a pressing need to manage improvement to land and resource, including biodiversity, and the vital task is to ensure protection for the massive contribution that the countryside makes to quality of life, respecting access to all for recreation, health and education, and also the countryside's economic contribution.

The role of government offices and agencies

These are the challenges facing enterprise in rural Britain, compounded by the simple fact that performance weakens the further you go from major urban centres. Could this also indicate a weakening of interest from the agencies and offices that are charged with furthering rural enterprise and initiative as you move further from those centres?

Lord Haskins, in his Rural Delivery Review, found a picture of bureaucratic complexity and customer confusion in rural delivery arrangements, which is borne out by Rural Regeneration Unit (RRU) experience. He stated that rural businesses, communities and their representatives are at the receiving end of the regulations, products and services that are designed to deliver the government's rural policies, but there is intimidation caused by the multi-plicity of organizations, products and services and numerous rules that inhibit access to these services. The general feeling of many is one of having things done **to** them rather than **for** them.

The role of the individual

How can anyone with this awesome advance of social and economic change in the countryside, with the pressures on their own time, enthusiasm and funds, find time to engage with and for their community, or to participate in the important process that acknowledges their good fortune in living with the benefit of such an important and valuable resource?

And, if despite the difficulties, they do create the time to help what should they expect? Many people, often both partners in a couple, now live in the country and work in the town; others live in the town and work in the coun-tryside, travelling to and from work, which limits severely those precious periods for family, relaxation and leisure.

Then there are the farms and rural enterprises, working in which also puts great pressure on family and leisure time. Nevertheless, all these groups and the rest of the population, irrespective of their social and economic circum-stances, expect the countryside to be at their disposal at all times.

Working together

Over the years, successive governments have sought to equalize delivery of services across the nation by centralizing control, noticeably in health and education but also in agriculture. Today, there is an increasing recognition that performance would be immeasurably enhanced by replacing this top-down solution by a bottom-up approach. Government has promised to devolve decision making, funding and delivery closer to those responsible, whether as deliverers or customers, but this will need massive changes in culture and structure which will take time.

However, it would be folly for rural enterprise and entrepreneurs simply to sit back with the expectation that this new promised land of devolved decision making and delivery responsibilities would see the Regional Development Agencies, local authorities and other agencies, like the three wise men, emerge from the desert bearing gifts.

If government intends that communities should help themselves through bottom-up solutions, then the leaders and businesses in those communities should ensure that their proposed activity recognizes various criteria. The proposal should:

☐ fit in with government policy – this would promote social inclusion and recognize the needs of the community and its visitors;
☐ ensure protection and enhancement of the environment;
☐ make sensible use of natural resources;
☐ aim for sustainable and enduring economic growth and employment;
☐ benefit the community and give access to local aspirations.

Taking social responsibility

If your are in business and want to help, ask yourself the questions: can I release my staff for more training; what if they should aspire to stand for local government election, or wish to attend parish or other community meetings; is it possible to make my office available for local groups or individual training with the use of fax, photocopier, etc?

There are many examples of good people who give an enormous and generous output of their time and energy, and only need some minimal use of the fax, the telephone or even a little space for files. Not only does supporting these people benefit the community but it helps to enhance the prestige of the cooperating company or organization within that community, and engenders personal satisfaction and well-being to the individual and those in the organization.

Rural businesses and other enterprises, large and small, should assume some responsibility and consider the role of community provider, as clearly those agencies charged with the responsibility of delivering anything from bus services to childcare provision cannot always deliver, or even have the means to. So think: How can I contribute? Such actions could even bring benefits; for example in planning applications, if you can demonstrate to the planners that the proposed activity will advantage the community (eg maybe you can show how the government's health initiatives are met locally by the proposal.)

The big enemy is the silo mentality of government that determines what things have to be done, but where planners and officials impose constraint. Surely it is not unreasonable to expect elected representatives to intervene on a constituent's behalf, and endeavour to address and resolve difficulties.

This wholly constructive approach can do two things: firstly, it could and should resolve your difficulty; and secondly, in doing so it should ensure that others avoid suffering the same pitfalls in the future. Often the agencies and authorities will welcome constructive approaches to the resolution of policy and funding problems, where they are only the reluctant deliverers of intentions that do the opposite to that which was intended, or at least where outcomes can be improved. Here, the elected MPs, MEPs and county councillors can at last earn their keep, by approaching ministers and their civil servants to argue for change and better understanding of policies and delivery mechanisms, especially as it is often the case that circumstances can vary regionally and even locally from parish to parish. Herein lies yet another weakness of centralist programmes, and the need for radical change so that programmes are accompanied by delegated authority that recognizes the need for flexibility.

THE WORK OF THE REGIONAL REGENERATION UNIT (RRU)

Since its creation in 2002, the RRU has been a beacon for sustainable and partic- ipatory activity in local rural communities, especially those that are disadvan- taged. The RRU devises and implements social and economic initiatives together with local government agencies and bodies and seeks funding for its diverse range of activities that will benefit these communities and the wider national population. The RRU is dedicated to finding practical solutions to the many problems facing rural communities, then designing, developing and implementing practical activities that have a directly positive impact on the rural economy and society.

In its broadest sense the RRU is an educational operation; it seeks to inform, enable and empower rural communities to be self-reliant and entrepreneurial. This is best done in partnership with urban communities, particularly those that are disadvantaged. In particular, we believe that the urban–rural divide is one of understanding that can best be bridged by projects that bring commu- nities together in a way that creates tangible and real benefits for both.

The RRU is action-oriented: action grounded in public policy that in turn it aims to shape, both through project implementation and policy advice capabilities. These facilities are underpinned by an extensive and pervasive interface with European, national, regional and local government and agencies offering exchange of information, advice, and self-help among rural communities across the UK.

The RRU is a not-for-profit company, politically and financially non-aligned, and its independence allows it to collaborate with all existing agencies and bodies, seeking funding for its diverse range of social and educational projects from all relevant public and private sector grant bodies, authorities and trusts. From the board, and throughout the RRU team, there is extensive experience of rural affairs, business management and European, central and local government. The RRU undertakes projects in rural communities that focus around the provision of local food and creating opportunities for underprivileged young people to benefit from access to the resources of the countryside.

A case in point

It is possible the RRU invented the new food cooperatives network, when it successfully catalysed urban communities to organize food-buying cooperatives. The RRU has gained the expertise to do this from its contracted success with Cumbria Health Action Zone, where over 6,000 scheme members still enjoy healthy food produced locally. RRU's Cumbrian experience has attracted a nationwide two-year pilot project for the Welsh Assembly Government to roll out cooperatives throughout Wales, and DEFRA have commissioned similar work in the English East Midlands.

In a press release of 10 March 2004, the Welsh Health and Social Services Minister claimed that there was growing evidence for the protective effects of fruit and vegetables against chronic disease. Eating at least five portions of fruit and vegetables each day could lead to a reduction of up to 20 per cent in deaths from diseases such as heart disease, stroke and cancer in Wales and the UK.

The success of these simple but effective schemes comes from connecting farmers, growers and communities, shortening the distribution chain and thus being able to provide healthy local food at prices attractive to all parties. This leads to a healthier diet and lifestyle for those in the communities, and viable trade to the farmer. These schemes are developed in ways sensitive to local businesses that are given the first opportunity to become suppliers to the food cooperatives.

2 The Management of Sporting Estates

David Steel, Smiths Gore

WHAT IS A SPORTING ESTATE?

A sporting estate by its very nature is difficult to define. This is principally due to the wide variety of sporting activities throughout the UK. Perhaps the four most helpful defining variables are: the number of different sporting activities to be found on the estate, together with its size, location and commerciality.

A sporting estate will most commonly encompass a number of different field sports, for example: a reared or wild pheasant or partridge shoot, grouse shooting in certain locations, fishing on rivers, ponds, lochs or reservoirs and deer stalking in either woods or on open hills. Equally, however, a sporting estate could be centred on only one activity.

Sporting estates vary greatly in terms of size. Estates can range from a single farm through to an estate, and from lowland chalk streams to heather moorland and hill.

The final defining variable is that of commerciality. Again the range of options is broad, and covers estates run on a non-profit basis for family and friends, to let sporting enterprises yielding impressive income returns, to rival those from other property asset classes on the estate.

As highlighted, sporting estates successfully exist and operate in infinite variety. However, there are common denominators to be found on all estates, and these will be examined and explored further.

OBJECTIVES OF SPORTING ENTERPRISES AND BALANCING CONFLICTING DEMANDS

When managing a sporting estate, it is important to understand that the sporting activity may compromise other activities. It is key to understand the estate's objectives and ensure that all the relevant interests agree how different objectives should be balanced and to work together.

Not all situations result in conflict. For example, if a grouse moor owner wants a reduction in sheep numbers to avoid over-grazing, any profits foregone by the farmer may be offset by entering into a 'Countryside Stewardship Scheme'/Environment Stewardship which can also offset having subsidy payments reduced.

Woodlands

The conflict here is between producing the best quality timber against providing the best possible habitat for pheasants and other game. This conflict will dictate not only the initial choice of tree species but also the future management of the woods. In addition, if quality stalking is provided damage will inevitable occur to woodlands and some potential timber profits will be lost.

Farming activities

Farming is another activity where clashes can occur. For example, when an estate owner requires land for game crops or woodland planting to an extent, the farming activity is affected. The ideal is for activities to work together, with the owner having reached a compromise. When planning activities, seek a compromise such as a release pen sited to minimize crop damage to the adjoining fields, or arranging for a day's shooting for the tenants.

Neighbours

Neighbour disputes on sporting estates do not solely apply to playing your stereo system too late at night. Placing feeders on boundaries or stepping in front of somebody fishing the opposite bank will certainly cause bad feeling. If relations are good, this will enhance both parties' enjoyment. For example, where each neighbour owns one bank of the river, he or she can agree to fish both banks every other day rather than his or her own bank every day.

Other activities

Many activities that happen on estates could conflict with sporting events: the activities of wind turbines, livery, paintballing, quad biking, canoeing, wind-surfing and sailing, to name a few.

Most of the conflicts already mentioned affect the internal user of an estate. However, some of the external conflicts are more difficult to resolve.

Public rights of way and the right to roam

The Countryside and Rights of Way Act 2000 (also known as the 'right to roam' legislation) and public rights of way are potentially disruptive. Once again the estate owner should look at what compromises are available. For example, holding a shoot day during the week when footpaths are less used or, on a grouse moor, providing well defined and surfaced tracks for walking away from the main drives. Section 22 of the CROW Act allows owners or occupiers to restrict access for up to 28 days per annum and also to apply for a five-year dog exclusion on grouse moors.

Anti-bloodsport saboteurs

This is an area of increasing concern to many. Ideally action plans should be drawn up to deal with saboteurs. Some specialist security firms not only provide this but also a presence on the day.

MAKING A SPORTING ENTERPRISE SUCCESSFUL

A golden rule is to achieve the maximum output from the minimum input. However, inputs that should never be minimized are time and effort. If time is not available for best management and environmental practice, the enterprise will be compromised.

General

Whatever the sporting activity, some management practices are common to all. They are: vermin control, access, habitat management and food. For grouse and wild bird shoots these are especially vital.

Released pheasants and partridge

For released pheasant and partridge shoots the aim, apart from producing high-quality sporting birds, is to maximize the percentage of birds shot to birds released:

- ☐ Put down good quality poults that are disease-free and healthy enough to withstand poor weather.
- ☐ Provide well-sited release pens on clean ground, ie not using the same area year after year causing disease and damage to understorey.
- ☐ Using a number of small scattered pens can minimize disease and is environmentally friendly.

☐ Dogging-in or pushing birds back into the centre of the estate to prevent them straying is important when your neighbours have more attractive woods.

☐ Well-managed woodlands provide good roost sites, shelter, feed and open sunny glades and game crops.

☐ Consider use of well-sited game crops.

Grouse

Managing grouse as a wild bird is a different challenge. The situation is complicated by the need to have a sufficient surplus left to provide for the following year's breeding stock but not too many birds as this encourages disease. Factors to consider are:

☐ Heather burning to ensure a mosaic of vegetation is essential.

☐ Sheep numbers must be managed to prevent over-grazing.

☐ Medicated grit should be made available for disease prevention.

☐ Rigorous vermin control at all times of the year.

Stalking

The number shot per season is dictated by the overall number of deer. Unlike in shooting, a stalker is also interested in the confirmation of the beast's head (for stags and bucks), the weight of the beast and, often overlooked, the scenery:

☐ Consider the provision of high seats for woodland deer control.

☐ Consider the number of deer needing to be culled to protect woodland.

☐ In the case of red deer, provide some winter shelter.

☐ Cull the old and weak and genetically poor beasts to leave enough food for better animals.

Fishing (game, coarse, lake and river)

Fishing is one of the most popular pastimes in the UK. Different areas provide different habitats and therefore provide a variety of coarse or game fishing, river or lake (loch) fishing, migratory or non-migratory. The management principles that apply to all aspects of fishing are:

☐ ensuring that gravel redds or spawning grounds are kept clear;

☐ ensuring that banks are not eroded;

☐ removal of excess overhanging vegetation as well as ensuring that some vegetation is providing dappled shade;

☐ weed management and weed control;

☐ netting of migratory fish at sea;

☐ pollution from upstream;

☐ abstraction;

☐ fish farms.

Some issues will be outside the control of the estate owner, such as the topography, value of the game and supply of beaters.

RISK MANAGEMENT AND HEALTH AND SAFETY

Health and safety is an increasingly important aspect of all activities. The activities undertaken on the sporting estate are varied and, therefore, the potential risks are very diverse. Any activity carried out, whether by an employee or not, must have its risk assessed and measures taken to minimize any risk identified.

Common sense can go part-way to accommodating health and safety. However, all tasks, even those done for years, can present a risk. For example, it is recommended that everyone should wear a crash hat when riding a quad bike. If you are an employer, you should insist that one be worn at all times.

In the event of an accident, injury or near miss that has occurred during the course of someone's employment, details need to be logged in an accident book. Any injury that results in the employee being hospitalized for 24 hours or more or off work for three days must be reported to the Health and Safety Executive, who will investigate the accident and will view your records. If you can demonstrate that your employee has been on the relevant courses and that any machinery was maintained correctly, then it may be deemed an unfortunate accident. If for example, the tyres on the quad bike had not been checked and logged regularly, then you as the employer are at fault and the punishments can be severe.

Remember, even if someone is not paid or does not work full-time or on a regular basis, anyone acting under the supervision and control of somebody else is an 'employee' and you as employer are liable for his or her safety.

Health and safety is a complicated issue with many rules. Professional advice can assist in working within 'best practice'.

HUMAN RESOURCES

HR is a very broad church but is at the heart of any business. A well-run estate is likely to have a HR strategy that is closely aligned to the overall business strategy. In the context of a sporting estate therefore you can expect to have made provision for the demand for extra labour at the height of the season and, of course, budgeted accordingly.

In respect of your permanent full- and part-time staff the employment relationship starts at the point at which an offer of employment is made. An employee has a number of basic rights and there are a corresponding number of obligations that you as an employer also have to comply with. This is not the medium to give detailed advice apart from saying that you must provide a contract of employment and that part-time staff are to be treated the same as full-time staff. That means that all aspects of pay and benefits must be applied to part-time staff on a pro-rata basis based on the entitlement of a full-time employee – and that includes public holidays.

The question that arises when organizing a shoot is how you engage and reward the casual workers required to ensure that the day goes smoothly and your paying guests feel that they have received value for money. You may decide that asking for volunteers from the local community is adequate or you may prefer to use the services of an employment agency and relieve yourself of any on the incumbent responsibilities for such staff.

If in any doubt when dealing with the complex and ever-changing area of employment law, you should seek advice from an expert.

COMPENSATION AND CROP DAMAGE

In the context of a managed sporting estate, compensation payable to third parties is most commonly associated with crop damage by game. More particularly, it is damage through loss of yield, which usually occurs where arable crops are grown adjacent to reared pheasant or partridge shoots.

A balanced, well-managed and sustainable rearing programme will generally result in minimal damage. More serious loss of crop, however, can occur where shoot enterprises are run on a more intensive basis. Another albeit less common occurrence of crop damage is that caused by deer to trees being grown for a commercial final crop, eg Christmas trees. Scottish Highland estates can also face claims where deer retreat from the hill in harsh weather to graze on low ground crops, or take shelter in woods.

For a sporting estate occupied and farmed 'in hand' by the owner, compensation claims will not be an issue. The potential liability occurs where the sporting rights are divorced from the occupation of the land.

In English and Welsh law there are statutory provisions protecting farming tenants' right to claim compensation from their landlord. These are set out in the Agricultural Holdings Act 1986 (section 20), where strict time limits must be observed. Farm tenancies in England granted since September 1995 are generally governed by the Agricultural Tenancies Act 1995. This Act contains no statutory provisions relating to game damage, but parties can contract by agreement that compensation will be paid where relevant. Generally, compensation will be settled by mutual agreement but costs can quickly run up for long-running unsettled claims. Therefore early professional advice is to be recommended for a potentially difficult claim. Compensation could be made in advance by way of a reduced or abated rent for any vulnerable land.

In Scotland the law is governed by the Agricultural Holdings (Scotland) Act 1991 which consolidates provisions applying to pre-1991 Act tenancies. Section 52 (as amended by the Agricultural Holdings (Scotland) Act 2003) states that compensation is payable to an agricultural tenant on the proviso that the tenant has no express and unqualified right to kill and take game from the land the tenant occupies (excepting his or her statutory right to kill and claim ground game under the Ground Game Act 1880). Again, any claim is subject to presenting timeous notice of the damage incurred, to be promptly followed up by a final notice of claim. Disputes over compensation are determined by the Scottish Land Court.

It is also important to note that compensation could also be due to tenants where damage is caused to crops by vehicles on shoot days, or where land is withdrawn from a tenancy for the growing of game cover crops, or for rearing operations and associated equipment storage.

MARKETING AND SALES

Marketing is one of the most important issues that affects the profitability of a sporting estate. Without a market for any product, no income can be achieved, either through the letting of sport or the sale of game. There are a few simple steps for a business to find suitable markets.

Identify your assets

Be clear on what an estate can offer and what would be attractive to potential customers, such as accommodation, transport or the assistance of a ghillie.

Identify a market

Markets are defined by price, quality and accessibility. Top prices demand the best service for clients. The key is linking sporting assets with suitable clients – rugged and energetic sports will be better suited to younger, fitter individuals while driven bird shooting is accessible to a much wider client base.

Marketing channels

A variety of methods are available to market a sporting asset:

- ☐ advertising through magazines or websites;
- ☐ attending shows such as game fairs;
- ☐ word of mouth.

Some options can be costly and it may be more effective to employ a professional firm to market your product.

Once interest has been expressed in any sporting opportunity an estate must secure the deal by producing a written and legally binding contract for signature and obtaining a deposit from the tenant.

A successful marketing campaign can be summarized as follows: identify your PRODUCT; arrive at a PRICE; PROMOTE the product through the best markets to produce a PROFIT for the estate.

ECONOMIC BENEFITS

The economic benefits of a sporting estate can be separated into two main areas:

☐   economic benefits to the owner;
☐   economic benefits to the local community.

Sporting estates are expensive business assets with potential profitability linked to owners' objectives and the availability of external investment. Estates can be separated between four main types and can be shown on a sliding scale of profitability.

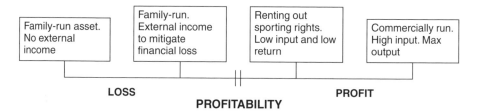

Figure 2.1 The economic benefits of a sporting estate

Sporting estates are valued directly through game records with currently every stag worth £25,000, salmon worth £4,000–£5,000 each and a brace of grouse worth £3,000. This only emphasizes the importance of maintaining annual records and the benefits that can be derived from letting sporting assets to paying guests.

Rural economies also benefit from sporting estates with 40,000 people directly employed in shooting alone. A recent survey conducted by the Countryside Alliance also found that £600 million is contributed to the rural economy through shooting each year. Further analysis in the north of England showed that £137,150 was spent on sourcing and preparing food, local hotels and bed and breakfast establishments profited from 3,704 bed nights valued at £644,690 with sales of shot grouse alone in that area contributing £160,000.

Contributions to the rural economy are best summarized by Labour's spokesman for shooting, Martin Salter, who was quoted as saying: 'We are supportive, not just because shooting contributes £1 billion to the economy every year, but, more importantly, because we see the benefits of encouraging an activity which gives great enjoyment and helps people to understand the countryside and actively to protect the environment.'

WILDLIFE AND BIODIVERSITY

The benefits to wildlife and biodiversity of various types of sporting estate have been widely investigated, with research proving that the management of land for sport can produce benefits not just for game species but also invertebrates, birds, mammals and plants. All major conservation bodies acknowledge that moors managed for grouse are also invaluable for birds such as the merlin, golden plover and curlew. A recent survey by the British Trust for Ornithology found further evidence of these management benefits with 29 per cent of farmland birds being found in only 1 per cent of the land – cover crops planted for shooting.

Habitat management also applies to aquatic ecosystems that can benefit from bank improvements, alterations to channel depth and flow and clearing of spawning grounds. Here again this management, designed to enhance habitats for trout and salmon, also helps to establish habitats for waders and marshland birds as well as rare mammals such as water voles and otters.

Grant funding is available to improve habitats through agri-environment and woodland management schemes. These schemes greatly benefit the management of sporting habitats by providing financial support for works that benefit wildlife but normally would be too uneconomical to undertake.

Advice on managing land and water to enhance sporting assets and biodiversity can be obtained from advisory bodies including the Game Conservancy Trust, the Atlantic Salmon Trust and the Wild Trout Trust or from land agency firms.

Thring Townsend's Agriculture Team

Appointed solicitors to the NFU in nine counties, including Berkshire, Hampshire, Wiltshire and Oxfordshire.

Specialist legal advice on:

> Agricultural disputes

> Buying and selling farms

> Environmental issues

> Farming and food businesses

> Farm tenancies

> Partnerships and other farm business structures

> Quotas and subsidies

> Rights of way and access to land

Call us at:

> Bath   01225 340000
> Swindon   01793 410800
> Frome Market   01373 831036

Thring Townsend
Solicitors

www.ttuk.com

Part Two:

The Development of Land and Rural Buildings

3 Planning

Andrew Pym

Almost everyone living in the country will be involved in planning applications or appeals, whether in respect of their own or neighbours' property or developments that affect the amenities and environment of the village or town in which they live. This chapter is intended as a preliminary guide only to the morass of complex issues and procedures that are likely to arise. The areas covered are:

☐ carrying out works;
☐ permitted development;
☐ change of use;
☐ enforcement;
☐ the environment;
☐ appeals.

CARRYING OUT WORKS

The question 'Do I need planning permission?' is likely to come early when starting or expanding a business; it may arise even after decisions have been made and works undertaken. This chapter is intended to explain the framework and answer some of the more usual questions; the primary aim is to stimulate readers into thinking about this issue in the round, in the hope that the pitfalls can be avoided.

Planning permission is required for any 'building, mining, engineering or other operation', which covers almost everything, but certain works are excluded because they are 'permitted development'. The General Permitted Development Order (SI 1995/418) gives automatic consent to a wide range of works that can be undertaken to residential, business, agricultural and other types of property without the need to apply for permission, but this automatic consent only applies when the conditions and limitations imposed by the Order are complied with.

Where planning permission is required, application must be made to the local planning authority (LPA), run by the district or borough council, or the unitary authority. To be valid an application must comprise:

☐ the application form with adequate location and detailed plans to show the proposed works;

☐ an ownership certificate to identify whether the applicant is the owner and whether there is any tenant with a lease of seven years or more to run, and an agricultural holdings certificate to identify whether any farm tenant is in occupation;

☐ the planning fee, for which there is a published scale available from the LPA.

Depending on the scale and nature of the proposed development, it may be necessary to submit additional information; a list of the LPA's normal requirements should be available from the planning office, and any additional requirements in a specific case can be discussed with the case officer. Such requirements may include:

☐ a 'design statement', explaining how the design for the new building or alterations has been decided in the context of the character and architecture in the locality;

☐ a 'green travel plan' to show how the development can be accessed by public transport, to reduce dependence on the motor car – a concept that can be difficult to achieve for small-scale business developments in many rural areas;

☐ an Environmental Statement (ES) based on an Environmental Impact Assessment (EIA), describing the local environment, the effects of the development and how these might be mitigated;

☐ a flood risk assessment.

Even when planning permission has been granted, there can be additional obligations. These are generally imposed by the LPA as conditions on the planning permission, and they are worded in such a way that the development cannot (or should not) be undertaken until the requirements have been met. These often include:

☐ submission of materials to be used for approval (eg bricks and tiles);

☐ submission of all hard and soft landscaping for approval, with an obligation to carry it out promptly when the development is completed and maintain all plants for at least five years;

☐ undertaking an archaeological assessment of the site before carrying out the development and submitting full details to the LPA;

☐ agreeing details of the foul and surface water drainage schemes with the relevant authorities.

When planning permission has been granted, it should be implemented within three years. If the permission is an Outline Consent, then there will be an additional obligation to submit the details of the scheme within a shorter time.

The next sections summarize the rules affecting rural businesses, but please read both the sections on enforcement and the environment as they put much of the planning system in context, and are important!

PERMITTED DEVELOPMENT

The General Permitted Development Order SI 1995/418 as amended (referred to as the GDO) covers a wide range of works, including:

☐ householder development: not a topic for this book;

☐ agricultural buildings: with rules for 'prior notification' of the LPA of proposed buildings with an area of up to 465 square metres and provisions for the LPA to satisfy itself as to the need and to address such matters as design and location; other limitations are imposed in some circumstances, for example a height limit within 3 kilometres of any airfield; tighter rules apply to works on individual units or separate parcels of land of less than 5 hectares;

☐ temporary uses: where there is a right to use open land (not in the curtilage of any building) for up to 28 days in each calendar year for a purpose that does not involve the carrying out of any works; this is limited to only 14 days if the use is for a market, or for car or motorcycle racing; additional restrictions apply on any Site of Special Scientific Interest (SSSI); use of any land as a caravan site is **not** permitted, unless it is exempt under the Caravan Sites and Control of Development Act 1960;

☐ temporary buildings: such structures can be erected on land in connection with the permitted use; examples are Portacabin offices, bale buildings for pigs, and marquees; where the building remains for long periods, full planning permission may be required, and the test is whether it is securely fixed to the land; in the Courts, a marquee erected for about 8 months in successive years was held to be a building that needed permission because it was (sensibly) securely fixed to the land;

☐ minor works to business premises: including extensions to industrial and warehouse buildings where floor area, volume and height limits are observed, where there is no change of use unless staff facilities are being provided, and where there is no material alteration in the external appearance; private access ways and hard standings can also be provided within limits;

☐ and there is lots more besides, mainly dealing with development by authorities and statutory undertakers which this chapter cannot record in full; it is important to check the rules in detail and, while there have been some changes to parts, the starting point is SI 1995/418 and this can be found at http://www.hmso.gov.uk/stat.htm.

But as with so much in planning, beware that:

☐ permitted development rights may be removed by an Article 4 Direction made by the LPA and approved by the Secretary of State; but this should be published and would be recorded on the Search when buying a property;

☐ permitted development rights are more limited in conservation areas; any work that may affect a listed building or be carried out within its curtilage requires listed building consent and/or planning permission;

☐ at some time, all LPAs are likely to be given formal power to vary the standard rules within all or parts of their local areas, although this power is not likely to be used widely.

CHANGE OF USE

Planning permission may also be required to change the use of land or buildings, and this is governed by the Use Classes Order (SI 1987/764) and the GDO. Where the use of premises is to change, the GDO can permit this without express planning consent being required but other changes will require consent.

The basic rules are summarized below but in the rural context it is important to note that any land may be used for agriculture or forestry without the need for planning permission – but see the section below on the environment!

Notwithstanding the move towards superstores and out-of-town retail, it is important to note that LPAs are generally concerned to keep shops open and to preserve the character and diversity of towns and villages. Unauthorized changes of use from retail to offices can be subject to enforcement action; the change of use of pubs to private houses can be resisted unless there is a second pub in the village; it is important to be sure of the planning position before committing capital and effort into a venture that might be frustrated.

The Use Classes Order defines the following categories of commercial property, and the GDO allows limited changes without express planning permission:

☐ Class A1 permits use for most categories of shop but the list is specified and includes the sale of cold food for consumption off the premises, A2 covers business and financial services, and A3 is for food premises, including any hot food take-away. Changes between these categories is limited to a move from A3 to A1 or A2, and from A2 to A1 where there is an existing display window on the ground floor; any change to A3 requires planning permission because of the potential smells and late night trade.

☐ Class B1 covers business use for office, research or any industrial purpose where the use is one that could be carried out in a residential area without upsetting the neighbourhood. B2 is the catch-all category covering all general industrial uses not suitable for a residential area and not covered by the special uses in B3–B7, which involve a range of special uses that could have significant impacts on the local area.

☐ Class B8 is a very broad category covering storage and distribution. Changes are allowed to class B1 from B2; where the B8 floor area concerned is less than 235 square metres changes may be made to or from B1 and B2.

☐ Class C deals with hotels, residential institutions and houses, a house is defined as a property lived in by one person, a family or by up to six people living as a single household; this serves to distinguish the property from a 'house in multiple occupation' where several people may have a room each and share facilities, but live separate lives; this is a use that is subject to increasing regulation and licensing. Where a dwelling house is made into two, planning permission is required, but this does not apply where two are made into one.

The Use Classes Order identifies the main types of use, but this does not cover everything and there are a lot of premises which have hybrid uses or are treated as *'sui generis'* uses – that is special uses, which are outside the standard rules and are more strictly controlled. There is scope for changing the proportions of use within such 'planning units' provided that the major use continues and there is no material effect on the appearance.

ENFORCEMENT

Although the legislation, regulations, national and local policy guidance and local development frameworks all add up to a huge amount of paper, there are many 'grey areas' in planning. It is always possible to ask planning officers whether planning permission is required but this involves revealing your intentions. It can be worthwhile to prepare for any such meeting by identifying the issues that may be relevant to any proposal, and taking advice, before talking to the LPA because he or she may express views or take other steps (eg listing a building you wish to demolish) and frustrate your plans.

It is also important to note that it is an offence to carry out works to special properties without securing permission. Special properties include listed buildings and SSSIs; listed buildings are protected but so are the buildings within their curtilage, and this includes buildings in the curtilage at the date of the listing, even if they have been sold off. Unauthorized works (eg installing plastic windows) on any such properties is an offence, and unlike other works, the passage of time does not bring immunity. Conservation areas also have special status limiting what can be done without consent.

Works to other properties can be carried out without planning permission but this can create problems and antagonism with the authorities and/or neighbours; the LPA has the right to serve an enforcement notice for any development that does not:

☐ have express planning permission;
☐ have the benefit of a permitted development right, and where this is subject to conditions or limitations, the right only exists where the requirements have been complied with.

On receipt of an enforcement notice, an appeal can be made (see the section below on appeals). One of the grounds of appeal is that planning permission ought to be granted, but a number of arguments can be put forward, and you can argue that no planning permission is required or that the works required to rectify the position are excessive or unreasonable.

An offence is only committed when an enforcement notice is upheld (by losing an appeal or not making such an appeal), and the requirements are then not complied with. Persistent or outrageous breaches of the rules can warrant a prison sentence, but this is very rare.

To date, LPAs have had the right to serve a Stop Notice to put a stop to any breach of planning control, being unauthorized development or use of land or buildings, but this can create a duty for the LPA to pay compensation if it is in the wrong. LPAs will shortly have the right to serve a Temporary Stop Notice which will take immediate effect to prevent work on land, or to stop a use from continuing; everyone must then comply, whether owner, occupier or contractor. This notice will only apply for a maximum of 28 days because it is intended to stop the activity while the position is being sorted out. This could be inconvenient if works are in progress and time is critical, but this shows how the rules on planning are being tightened up.

LPAs have the right to serve a Planning Contravention Notice to establish the owners and occupiers of land and the use to which it is being put. This is a statutory notice and a reply must be given or penalties apply. The purpose is to allow the LPA to establish who is doing what on the land, and if there is a breach of the rules it can serve a notice on the right party.

LPAs can also review any development that has been implemented and if it is found that one or more of the conditions set out on the planning permission are not being complied with, the LPA can serve a Breach of Condition Notice. There is no defence against such a notice unless it can be shown that the condition is being complied with or that the breach is now immune from enforcement action.

Immunity from enforcement action arises after two specified periods:

☐ Any building, engineering or other operation is immune from enforcement action four years after it was substantially completed; this also applies to the change of use of any building to a private dwelling house.

☐ All other development, ie changes of use or development in breach of a condition, is exempt from enforcement after 10 years: this might apply to an occupation of a house in breach of an agricultural occupancy condition or business premises that were granted a personal occupancy condition.

Two other processes exist which can be of benefit: a Certificate of Lawfulness of Use or Development can be sought 4 or 10 years after the relevant works or use have been in place: evidence should be supplied to the LPA and if it is satisfied that the works or change did take place, it must issue a certificate. It does not matter if this is contrary to policy, because the decision is based only on the facts. Where you intend to put land or buildings to a particular purpose and, perhaps buy the property, it can be very important to be sure that this is allowed: application can be made for a Certificate of Lawfulness of Proposed Use or Development to confirm the position.

Other restrictions can exist: one example is a Tree Preservation Order (TPO). It is a strict (court appearance) offence for anyone, whether owner, agent or contractor, to carry out unauthorized works to a tree covered by a TPO. To illustrate the need for careful preparation, a council can impose an emergency TPO on any trees on the signature of a senior officer, where it has reason to believe that one or more trees are at risk of being cut down. The emergency TPO lapses after six months if it has not been confirmed, a process that allows the people affected to put forward their arguments for or against this level of protection.

THE ENVIRONMENT

While the question of planning permission used to be the more important, the environmental rules are now the greater and more serious. A breach of environmental law is usually a strict one, and can result in a court appearance. Waste transfer and disposal are clear examples, where the rules for transfer notes and the like should be complied with. Even if involved in business in a small way, it may be necessary to register part of the premises as a waste transfer station, eg where builders bring material back to the yard from various sites and then dispose of it, perhaps using a skip in the yard.

Consents can be required for a whole range of activities and the Waste Management Licensing Regulations 1994 (SI 1994/1056) are important. Schedule 3 includes a long list of activities that are exempt from licensing; as an example, it provides for burning waste products for energy production, composting, and some demolition waste with specified limits on each.

Particularly important is the need to consider whether an EIA is required before undertaking some types of work. Failure to do this can, again, result in prosecution, fines and a requirement to reinstate the land. Rules apply to a range of activities, including:

☐ the intensification of use of semi-natural or uncultivated land: this can apply to putting more animals on a field, the application of fertilizer or the ploughing of long-term set-aside, draining a wet corner or pushing in a shallow pond or scrape; there is no minimum size for the area involved;

☐ the new planting of more than 5 hectares with trees, but the rules apply to 2 hectares in a National Park or Area of Outstanding Natural Beauty, and to any area of planting in an SSSI;

☐ the carrying out of drainage works or extracting water for irrigation purposes.

This is another area where it is good to think and plan ahead, taking expert advice before cracking on and carrying out works without adequate preparation.

APPEALS

If planning is refused, you can always appeal. This can be done in three ways:

☐ using written representations – where the evidence is all submitted in writing – you see and can comment on the arguments made by the LPA and any other party, the inspector visits the site and then decides the appeal based on what has been read and seen;

☐ via an informal hearing: the same process is followed, but then there is a round table discussion to explore the key issues in conversation, so the inspector can understand everyone's case fully;

☐ via an inquiry: this is more formal with written evidence followed by a formal session with cross-examination of witnesses; this is appropriate in large or contentious appeals, but is the most expensive method.

The appeals system is administered by the planning inspectorate, which also makes a lot of information available on paper or on the internet. It can be contacted at http://www.planning-inspectorate.gov.uk .

Policy and other information is also published by the Office of the Deputy Prime Minister. This can be found by accessing http://www.odpm.gov.uk and clicking the 'in the Planning' section.

4 Compulsory Purchase and Compensation

Andrew Pym

For ease of understanding, this chapter focuses on the five key areas relating to the compulsory purchase of land and compensation of which all rural property owners should be aware:

☐ procedure;
☐ blight;
☐ compensation;
☐ no land taken;
☐ the Lands Tribunal.

PROCEDURE

Government has the power to allow its agencies and other public and private organizations to acquire property for many different purposes, ranging from new roads and airports to the provision of utility services and urban renewal. Compulsory purchase orders (CPOs) are normally used to facilitate schemes of public benefit, but they have a direct effect on those whose property or business is affected; if threatened it is important to understand the framework and secure advice at an early stage from an expert with a good track record. This chapter provides a short overview of the system to help people who are subject to a CPO to understand the principles.

The law relating to CPOs and compensation is complex and the current statutes date from 1845 to 2004. The language is arcane and difficult to interpret, and case law has developed to introduce some sense to the more difficult issues. A complete review of the law has been undertaken by the Law Commission, which has issued two substantial reports on Procedure and Compensation, but it is not clear when a new Act might implement the recommendations; they would do much to improve the whole system. Importantly, the present law and practice can create difficulties for property owners, and businesses in particular.

It is a fundamental principle of law, including the Human Rights Act 1998, that there is a right to acquire private property where there is a need in the public interest, provided that:

☐ the owner has the right to object and be given a fair and impartial hearing;
☐ proper compensation is paid.

Before a CPO is to be sought, the acquirer promoting the scheme of works should establish the need for it and the prospect of being able to carry it out (including the likelihood of getting planning permission and finance). It should also attempt to buy the necessary properties by negotiation with the owner, unless they are too numerous in which case the CPO can be sought at the outset, but the acquirer should still pursue negotiations in parallel whenever the property owner is willing to discuss terms.

Without recording all the technical processes, which can vary for a number of reasons, the CPO process can be summarized as follows:

☐ The CPO is published in draft and served on everyone with an interest in any part of the affected property, whether as owner or tenant, save for some short-term tenants and licensees.
☐ A statement of reasons explaining the scheme and the need for the CPO should be provided at the same time.
☐ There is a specified time within which formal objections can be made.
☐ If any objections are not resolved by discussion, there is an inquiry, at which an independent inspector will hear the arguments and then report to the relevant Secretary of State with recommendations on whether or not to confirm the CPO.

The CPO may include the whole of an owner's property, or only a part of it, or may only seek a right in the property, for example to lay a drain; a CPO may also include the right to take and occupy land for a limited period, eg during the construction of a new road; in this case the land is returned to the owner in due course.

Where a CPO proposes to acquire part only of a 'house, building, manu-factory, or of a park or garden occupied with a house', the owner can insist that the whole of the property is taken, unless the acquirer objects and the Lands Tribunal agrees to a purchase of the part. The same can apply to inconvenient areas of less than half an acre of undeveloped land; if part of a farm is to be taken and the remaining land is not reasonably capable of being farmed, the owner can oblige the acquirer to take all the land, provided a Notice to Treat has been served and before entry is taken (see below).

The cost of objecting and presenting a case at inquiry falls on the property owner but some or all of the costs may be recovered if an objection is presented at an inquiry and the CPO is not confirmed on the owner's land or a part of it.

Costs cannot be recovered for any objection where the affected land or the whole CPO is withdrawn before the inquiry.

If the CPO is confirmed, the acquirer can take one of two courses:

- ☐ Within three years of the CPO being confirmed he or she can serve Notice to Treat (which invites details of the owner's interest in the land and the compensation sought) and within a further three years of that date, he or she can serve a Notice to Enter and then take possession.
- ☐ He or she can make a General Vesting Declaration (GVD) which specifies a date on which all legal titles to the property will be taken; this generally applies where there are a lot of individual properties, or where the owner is unknown.

There are several very important points to note:

- ☐ Only when the Notice to Treat is served are the owners' interests in the property fixed. Up to this date, owners can continue to transfer the property or take other steps to protect their financial position; this can include the transfer of some other property of theirs, which may increase in value as a result of the scheme, into different ownership in order to maximize the compensation and avoid a deduction for 'betterment'.
- ☐ Short-term tenants, eg assured shorthold tenants and business tenants with only a short period of the lease left, may be excluded: the acquirer can take over the landlord's interest and then serve notices to secure possession under the lease or as permitted by law in the normal way.
- ☐ When the acquirer serves a Notice of Entry, he or she has to give a minimum of only 14 days' notice. This is unusual where a house or buildings used for business are concerned but this is the legal minimum, making it very important for owners and occupiers to maintain a dialogue with the acquirer throughout the process, and to plan ahead.
- ☐ Even when a CPO has been confirmed, the acquirer is under limited obligations and can decide not to implement the scheme; in effect the CPO can expire if no Notice to Treat is served within the three years or if no Notice to Enter is served thereafter; then no property is acquired and the power to do so in future is lost, but the owners cannot be sure of the position during each three-year period.

Where there is a restrictive covenant or an easement (eg for a water pipe or an access) the acquirer takes the land subject to those rights and statute gives him or her the power to override them. The person with the benefit of these rights can only seek compensation for his or her loss – but if these rights are not surrendered he or she can apply again if and when the land ceases to be used for a purpose authorized by statute.

BLIGHT

When any public scheme is announced, there can be immediate concerns; this can make residential property difficult or impossible to sell. House values can fall and this can affect business owners if their house has been used to secure a loan. There are rules allowing some owners to oblige an acquirer to purchase property in advance of a scheme but the rules do not cover everyone, and they do not apply from the time a scheme is first announced.

A blight notice may only be served by:

☐ the owner-occupier of a residential property;
☐ the owner-occupier of any rateable hereditament where the rateable value is less than the prescribed limit, which at 1 January 2005 was £24,600;
☐ the owner-occupier of an agricultural unit.

The notice can only be given for specified types of scheme, although the list is quite extensive. The detail of each case must be considered carefully but properties can qualify where they are affected by:

☐ designation in an approved or deposited draft development plan for development for a purpose of a public authority, or included for this purpose in any other plan approved by the local planning authority;
☐ a New Towns order or an urban development area;
☐ a clearance or renewal area;
☐ a highway scheme or associated mitigation measures as shown in a development plan, council resolution or the like;
☐ a private Act of Parliament or a confirmed CPO, but only before Notice to Treat is served (after which the acquirer controls the time of entry and purchase).

There are further rules allowing the acquirer to serve a counter-notice with provision for disputes to be resolved at the Lands Tribunal.

COMPENSATION

With the help of some constructive interpretation by the courts, the law seeks to provide fair compensation so that any person who has property acquired under a CPO receives an amount equal to his or her loss. That is easily said, but much less easily achieved.

The basic principles are based on payments for:

☐ the market value of the property taken: statute requires this assessment (1) to take no account of the fact that the acquisition is compulsory, (2) to assume that the property is being sold in the open market by a willing seller, (3) to ignore any special suitability of the property if that relates only to a purpose which can be pursued with compulsory powers or for which there is no market other than for a purchaser with CPO powers, and (4) to ignore any increase in value that exists contrary to law (eg a use that does not have proper planning permission);

☐ the additional loss caused to any neighbouring property held by the same owner arising from 'severance' or 'injurious affection': usually these two heads of claim are addressed together but severance refers to the reduction in value of adjoining land which the owner retains because it is worth less after the other land has been taken; injurious affection refers to the reduction in value caused to that land because of the effects of the works (eg the noise from aircraft when a runway is built);

☐ any other loss arising directly from the acquisition of the property provided it is not 'too remote';

☐ an additional payment either as a 'home loss payment' (see below) or since 2004 an additional 10 per cent on other acquisitions subject to a maximum payment of £100,000; where a property is let, the maximum for an owner is £75,000 and for the occupier £25,000.

In assessing market value, the valuation date is the earlier of the date of agreement or the date of entry onto the property. The date of entry is the latest date although it can take a long time to establish the full losses and then settle the full payment. If the matter remains in dispute, the claim must be referred to the Lands Tribunal within six years of the date of entry; save in exceptional cases, after the six-year deadline has passed, the matter can only be settled by agreement or the right to compensation can be lost.

Also in assessing market value, proper account must be taken of all relevant facts. For example, where there is a proper prospect of buying in an interest (eg a lease) an owner may take account of the additional value he or she would obtain by doing this and profiting from the 'marriage value' on resale. Where a piece of land would be required to provide access to a development site, the owner can claim for the 'ransom' value he or she could obtain from the developer. The market value should take account of any existing planning permission, the purpose to which the land will be put by the acquirer (unless it is so special that the statutory rules preclude this), and any additional planning permission which would have been granted in the absence of the scheme.

Where a property is used for a special purpose and there is no proper market for such property, the rules provide for compensation based on the cost of equivalent reinstatement. This is comparatively rare but can protect some owners with special uses (eg where a place of worship is involved).

When assessing the loss in the value of other land, however, the acquirer can offset this against any increase in the value of neighbouring land which the owner will retain where that increase arises directly from the acquirer's scheme. This is called 'betterment' but it has the potential to be unfair, given that other owners who do not have any land taken may also benefit from an increase in value without suffering any recoupment by the acquirer; this is akin to the possible tax that is being discussed for property which increases in value on the grant of planning permission. It must be remembered, however, that the owner can transfer his or her retained property into other ownership, including a Trust, and so protect himself or herself from betterment provided this is done before Notice to Treat is served.

A 'home loss payment' is paid to all occupiers of residential property to reflect the unquantified costs of moving to a new property and the general stress and time involved. An owner-occupier or a tenant with more than three years of a lease to run will receive 10 per cent of the value of their interest within prescribed limits (at 1 January 2005 these are a minimum of £34,000 and a maximum of £3,400); a tenant receives a fixed sum (currently £3,400).

Compensation for disturbance can be claimed by the owner or tenant in occupation of business premises (including farms) where the valuation is based on the existing use: this is intended to cover the costs of finding replacement premises and moving the business, together with all associated costs. If the new premises are larger or more expensive, it will be held that the owner will have value for money and therefore will not be entitled to compensation, unless there are exceptional reasons.

If the market value of the CPO property is based on development value and that value could only be achieved by the owner giving up possession and moving, he or she cannot claim for disturbance as well; he or she would have to move anyway to secure that value.

Claims for disturbance to a business can include (1) goodwill, as the level of business may be reduced on relocation, (2) loss of profits not reflected in the open market value, eg where a crop in the ground cannot be harvested, (3) the costs of making customers and others aware of the relocation, and (4) removal expenses and fees.

An acquirer can also carry out 'accommodation works' that will reduce the impact of his or her scheme on the owner's retained land, eg he or she may lay a new water pipe to land, or build a bund to reduce the noise and visibility of a road. There is no duty on the acquirer to provide these unless it is a condition of the planning permission, but owners can suggest and negotiate for such works. If provided, they will be taken into account in assessing the compensation. Where such works are undertaken on the owner's retained land, and not on the land taken, all the terms should be agreed and recorded in writing as these works will be outside the scope of the CPO and if there is a subsequent dispute the arrangement will be treated simply as a private agreement between the two parties.

Two particular points to be aware of are as follows:

☐ A major issue can arise over abortive costs: an owner must prepare for the purchase of his or her property, particularly as a Notice to Enter can give as little as 14 days' notice. It is never clear whether an acquirer will actually take the land until a Notice to Treat and then a Notice to Enter are served, or a General Vesting Declaration is made. Yet if the owner does not prepare, he or she may be put out of business. Costs incurred after confirmation of the CPO in locating new premises can be claimed provided they are a reasonable and natural consequence of the CPO and provided the acquirer serves a Notice to Treat, even if he or she does not then complete the acquisition. If no Notice to Treat is served, the owner will retain his or her property but will have no right to recover these costs.

☐ Where an acquirer engages a reputable contractor to carry out the works, the acquirer is not responsible for the contractor's actions. This can mean that if the contractor causes damage to land which is not covered by the CPO, the owner has a claim against the contractor and not the acquirer. Where several contractors and subcontractors are working on a site at the same time it can be almost, if not wholly, impossible to prove who caused the damage, and when each contractor denies responsibility the owner is often left without any compensation.

NO LAND TAKEN

Where an owner-occupier (including a tenant with a lease of a house but not business premises and at least three years remaining) is affected by the **use** of public works but has no land taken, he or she is entitled to claim compensation for the loss in value of his or her property caused by the noise, smell, fumes, smoke, vibration and artificial lighting arising from the use of the public works. This right replicates the rules that normally apply to a nuisance at common law because statute protects an acquirer, acting reasonably, from an action in nuisance when building and using the authorized works. Claims can also be made where existing works are altered.

More complicated rules apply to people affected by the **construction** of public works: these allow compensation to be sought where the works:

☐ are authorized by Parliament;
☐ would be actionable in the courts if done without Parliamentary authority;
☐ interfere with a public or private right that the owner can use;
☐ cause damage from their construction (not their subsequent use).

Compensation can be claimed but this only reflects the reduction in the market value (ie rental value) of the property, and not the loss of profits. It is important to note that this is a difficult claim to pursue.

Losses can also arise from works in the highway: works to repair or rebuild roads are not compensated as this is a necessary and natural act to maintain the network. Utility companies often carry out works in the highway. Some companies pay compensation for loss of business where this can be substantiated; others do not, and some pay compensation in some (limited) cases and not in others. If affected to a material extent by the nature of or time taken for the works, the relevant company should be approached and proper advice should be sought.

THE LANDS TRIBUNAL

This is the official body with powers to resolve disputes over compensation or some counter-notices (eg blight notices). It operates like a court, with formal procedures laid down, including rules on the submission of evidence, time limits and the like.

It is permitted for owners to conduct their own cases, without professional help but this is rare – and risky. If the dispute is substantial enough and well founded it is undoubtedly best to have a good professional team.

5 Agricultural Tenancies and Diversification

Duncan Sigournay, Thring Townsend

INTRODUCTION

Agricultural land within England and Wales is occupied in a number of different ways. These range from owner-occupation through to different types of letting arrangements such as farm business tenancies (governed by the Agricultural Tenancies Act 1995) or protected tenancies (under the Agricultural Holdings Act 1986), as well as share farming and other contractual arrangements. Indeed, many farmers occupy land under a combination of these arrangements.

Given the current state of the rural economy, and in particular the agricultural sector, both owner-occupiers and tenants alike are increasingly looking towards non-agricultural activities to generate much-needed income. That is not to say that diversification will be the solution for everyone but it is certainly an avenue worth considering.

In this chapter diversification in the context of let agricultural land will be considered – from both the landlord's and the tenant's perspective. Accordingly, the following issues will be addressed:

☐ agricultural tenancies – an overview;
☐ agricultural holdings under the Agricultural Holdings Act 1986:
  – characteristics;
  – security of tenure;
  – Notice to Quit of whole;
  – Notice to Quit of part;
  – compensation;
  – diversification by tenant under the 1986 Act;
☐ farm business tenancy under the Agricultural Tenancies Act 1995:
  – characteristics;
  – termination;

- break clauses;
- compensation;
- diversification by tenant under the 1995 Act;
☐ imminent reforms;
☐ Code of Good Practice;
☐ Diversification and the farm Single Payment scheme;

AGRICULTURAL TENANCIES – AN OVERVIEW

By virtue of the Agricultural Tenancies Act 1995 agricultural tenancies can now effectively be divided into two separate legislative camps: those granted on or after 1 September 1995, which will typically be farm business tenancies – save in a number of limited circumstances – and those agreements preceding that date, which will be governed by the Agricultural Holdings Act 1986.

Since the two governing statutes are quite distinct and adopt a totally different approach to the letting of land, it is imperative that the parties are aware of the status of their agreement. The legislative differences impact greatly upon landlords and tenants wishing to diversify away from traditional agricultural activities. Accordingly, if in any doubt, professional advice should be sought.

AGRICULTURAL HOLDINGS ACT 1986

The 1986 Act effectively provides security of tenure for the tenant as well as imposing certain conditions on the parties, in particular, in relation to compensation. Furthermore, agricultural tenancies entered into prior to 12 July 1984 will typically benefit from succession rights – that is not automatic succession for close members of the tenant's family but merely enabling such members to apply for succession with all the incumbent qualifying criteria. Therefore although new 1986 Act tenancies cannot be created, the succession provisions will ensure that such tenancies will endure for some time to come.

What is an agricultural holding?

Essentially an agricultural holding is a letting of agricultural land that is used for a trade or business. However, that is not to say that the land must be used exclusively for agriculture – the main criterion is that the actual use of the land at its commencement and subsequently is predominantly agricultural. As will be seen later, with farm business tenancies there is scope within agricultural holdings to diversify into non-agricultural commercial activities without the tenancy necessarily losing the protection afforded by the 1986 Act.

Diversification by landlord – security of tenure under the 1986 Act

The security of tenure provisions within the 1986 Act effectively treats most agricultural holdings as yearly tenancies. Furthermore it imposes restrictions on the operation of notices to quit. As such it can often be quite difficult for landlords to regain possession in order to pursue their own diversification objectives.

So what can be done by the landlord when a development potential arises (eg a change in the local plan)? In the absence of a negotiated surrender by the tenant, the landlord will be faced with having to serve a Notice to Quit on the tenant based upon one of the statutory grounds.

Incontestable notices to quit

The 1986 Act prescribes a number of circumstances in which a valid Notice to Quit of the whole of the holding can be served on the tenant without the tenant having a right to serve a counter-notice. Indeed, the only action available to the tenant in such circumstances is to challenge whether the ground stated in the Notice to Quit in fact exists. The statutory grounds for incontestable notices comprise:

☐ Case A – retirement from smallholding where suitable alternative accommodation is available;

☐ Case B – the land is required for a non-agricultural use for which planning permission has been obtained;

☐ Case C – a Notice to Quit is served within six months of a certificate of bad husbandry having been granted by the Agricultural Land Tribunal;

☐ Case D – non-compliance with either a notice to pay rent or notice to remedy;

☐ Case E – the landlord has been materially prejudiced by a breach of the tenant not capable of being remedied;

☐ Case F – insolvency of the tenant;

☐ Case G – death of the tenant – though such a notice does not prevent a close relative applying for succession where qualifying criteria and procedural steps have been fulfilled;

☐ Case H – Minister's amalgamation scheme.

In practice, the statutory ground most likely to be used by the landlord in order to gain possession in pursuit of developing the land will be Case B since it is particularly concerned with non-agricultural activities. However, in certain circumstances other statutory grounds may also be appropriate.

Case B Notice to Quit

Landlords must be aware that the planning permission must be obtained prior to the service of the Notice to Quit. Furthermore the Notice to Quit must relate to the whole of the holding and not just part of it unless the landlord can show that he or she has the ability to serve a Notice to Quit of part.

Notice to Quit – length

On the basis that the landlord has a planning permission for non-agricultural use, what is the timescale involved? In essence, the Notice to Quit would terminate the tenancy 12 months from the end of the current year of the tenancy. However, there are exceptions to this general rule. Consequently, timing can be crucial with a landlord possibly having to wait a further year for possession if the notice is not served before the end of the tenancy anniversary. The matter is further complicated by the fact that many agricultural tenancies are oral in nature and therefore there may be some confusion as to the actual anniversary date.

Notice to Quit of part

If the holding is large and the permission only relates to part of it then there are three circumstances in which a Notice to Quit of part can be valid:

☐ It can be valid where there is an express provision within the agreement. Importantly, such a provision will not be implied into a tenancy agreement.

☐ Section 31 of the 1986 Act sets out certain statutory exceptions allowing notices to quit of part. This section contains a collection of socially desirable objects for which the landlord should be entitled to resume possession of part only of the holding (eg erection of cottages or other houses for farm labourers, provision of allotments, adjusting boundaries between agricultural units).

☐ It can be valid where there has been a severance of the landlord's reversion, ie the freehold owner of the land sells off a part of the freehold to another legal entity. There still exists only one tenancy, although in practice the tenant would be paying two landlords apportioned rent.

Enlargement of notice

One point that must be borne in mind is where Notice to Quit of part is served arising out of either a severed reversion or under section 31 of the 1986 Act, the tenant would be entitled to enlarge the notice to cover the whole of the holding, not just that part of the holding mentioned in the Notice to Quit. That may or may not be desirable to the landlord.

On the basis that such a Notice to Quit was valid the tenant would have very little recourse but to submit a claim for compensation. Although not applicable to all scenarios, compensation can be based upon disturbance, improvements, tenant right matters and other miscellaneous issues.

In October 1999 a joint Guidance note was issued by the Country Land & Business Association, Tenant Farmers Association and the National Farmers' Union in relation to compensation and Case B notices to quit. This is available from the respective organizations.

Disturbance compensation formula

In the event of a successful Case B Notice to Quit the disturbance compensation formula would be one year's rent, and possibly up to two years' rent if additional loss can be proved, and in some circumstances a further four years' rent on top of the one or two may also be allowed.

Diversification by tenant under the 1986 Act

As highlighted earlier, provided the character of the holding remains 'predominantly' agricultural the tenancy will continue to fall under the provisions of the 1986 Act notwithstanding that non-agricultural activities take place on the land. Many landlords have granted consent to tenants with 1986 Act tenancies to undertake limited diversification activities, such as bed and breakfast in the farmhouse, or a camping site on the farm.

Even though the 1986 Act provides a suitable framework in which modest diversification proposals can be incorporated, tenants must be aware of any 'user covenants', which are commonly applied within their tenancy agreements, that restrict the use of the land to a particular purpose (eg agriculture, dairy farming). Such covenants will be binding on the parties and, therefore, in such circumstances the tenant will need to seek his or her landlord's consent to the diversification proposal.

Although tenants may be reluctant to approach landlords for such consent they should not assume that consent will not be forthcoming. Generally landlords want their tenants to be successful; success brings the incentive that the landlord may also benefit from enhanced rent and the knowledge that his or her tenant's business is more viable. The fact that many owner-occupiers have also benefited from diversification projects often makes them more predisposed to consider such approaches from their tenants.

The landlord may welcome the tenant's proposals; alternatively he or she may have legitimate concerns about it – in which case some conditions may be attached to the landlord's consent. On the other hand the landlord may consider that the proposal is not suitable or even that such a project, if implemented, should not remain under the provisions of the 1986 Act. The landlord may be able to argue legitimately that the matter would be better suited to a surrender of the particular building or land with an immediate grant of a business tenancy to the tenant under the provisions of the Landlord and Tenant Act 1954.

Even with the recent introduction of the Code of Good Practice there is still no mechanism in place to force the landlord to grant consent where the tenancy agreement contains a covenant restricting the type of activity on the holding. The Code does not override the tenancy agreement – instead it attempts to encourage landlords to take a more measured and objective approach to the issue of granting consent for diversification.

AGRICULTURAL TENANCIES ACT 1995

The essence of the Agricultural Tenancies Act 1995 is freedom of contract and in only limited areas – fixtures, compensation, rent and certain elements of dispute resolution – is compliance with statute mandatory. There are other areas in which the Act provides a fallback should the parties not make other arrangements but, generally speaking, there is far greater scope for the imagination than was the case under the Agricultural Holdings Act 1986.

Tenancies under the 1995 Act do not carry security of tenure, other than for the term contained within the tenancy agreement, nor do they grant succession rights to agricultural tenants.

One of the main aims of the Act was to encourage landowners to let land where previously they were inhibited from doing so by the strictures of the former regime. This has broadly been achieved, and owners are increasingly adopting the 1995 Act.

Although farm business tenancies can be created orally, the lack of statutory default provisions makes such an approach hazardous and it is certainly not recommended.

What is a farm business tenancy?

Under Section 1 of the 1995 Act a tenancy (whether oral or written) beginning on or after 1 September 1995 will be a farm business tenancy (FBT) provided that it satisfies the 'business' conditions and either the 'agriculture' or 'notice' condition.

The 'business' conditions require that at least part of the land must be farmed for the purposes of a trade or business and must have been so farmed since the beginning of the tenancy. 'Farming' is defined to include 'the carrying on in relation to land of any agricultural activity', and 'agriculture' has the same definition as in the Agricultural Holdings Act 1986.

There is a rebuttable presumption that if the land is farmed by way of a trade or business at the time the status of the tenancy is challenged it has been so farmed since the beginning of the tenancy. In other words, the burden of proof is on the party that claims that the condition is not fulfilled.

The 'agriculture' condition requires that the character of the tenancy is primarily or wholly agricultural. Unlike the 'business' conditions, the 'agriculture' condition needs only to be satisfied at the time of challenge to the tenancy's status.

The 'agriculture' condition can be avoided by compliance with the 'notice' conditions. These require that the landlord and tenant exchange notices on or before the date they enter into the tenancy agreement or, if earlier, the date the tenancy begins. The notices must identify the land to be comprised in the proposed tenancy and confirm the intention of the parties that the tenancy is to be and remain a farm business tenancy. The character of the tenancy must be wholly or primarily agricultural at the outset.

Two points arise from the 'notice' conditions. First, the notices must be exchanged; it is not good enough that one of the parties serves a notice on the other. Secondly, they must be exchanged on or before the earlier of the date of the agreement creating the tenancy or the date on which the tenancy begins (ie the date on which the tenant becomes entitled to enter into possession of the holding); the condition is not satisfied by a notice contained in the contract of tenancy itself.

If the 'business' conditions fail at any point in the term and the business use later recommences, the result (subject to what is said below) will be not a farm business tenancy but a tenancy protected by the Landlord & Tenant Act 1954, Part II. Similarly, if neither the 'agriculture' nor the 'notice' conditions are fulfilled, the tenancy will not be a farm business tenancy. If the land is used for business purposes, it will be protected by Part II of the 1954 Act; if there is no business use, governance will revert to the common law.

In assessing the status of the tenancy, use in breach of covenant is disregarded, except where the landlord or a predecessor of his or hers has consented to the changed use or the landlord personally has acquiesced in it. It is, therefore, advisable to import obligations as to user that will assist in maintaining the status of the tenancy as a farm business tenancy.

Termination of farm business tenancies

A farm business tenancy for a fixed term of two years or less expires automatically on the term date and therefore no notice need be served by either party to bring it to an end.

However, for a tenancy for a fixed term of more than two years to be terminated notice of between 12 and 24 months must be served. If neither party serves such a notice, the tenancy will continue as a tenancy from year to year.

Under the TRIG reforms (see later) the 24-month upper limit on notice periods is to be removed.

A yearly tenancy, whether granted initially or arising after a fixed-term tenancy, can be terminated only by a notice of between 12 and 24 months. Tenancies based on a period other than a year (eg weekly, monthly or quarterly tenancies) are terminated in accordance with common law rules by notice equating to one period of the tenancy (a week, a month or a quarter as the case may be) and expiring at the end of a period of the tenancy.

Break clauses

A break clause in a fixed-term tenancy for more than two years will operate only if notice of 12 and 24 months has first been served. A break clause in a fixed-term tenancy of two years or less can be operated on whatever period of notice the parties agree.

Compensation

The tenant is entitled to compensation for improvements that add to the letting value of the holding at the termination of the tenancy. Improvements are defined to include physical improvements and intangible advantages such as planning permission. In order to be eligible for compensation the tenant must have obtained the written consent of his or her landlord or the arbitrator to make the improvement.

There are special provisions dealing with compensation where there are successive tenancies, and where the landlord has resumed possession of part or there has been a severance of the reversion.

Diversification by tenant under the 1995 Act

Clearly the effect of the various interrelated qualifying criteria for a farm business tenancy ('business', 'notice' and 'agriculture' conditions) is to create a multitude of possible scenarios for the actual status of a tenancy during its lifetime – dependent upon the activities being conducted on the holding at any particular time. Typically these would involve changes in either the 'business' nature of the holding or a move away from traditional 'agricultural' activities.

Indeed, provided the 'business' condition and the 'notice' condition are satisfied, the status of the tenancy would only change were the agricultural activity on the holding to amount to nothing more than *de minimis*. On the other hand if the 'notice' condition had not been satisfied, one would be relying upon the 'agriculture' condition requiring the holding to be 'primarily or wholly agricultural'. Accordingly, farm business tenancies can often be used or retained when diversification or non-agricultural activities are planned on the holding.

This highlights one of the key, though often overlooked, advantages of farm business tenancies, namely their suitability to diversification: indeed, the 1995 Act was drafted with the changing nature of agriculture in England and Wales in mind. The fact that more use of its flexibility has not been made is not necessarily the fault of the 1995 Act itself but the lack of appreciation of its flexibility by professionals, tenants and landlords alike.

User clauses

As with the case of 1986 Act tenancies, the tenant should be familiar with the user covenants contained within the agreement. Any proposal that does not comply with such clauses will require the landlord's consent. In particular, where the investment into a scheme is large it is imperative that the landlord is involved at an early stage.

IMMINENT REFORMS

In November 2002 the Tenancy Reform Industry Group (TRIG) was re-established. TRIG is a cross-industry group charged by DEFRA to look into possible areas of reform to both agricultural tenancy legislation and fiscal issues affecting the agricultural sector. It was first used to great effect in the formulation of the Agricultural Tenancies Act 1995.

Its re-establishment follows the 2002 study by the University of Plymouth into the 'Economic Evaluation of the Agricultural Tenancies Act 1995' as well as the Report of the Policy Commission on the Future of Food and Farming in January 2002. Both reports highlighted issues relating to diversification on tenanted holdings as well as other matters affecting agricultural tenancies.

The proposed reforms to the 1986 Act include:

☐ extending the definition of 'livelihood' within the succession provisions so that non-agricultural income derived on the holding counts towards an applicant's 'farming' income;
☐ modernization of the existing arbitration provisions.

The proposed reforms to the 1995 Act include:

☐ giving greater flexibility on rent review formulae for farm business tenancies;
☐ relaxing the provisions concerning compensation so as to give both parties greater certainty;
☐ removal of the 24-month upper limit on notice periods.

Following publication of the TRIG Final Report in June 2003 and the subsequent government response in December 2003 all of TRIG's legislative recommendations have now been incorporated into a Regulatory Reform Bill, which should ensure that they come into force towards the end of 2005.

CODE OF GOOD PRACTICE

Of all of TRIG's recommendations the one that potentially will have the greatest impact on the issue of diversification is the introduction of the Code of Good Practice for agri-environmental schemes and diversification projects within agricultural tenancies (the Code). The Code was launched by DEFRA in October 2004.

The Code sets out the procedural steps to be taken by each party when such consent is sought for diversification where otherwise it is precluded by the tenancy agreement. These steps propose:

1. Early consultation between the parties once a project starts to be planned.
2. Agreeing a timetable during which the landlord and tenant seek to agree terms.
3. Preparation of detailed proposals with a guide as to information that might be relevant depending upon the nature and scale of the project.
4. Issues to be addressed in considering the proposals and the need for a written response.
5. Preparation of a formal agreement between the parties.

It is intended that the Code will create an environment where both parties give serious and pragmatic consideration to the proposal.

Linked to the Code is the proposal that a non-binding adjudication scheme be established to deal with cases where consent has been refused or where, in the opinion of the tenant, unreasonable conditions have been imposed in return for consent being granted. The adjudicator would then consider whether the refusal to grant consent, or indeed the conditions to be attached to consent, were reasonable in the circumstances. Given the non-binding nature of the adjudication scheme, the supremacy of the tenancy agreement and hence any user covenants therein remain unaffected.

It is intended that the existence of the Code of Good Practice will promote greater communication and cooperation between landlords and tenants, thereby creating an environment where both parties give serious and pragmatic consideration to any diversification proposal.

DIVERSIFICATION AND THE SINGLE PAYMENT SCHEME

In January 2005 a completely new European subsidy regime known as the Single Payment Scheme was introduced. As such tenants must ensure that due consideration is given to the impact of the diversification project on payments they receive under the Single Payment Scheme. In particular the regulations surrounding 'cross compliance' and the need to keep land in 'good agricultural and environmental condition' must be considered so that payments are not jeopardized.

6 | Farm Single Payments

Peter R FitzGerald and Philip D Whitcomb, Wilsons

SUBSIDIES IN TRANSITION

The most recent reforms of the Common Agricultural Policy (CAP) have been described as the most fundamental change to impact UK agriculture since entry to the EU or the repeal of the Corn Laws. Farm support will no longer be conditional upon producing crops, meat or milk. The new single payment entitlement will replace all the existing claims such as the Arable Area Payment Scheme, Set-Aside, Suckler Cow Premium and Sheep Annual premium. Instead the farmer will receive from 2005 payments in return for land management on condition that he or she can match certain criteria.

The new scheme will be phased in over an eight-year period with a deadline of 1st May 2005 for registration. The proportion of total payments in farm support under the old scheme on cropping and livestock support will dwindle from 90 per cent in 2005 to 10 per cent by 2012, while the proportion paid under the new farm Single Payment will rise incrementally from 10 per cent in 2005 to 15 per cent in 2006, 30 per cent in 2007, 45 per cent in 2008, 75 per cent in 2010 and finally 90 per cent in 2012. The basis on which the cropping and livestock support element will be calculated will be the average of the payments made over the three-year period 2001 to 2003.

TIPS AND TRAPS

☐ Farm Single Payments are personal to the occupier of the land. They are clearly not an item of land and it must be open to doubt as to whether they are farm stock. It would be wise for any person in receipt of farm Single Payments to add a Codicil to their Will to clarify who should receive it.

☐ Grazing Agreements – only one party can establish an entitlement to farm Single Payments on each eligible hectare of land. Entitlement will depend on occupation for 10 months of the year. A traditional five- or six-month Grazing Agreement probably means that neither landowner nor grazier will qualify. A decision needs to be made as to whether a farm Single Payment is to be received by the landowner or the grazier. If the former, very careful drafting is needed so that the landowner is deemed to be occupying the land throughout the period and simply selling a right of herbage. At the least the owner will need to be responsible for fencing, fertilizer, etc and is probably right that he or she cannot be licensing the grazier to mow. Conversely if the grazier is to receive the farm Single Payment he or she will need a term of 10 months and the landowner should impose an obligation that on request the grazier should be obliged to transfer any farm Single Payment entitlement back to the landowner.

On paper it seems that it is clearly in the landowner's interest to receive the farm Single Payment but if he or she does, will he or she find a grazier at all?

☐ DEFRA have now clarified that farmers with common rights can receive farm Single Payment. However, they must be engaged in production on the common land and keeping the land in good agricultural and environmental condition. It seems that this may be achievable even if they do not actually turn stock on to the common.

☐ The occupier of land used predominantly for grazing horses can be eligible for payment in just the same way as any farmer. It will be important for the owner to register his or her holding fairly urgently so that it appears on the Rural Land Register. The owner will of course be liable for the same cross-compliance provisions as for any other farmer. The owner will also need to be occupying the land himself or herself for at least 10 months of the year.

7 | Capital Gains Tax and Inheritance Tax Issues

John Skinner, Whitley Stimpson

Capital tax planning can be a very complex area and equally difficult to cover in a comparatively short chapter. But, especially with inheritance tax (IHT), it needs re-addressing as circumstances change. Get professional advice at an early stage and you should benefit in the long run.

IHT is currently a hot political potato – even with signs of stagnation in the housing market, increases in property prices have easily exceeded the paltry inflation-based rises in the 'nil rate band' (ie the amount above which tax is paid on a person's estate). In the 2004/05 tax year this band is £263,000, which can easily be eaten up by the value of a modest family home, leaving the rest of an estate subject to tax at 40 per cent.

Added to this, at the 2004 budget the chancellor introduced draconian measures to combat various schemes that had been set up to remove assets from ownership (and hence not liable to IHT) by an individual while he or she still benefited from it. This so-called 'pre-owned assets' legislation was roundly criticized for its retrospective effect and the level of doubt it generated.

For instance, it was suggested to the Inland Revenue that the legislation could be interpreted to mean that even equity release schemes, whereby a building society would lend money secured against the (mortgage-free) capital value of a house, with the loan and subsequently accrued interest, being repaid from the sale of the house on the death of the occupants, would fall foul of the law. The Inland Revenue's response was that this suggestion was 'scare mongering'.

CAPITAL GAINS TAX (CGT)

CGT has been with us since 1965 as a tax on the gains generated from the sale of capital assets. All forms of property are chargeable to CGT unless specifically exempted by the legislation, eg:

☐ cars;
☐ your only or main home – subject to various conditions;

☐ 'wasting asset chattels' – ie tangible moveable property with a life of less than 50 years where not used in a business;
☐ non-wasting assets sold for less than £6,000;
☐ government securities, prizes, betting winnings and currency.

There are others, but the list gets more esoteric – as if the above was not bad enough.

The tax applies to individuals as well as companies, although a company's gains would be subject to corporation tax rather than CGT. Individuals benefit from an annual exemption (£8,200 in 2004/05), which works in a similar fashion to the personal allowance for income tax, whereas no such allowance exists for companies.

A common assumption is that CGT is paid by an individual at 40 per cent (the highest rate of tax), but this is not necessarily the case. The rate of tax depends on the amount of unused income tax bands – if, in 2004/05, you have not used all of your £31,400 of starting and basic rate bands, any unused element will be applied to the taxable gain, so that part of the gain may be taxed at 20 per cent, or maybe even 10 per cent if you have had no income.

Calculating the gain

A capital gain or loss is calculated on the disposal of an asset by deducting from its sale proceeds (or market value in the event of a gift):

☐ the asset's original cost (or market value at March 1982 if held at that date);
☐ subsequent expenditure that increased the asset's value (eg a property extension);
☐ costs of disposal (eg solicitors' fees);
☐ 'indexation allowance' and/or 'taper relief'.

The indexation allowance is given as an attempt to counter the effects of inflation and is calculated based on the retail price index. However, it is restricted so as not to create or increase a loss.

This allowance was frozen in April 1998 for individuals but continued for companies, and was replaced by taper relief, which comes in two varieties, depending on whether or not the asset in question meets the criteria of being a 'business asset'. Business asset taper relief is a very attractive proposition as it reaches a maximum of 75 per cent after two **complete** years of owning an asset, whereas non-business asset taper relief reaches only 40 per cent after ten years. A sliding scale exists for assets held for less time.

The following assets qualify as 'business assets':

☐ Assets used in the taxpayer's trade (either solely or in partnership with others) or by a 'qualifying' company.

55

☐ Assets held by an employee for use in his or her employment by a trading employer.

☐ Shares or securities in a qualifying company, ie a trading company, or the holding company of a group of trading companies, that is unquoted (or, if quoted, where the taxpayer is a director, secretary or employee), in which he or she holds 5 per cent or more of the voting rights (*not* necessarily shares).

☐ A company, or holding company, where the taxpayer is a director, secretary or employee and has no 'material interest' in the company or its controlling company. A material interest arises when an individual, and those people connected with that individual, controls more than 10 per cent of a company's shares or its voting rights, or would be entitled to more than 10 per cent of the company on a winding up or complete distribution.

These rules may seem insanely complicated and the Inland Revenue has issued detailed guidance on its interpretation of the meaning of 'trading company', but they do become important, for instance in family companies, where the shares may be held by a number of family members for whom their shareholding does not entitle them to business asset taper relief.

Planning points and reliefs

☐ Matching – all capital disposals in a given year are initially 'matched' with each other, so that if you sell an asset that generates a gain, but are also aware that another asset you hold would generate a loss, sell the latter asset in the same year to reduce the gain on the former asset. Do not forget your annual exemption though, which will be set against any gains that you have and may allow you to hold on to the asset 'pregnant' with loss to a later year.

☐ Accumulated losses from earlier years – where the above matching process generates a loss position (ie total losses have been greater than total gains), the losses are carried forward to be set against gains in future years.

☐ Transfers between spouses – both husband and wife are entitled to an annual exemption and a transfer of an asset, or in part, between the two if done in such a manner that the recipient is treated as if they owned the asset from its original purchase date. This is a very useful planning tool, especially where one spouse has their basic rate tax band available. Spouses do have to be living together though to take advantage of this relief.

☐ Minimize your income – if you can legitimately minimize your taxable income in the year of a capital disposal, the tax rate on the gain could be cut from 40 per cent to 20 per cent.

☐ Timing – if you are faced with agreeing an exchange date on a disposal (which will trigger the gain, rather than the date you actually receive the money) late in a tax year (say January to March), see if the buyer is willing to delay exchanging contracts until after 5 April. This will buy you another 12 months before you have to pay the CGT.

☐ Rollover relief – if you re-invest all the disposal proceeds from the sale of one 'qualifying' business asset into the purchase of another similarly qualifying asset, the gain is deferred until the new asset is sold. There is a specific timescale in which the reinvestment asset must be bought. The relief applies to land and buildings (but only when **used** in a trade, eg workshop and yard), goodwill, milk and potato quotas, ewe and suckler cow premium quotas, and, should you be considering buying them, satellites and spacecraft.

☐ Enterprise investment relief – this involves using the proceeds from a disposal and buying shares in a company that is carrying out a qualifying trade. Again, this merely defers the CGT until the shares are sold, but so long as certain criteria are met, the gain on the sale of the new shares can be completely exempt from CGT.

☐ Gifting assets – there may be circumstances where you agree to gift a chargeable asset, or sell it at less than its market value. For CGT purposes, a gain still arises for the donor and is computed using the market value, so you would face a tax bill without having received any money to cover it. However, where the gift is of a business asset, the donor is not charged to CGT where the recipient of the gift agrees to acquire the asset at less than the market value less the value of the donor's gain. The recipient therefore has a larger gain on which to pay tax when the asset is subsequently sold.

☐ Principal private residence – the general rule is that the disposal proceeds for your home are tax free, but there is a whole raft of caveats. For example, the grounds attached to the house are restricted to 1.25 acres, or larger if appropriate to the size and character of the house. Care needs to be taken if part or all of the house was rented out, although there is a 'lettings' relief available. If you own more than one house, you can elect which is your 'principal private residence' and if the other is let as a holiday home, rollover relief is certainly available, as well as the lettings relief as long as the criteria are met.

IHT

As mentioned above, IHT is paid at 40 per cent on the element of your estate that exceeds the 'nil rate band', (£263,000 in 2004/05). However, it can also be charged on certain gifts while you are still alive and on certain transfers into and out of trusts. There is also interaction with CGT, especially when it comes to gifting assets.

The key to IHT planning is to review your possessions, and your will, on a regular basis, or as your circumstances change. If you do no planning, or die with no will or one that was so out of date to be meaningless, your beneficiaries will not thank you, as they will likely as not have to share your estate with a beneficiary who was not named in your will – the Chancellor of the Exchequer.

Planning should look at three key issues:

☐ What reliefs are available on the assets in my estate?
☐ Can I pass on any assets while I am still alive ('lifetime gifts') or on death?
☐ How can I mitigate any tax that is unavoidable?

Planning can be as simple as gifting money – there is a specific annual exemption of £3,000 as well as any amounts you can afford to make each year 'out of income' (ie that forms part of your normal expenditure and does not reduce your normal standard of living). Or, you could take out an insurance policy to cover the tax on your estate. Great care should be taken to make sure that you are not the beneficiary of the insurance policy, as this merely forms part of your estate on death and defeats the object completely.

However, if you have not identified that you have got an IHT issue until you are late on in life, the premiums on the policy may preclude this as a viable option. So the advice remains: plan early and review regularly.

As with CGT, a husband and wife are chargeable to IHT separately, so that any available exemptions apply to each of them and each can make transfers free of tax up to the nil threshold.

Lifetime gifts

Various exemptions exist to exclude some gifts from being chargeable to IHT (the annual exemption and gifts from income mentioned above), but others include gifts in consideration of marriage (£5,000 per parent and less for others), and capital transfers for family maintenance.

Where gifts are made that have no exemption, a running total is required of 'chargeable' lifetime transfers (CLTs) and once these exceed the £263,000 threshold, IHT becomes payable.

To encourage lifetime giving, CLTs above the threshold are only taxed at 20 per cent (unless the gift is within seven years of death).

IHT works in seven-year cycles and CLTs are removed from the running total on the seventh anniversary of the original gift. Although, as explained below, gifts in the previous seven years can be re-instated, making it really a 14-year cycle.

Unless you are extremely wealthy, it is quite probable that transfers in your lifetime will be completely exempt, or 'potentially exempt', ie they will only be subject to tax if you die within seven years of the transfer. But dying within seven years of making a potentially exempt transfer (PET) will make that gift chargeable and would make any PETs in the previous seven years also come back into charge.

Where a PET comes back into charge because of death within seven years of its transfer, it is included in the estate at the time of the gift rather than the death. Consequently, where an asset is growing in value, it would be advisable, for IHT purposes, to make a lifetime gift of it as any subsequent gain in value is in the hands of the recipient and not the donor.

However, the CGT effect cannot be ignored – a gift of an asset chargeable to CGT would generate a tax liability unless gift relief is available (see previous section).

As a lot of people's major asset is their house, various schemes have been dreamed up to try and remove their house from their possession and yet still allow them to live in it. But legislation from 1986 addressed this issue making 'gifts with reservation of benefit' treated as still belonging to the donor and hence no gift at all.

You can gift your house to your children should you so wish to remove it from your estate, but you would then have to pay rent (that the children would be taxed on) at a market rate for the rest of your life to remain in the house. And it has not been unknown for children to evict parents.

Various schemes of far greater complexity have been devised in recent years regarding the removal of a home from an estate, but these have now been thwarted since the 2004 Budget with the introduction of the 'pre-owned assets' legislation. This new law imposes an income tax charge on anyone that has dispossessed themselves of any asset but has contrived to retain the right to benefit from it.

Although many lifetime transfers are PETs, the main category of transfers that are immediately chargeable to IHT is transfers to discretionary trusts – but tax is only paid if the nil rate band is breached. A discretionary trust is where no one has a specific right to income from the trust and it is the trustees who decide how much income to pay to the beneficiaries.

Position on death

Death is effectively treated as the ultimate transfer of your whole estate, plus any PETs and chargeable lifetime transfers from the previous seven years. A sliding scale is applied to the value of the transfers within the seven years, reducing to 20 per cent by the sixth year.

Assets are valued as if sold on the open market and various reliefs are available:

☐ Business property relief – the rate of relief depends on length of ownership, but the relief covers a business or interest in a business, unquoted share-holdings, and land, buildings or equipment used in a company controlled by the deceased, or the deceased's own business or partnership.

☐ Agricultural property relief – this applies to agricultural land and buildings ancillary thereto, including the farmhouse. There are specific time limits, but the property must have been occupied for agricultural purposes by the deceased or a tenant, thus enabling the relief to apply to agricultural investment property.

8 | Converting Farm Buildings

Rupert Clark, Smiths Gore

This chapter, in the form of a case study, aims to take the reader through the step-by-step process of taking a development site through the development process – transforming it from a potential asset to a real one.

BACKGROUND

In this case study, it is assumed that we are looking at a range of listed farm buildings set in a rural location that are considered to be redundant for the purposes of modern-day agriculture. There is good access to the site via a farm track that leads off an 'A' road and visibility in both directions is good.

The buildings themselves are in a relatively poor state of repair and would require in the order of £20,000 spending on them within five years to ensure that they are kept in a wind- and weather-tight condition and are preserved for the future. At present, the buildings represent a liability and, without investment, have no potential for generating an income sufficient to meet that liability.

The owner has considered selling the buildings in their current condition to rid himself of the liability and has been advised that in their current state and subject to agricultural use, they are worth about £150,000. He has however rightly decided to consider the alternative options open to him prior to making any final decisions to sell. His options and the process in reaching a decision on the conversion of the buildings are the subject of this case study.

METHODOLOGY

A logical approach is required to assess the opportunities and feasibility for the conversion and change of use of a range of buildings of this type. The following sections set out the order in which such a study should be made and outline the issues that need careful consideration prior to drawing the appropriate conclusions and should be tackled.

The aim is to produce a feasibility study that provides a detailed analysis of a planned development or the options for a site. It should provide all the information required to allow a reasoned decision to be taken as to which option to pursue or whether or not to proceed.

PLANNING

There would be no purpose in spending further time on this matter if the planning prognosis was poor. Therefore a careful investigation of the planning issues by consulting the Planning Authority's Local Plan and understanding their new Local Development Framework, or the progress that they have made towards the preparation of one, is essential. In addition a discussion with the Local Highways Authority representative should indicate whether or not the intended development would result in an intensification of highway use that would cause them to either support or object to a planning application. Their support is essential to the success of such an application.

Other issues to consider are the effects on wildlife and landscape, sound and light pollution, provision of services to the development and any designations that affect the buildings and their surroundings.

The primary changes of use that are likely to be considered are a residential conversion, conversion to offices or workshops (B1 of the Use Classes Order) or conversion to storage or warehousing (B8). While the Planners will favour the B1 or B8 option as they are directed to do so by central government guidance (Planning Policy Statement 7), the residential option should not be discounted at this stage.

Even at this early stage, it is important to approach the planning officers in a professional manner. For example, showing them professional schematic drawings of what you are proposing in terms of access, car parking, landscaping and the conversion work required will demonstrate that you have thought the proposals through and will assist your case. Establishing a professional relationship will pay dividends later.

INITIAL DESIGN AND DEVELOPMENT ASSESSMENT

Assuming that all planning implications are positive, the next stage is to have a detailed measured survey of the buildings undertaken and from that, an initial draft scheme drawing prepared. Although there are firms that can produce these kinds of drawings at low cost, it is recommended that an experienced architect or building surveyor do this for you where the conversion of an old building is concerned. They will be able to provide you with advice and an assessment on how best to approach the physical conversion of the building. It will also provide an initial indication of the net internal area (NIA) of the building, from which an assessment of the potential rent can then be made.

At this point, practical issues such as the provision of services, car parking and security need to be considered as these can lead to considerable expense in some cases where, for example, a new electricity mains supply is needed. Lack of initial research can lead to a painfully expensive discovery later on when it may be too late to stop.

Investigation should also be made into whether a broadband internet connection is available and, if not, when it might be available. This has become a prerequisite for many commercial tenants. Lack of broadband will hinder marketing and impact on rent.

THE MARKET

An assessment of the local rental markets for the various conversion options must then be made. This will lead to an estimated rent that may be derived from the development. Consideration should be given as to the anticipated robustness of the market over the coming months.

At a later stage in the feasibility study, one will need to decide whether to develop speculatively (ie without a tenant for the property arranged in advance) or develop on the basis of having agreed a contract with a tenant to occupy the buildings before they are built. This is known as a pre-let agreement. This means that prior to investment, development, and risk taking, one has contracted with a tenant to an agreed form of lease and to development being undertaken to an agreed specification and deadline for completion (and the property therefore has a known occupier). The advantages and disadvantages of a pre-let agreement are illustrated in Figure 8.1.

Points in favour of a pre-let agreement	Points against a pre-let agreement
Certainty of income	Strict time frame for development
Easier to secure borrowing (banks like certainty)	Reliance on the contractor to perform
No gamble on the fortunes of the rental market	No account taken of growing rental market
No risk of void post-development	Impact of cost increases on development performance

Figure 8.1 Advantages and disadvantages of pre-let agreements

DEVELOPMENT COSTS

An assessment of the budgeted development costs needs to be made. Depending upon the scale of the development it may be wise to engage a quantity surveyor to provide this assessment and to ensure its accuracy. Standard conversion costs are available from a number of sources (for example, the Building Cost Information Service of the Royal Institution of Chartered Surveyors) but a quantity surveyor will be able to provide more accurate costings and assumptions.

If the building is listed, the Planning Authority is likely to want to influence the building materials used. Costlier materials are inevitable and should be budgeted for. Listed building consent will also have to be applied for which has time and cost implications. Again, using an experienced surveyor will allow you to accurately take these costs into account.

Careful consideration needs to be given to the level of specification to be employed. A high or low specification will have an impact on rent. For example, is an air conditioning system to be incorporated or is the building to be heated by night storage heaters? These kinds of decisions will impact on the attractiveness of the development to potential tenants and will also affect the rent that can be charged.

A view needs to be taken on the timing of the development and adjustments to the budgetary development costs will need to be made as appropriate to reflect anticipated build cost inflation.

FUNDING

Is the development to be funded using cash, by bank borrowing or by a combination of the two? Or is a joint venture party to be sought who will assist financing the development and share in both the risk and reward? Decisions need to be taken as the performance and potentially viability of the development could be at stake.

Grant aid should be investigated. Both Regional Development Agencies and DEFRA (Rural Enterprise Scheme) offer grant aid for this type of development. However, the criteria for success are tightly drawn and the application in both cases will require a planning consent to be in place and tender prices obtained in advance of submission. Therefore, a considerable amount of work and investment will be required in advance with no certainty of success.

OPPORTUNITY COST

The opportunity cost of the development should be assessed. You should account for the liability for future repairs to maintain the building should development not be undertaken as well as the returns available from other uses of the development money.

APPRAISAL

Armed with both the rental information and budgetary development cost together with a decision as to how the development is to be funded, one can then proceed to analyse the potential performance of the development. This is worth undertaking in two ways.

Cash on cash

Firstly, you could look at simple cash on cash return on the investment. This is simply a function of the rental return over the development cost providing a percentage return. It represents a simple snapshot in time providing a form of analysis that is easy to understand and is favoured by many.

Internal rate of return

The second method is more complex and provides a timed analysis of the investment return in the form of an internal rate of return.

This is calculated by assessing initial site value, the flow of rental income over the life of the development (this flow is discounted to allow for the eroding effect of inflation on the rent due in the future) and the sale value of the site at the end of that period. These combine to give an overall return or internal rate of return for the development.

Smiths Gore has developed a Rural Development Appraisal model that can make such a calculation, allowing for a wide range of variables. It will give an internal rate of return calculation, including and excluding opportunity cost and over a number of different timescales (normally 5, 10, 15 and 20 years). In addition, the appraisal will indicate the loan repayment period (assuming borrowing is used to fund the development), and will provide an assessment of post-development value.

COLLATERAL IMPACT

Consideration should be given to the impact of a conversion on the neighbouring property or the remainder of the farm. Often owing to the current state of farming, this form of diversification will be seen as a welcome form of diversifying income and spreading risk between markets. However, if a sale is being contemplated then it may be to the detriment of the remainder of the farm. Traffic and the increased number of people on the site are the most obvious impacts but there are others. Also think about other current uses of the property. For example, if the conversion is near an important pheasant shoot, can the shooting continue?

Or if the site is close to the owner's house, will the owner and his or her family put up with the noise and other disturbances that such a development will generate? Will the development impact on security?

OPTIONS

Using the above framework, an analysis for each of the development options can be undertaken. The outcome of these analyses can then be compared and a conclusion drawn as to which approach to take.

RISK

In undertaking a development of this nature, one is inevitably exposed to risk, including:

- ☐ a downward turn in the rental market;
- ☐ significant build cost inflation;
- ☐ risk that the building contractor's business fails part way through the development;
- ☐ not finding a tenant and so having void periods.

An assessment of the risks needs to be made and where possible these need to be managed or limited. They can be factored into your appraisal through the use of sophisticated models like the Rural Development Appraisal model.

MAKING A DECISION

Having drawn together all issues summarized above and with the development analysis at hand, a reasoned decision can then be taken as to whether or not to proceed to the next stage, the planning application.

RE-ASSESSMENT

Barn conversions rarely happen quickly and during the preparation and development phases, markets will change. It is therefore important to review the analysis at each stage and particularly prior to taking a decision to incur significant cost and proceed with development.

If there are likely to be further development opportunities, then it is also worth undertaking a post-development appraisal from which mistakes can be identified and lessons applied next time.

In our experience, the key to successful development is control – control of the planning process, appointing the right contractor, control of the contractor's work, control of costs and leasing to the right tenants once the property is converted. With control, this type of development can be a profitable, complementary part of a farm or estate.

9 VAT on Listed Buildings and other Residential Conversions

Phil Salmon, haysmacintyre

Probably one of the biggest myths surrounding VAT is that it does not apply to listed buildings. Unfortunately, the reality is that the VAT relief that is available in connection with work on listed buildings is far more limited. This chapter aims to set out the true situation, so that unexpected VAT costs can be avoided. It will also cover the VAT provisions surrounding the conversion of buildings into residential accommodation.

WORK ON BUILDINGS THAT ARE LISTED

The first point to address is the position surrounding listed buildings, and the first myth to de-bunk is that all listed buildings qualify for full VAT relief. The legislation refers not to a listed building, but to a 'protected building', and a protected building is defined as a listed building that is intended to remain as, or become a dwelling, or a building that will be used solely for a relevant residential or relevant charitable purpose. The meaning of these last two categories will be covered later, but the key point is that if the building that is listed is intended for use for a commercial purpose, then no relief is available.

The second key point to bear in mind is that, even if the building is 'protected', ie listed and to be used as a dwelling or for relevant residential or charitable purposes, not all works qualify for the relief. In order to qualify, the works must be an 'approved alteration' to the building in question.

In order to be approved, the work that is being carried out must have both required and received listed building consent. Crucially, that consent must have been granted in writing before the works commence, and one common pitfall is commencing work prior to the consent having been granted. Even if a resolution to grant the consent has been given, if you commence the work before the written consent is actually given, you will lose the VAT relief.

The next logical question is what constitutes an alteration. Essentially, the word bears its ordinary, everyday, meaning. The VAT legislation specifically rules out works of repair or maintenance from being regarded as alterations, except where those repairs or maintenance arise only because of an alteration, for example, re-plastering walls surrounding a new opening in a wall.

It follows from that example that HM Revenue & Customs do not view an alteration as being restricted to the external view of the building, and indeed they regard an alteration as any works to the fabric of the building that alters it in a meaningful way. The fabric of the building would include walls, roofs, stairs, floors, the plumbing and wiring, so a building could remain externally unchanged, but have a completely new internal layout, and this could qualify as an alteration.

There have been numerous VAT tribunal cases on the question of where the borderline lies between what is an alteration, and what is a repair, but things like replacing rotten windows with new ones would probably be regarded as a repair, even if the new windows looked visibly different from the old. This is because the need for replacement came before the desire for an alteration.

For the avoidance of doubt, the zero rate only applies to the services supplied by the building contractor(s) involved. It does not apply to the work carried out by any professionals involved, such as architects, or surveyors. Nor are goods (eg new window frames) zero-rated unless they are fitted by the contractor who sells the goods to you.

So we have outlined what qualifies for the zero rate, but not mentioned how the relief is obtained. Quite simply, the contractor who is providing the service does not charge VAT, so there is no VAT to reclaim from HM Revenue & Customs. If you are contemplating carrying out such alterations, then it is always sensible to discuss the question of VAT when selecting a contractor, and to ensure that they are aware that the work qualifies.

From the contractor's point of view, he or she is the person taking the risk that HM Revenue & Customs could later say that the work should have had VAT added, so he or she would be well advised to obtain a copy of the listed building consent, and to take photographs of the work as it progresses to demonstrate that it is an alteration.

The sorts of work that would typically qualify for the zero rate, in addition to straightforward alterations to existing houses are the conversion of listed farm buildings, often barns, into a dwelling. As mentioned above, relevant residential and relevant charitable buildings also qualify for this relief, and such buildings are defined as follows. A building is a 'relevant residential' building if it is intended for use for, essentially, institutional accommodation, such as a children's, or an old persons' home.

A building is intended for use for a relevant charitable purpose if it is intended to be used either as a village hall, or something very similar that provides social or recreational facilities for the local community; or if it is to be used by a charity in carrying out activities that are either provided free of charge, or for a charge that is below cost and well below what would normally be charged by a commercial organization carrying on the same activities.

This last category has proved the most problematic with HM Revenue & Customs applying a very narrow interpretation of what can be regarded as being used as a 'village hall', or for other 'relevant charitable purposes'. There is enough case law on this point for a separate article, so if you believe you may qualify to obtain the zero rate under the relevant charitable heading, you should seek professional advice on the circumstances of your own particular case.

WORK ON BUILDINGS THAT ARE NOT LISTED

There are rules that provide a similar relief if one is converting a building into residential accommodation and it is not listed. In such circumstances, the construction services do not qualify to be zero rated, and will bear VAT.

If you are carrying out such a conversion as a developer, and intend to sell either the freehold, or a leasehold interest of more than 21 years, then the first such grant of a building can itself be zero rated. The significance of this is that, if you register for VAT, you can recover most of the VAT you incur on the conversion costs, but will not have to charge the purchaser VAT.

This treatment only applies to buildings that are converted into dwellings or buildings that are used for relevant residential purposes. It does not apply to buildings that are converted into ones to be used for relevant charitable purposes. Nor does it apply to any subsequent sales or lettings and, most importantly, it does not apply to any sale or letting for a period of up to 21 years. For the avoidance of doubt, I should point out that the rules given here apply to England and Wales only, as Scottish land law has different (though similar) definitions.

If you carry out such a conversion, and use the building for short-term lettings, then such lettings are exempt from VAT, and unlike a zero rated supply, exemption does not allow you to claim back the VAT on costs.

It is stated above that registering for VAT allows you to claim back most of the VAT you incur, and this is because the VAT on certain items, most notably 'white goods' and most fitted furniture (kitchen units being a notable exception) cannot be recovered.

DOING IT YOURSELF

If you plan to convert a barn, or some other non-residential building into a dwelling for yourself, then there is a mechanism which allows you to reclaim the VAT you will incur to put you in the same position as if you purchased such a conversion from a developer. This is called the DIY Builders and Converters Scheme. It applies to the conversion of a building into a dwelling, and also a building that will be used for relevant residential purposes. It can also be used in connection with a building intended for use solely for a relevant charitable purpose, but only in the context of constructing a brand new building, as opposed to the conversion of a pre-existing building.

The scheme is something of a misnomer in that you do not have to physically 'do it yourself'. It does apply if you employ a contractor, and involves the submission of a claim to HM Revenue & Customs to recover the VAT that has been charged. Only one such claim can be made when the work has been completed, so there is a significant cash flow disadvantage compared with, say, a developer making quarterly reclaims through his or her VAT returns.

In addition, the claim must be made within three months of the date of the certificate of completion from the local authority. This tends to be adhered to rigorously by HM Revenue & Customs, so the advice here is to get into the habit, from day one, of making sure that you have a complete set of VAT invoices from the contractor, so that you can submit a timely claim.

The claim form must be accompanied by original invoices, the certificate of completion, and a copy of the planning consent. You cannot recover VAT on 'white goods', fitted furniture, carpets, or other items that are not seen by HM Revenue & Customs as being ordinarily incorporated within a building.

VAT RATE

The previous two sections mentioned that construction services that do not fall within the zero rate will bear VAT, but, since 2001, some work may qualify for VAT to be charged at a reduced rate of only 5 per cent, as opposed to the standard rate of 17.5 per cent. This rate applies to what are referred to as qualifying services supplied in the course of certain residential conversions.

The provisions are complex, but essentially apply when a building will be used for residential purposes which are not the same after the conversion as they were before it, or where a different number of residential units are created. For example, when a house is renovated, it remains a house after the work, and the 5 per cent rate does not apply. But, if a house was converted into flats, or a relevant residential building, then the reduced rate does apply because a different number of dwellings, or a different type of residential accommodation have been created.

Similarly, if the building had never previously been lived in, and was converted into a house, or a relevant residential building, or some other type of multiple occupancy dwelling, the reduced rate applies, because one has created residential accommodation where none previously existed. In addition, if a building has not been lived in for the previous three years, and is renovated or altered, the reduced rate can also apply.

The types of service that can be supplied at this 5 per cent rate include works to the fabric of the building, and also works within the immediate site of the building that are connected with providing water, power, heat, drainage, waste disposal, security or access to the building.

From the above, it can be seen that the rules regarding VAT and construction are far from straightforward, and it is perfectly possible to have projects where some work is zero rated, some reduced rated, and some standard rated. The aim of this chapter is to alert you to some of the potential problems, and if there is one key piece of advice, it is that it is far better to take professional advice before embarking on a project than after work has begun.

haysmacintyre  | vision through partnership

Looking at tax efficient wealth and income generation from your estate?

Whether you are considering wealth or income generation from your estate through lease, development, change of use or sale, we have the specialists to provide the necessary financial and tax advice (particularly if listed buildings are involved). For an informal and confidential discussion, please contact our landed estates team.

VAT

Graham Elliot (Partner) 020 7969 5610
gelliot@haysmacintyre.com
Phil Salmon (Senior Manager) 020 7969 5611
psalmon@haysmacintyre.com

**Tax and
other issues**

Alastair McDonald (Senior Partner) 020 7969 5501
amcdonald@haysmacintyre.com
George Crowther (Partner) 020 7969 5547
gcrowther@haysmacintyre.com

Fairfax House
15 Fulwood Place, London WC1V 6AY
T: 020 7969 5500   F: 020 7969 5600
marketing@haysmacintyre.com
www.haysmacintyre.com

haysmacintyre Chartered Accountants provides auditing and assurance, business and personal taxation, corporate finance, financial services and business support.

Part Three:

The Operation of Rural Businesses

10 **Business Tenancies**

Duncan Sigournay, Thring Townsend

INTRODUCTION

In seeking to generate more income from rural property, there are often opportunities to let buildings (and indeed other land) for non-agricultural commercial uses. These opportunities may range from letting out a building to a farming contractor to store his or her machinery, to a multi-million pound conversion of existing farm buildings to create a rural business park.

When considering such diversification, landowners must be careful not to fall foul of the regulations that govern the conversion and use of buildings. Similarly, they must also be aware of the legislation that governs such business lettings.

This chapter sets out the issues that must be considered in relation to such lettings and reviews the problems that can arise during the tenancy. In particular the following matters will be considered:

- ☐ the initial appraisal;
- ☐ the basic provisions of the Landlord and Tenant Act 1954;
- ☐ termination of a business tenancy;
- ☐ compensation issues;
- ☐ 'contracting out' of the 1954 Act;
- ☐ stamp duty land tax;
- ☐ registration;
- ☐ alternative contractual arrangements – licences, tenancies at will.

THE INITIAL APPRAISAL

A building may become available for commercial letting in a number of ways: the farmer may have no further use for a building; an approach may be made by a commercial business; or, in a drive to generate more income within an existing business, management changes may result in the present activities being housed in fewer buildings, releasing space for other uses. Traditional buildings are often left unused because they are awkward, labour intensive and, perhaps, the livestock that used to occupy them may have disappeared. If in a sound condition, such buildings can be upgraded by conversion to provide useful commercial space.

Before embarking on a planning application or investing money to facilitate the letting, a detailed appraisal needs to be undertaken. It is important to assess the following factors at the outset:

- [ ] the nature of the uses to which the building may be put;
- [ ] the effect that any new activity will have on the farmhouse, on the enjoyment of the property and on the day-to-day running of the farm;
- [ ] the potential market for a tenancy of the building;
- [ ] the costs to be incurred in seeking planning permission and the project costs to repair and improve the building so that it is fit for its new use;
- [ ] the rental value that can reasonably be expected;
- [ ] the capital cost against the capital value of the scheme as completed.

If an analysis of these issues shows that there is relatively little impact on the existing business, that only a modest investment is required and that there is a reasonable prospect of letting and in due course re-letting the building, the owner may have confidence to proceed.

If an owner is a little uncertain but believes that there is a market for the building, it may be appropriate to go through the planning process to secure permission; thereafter the owner can look for a tenant and grant a lease on what is referred to (by surveyors) as a 'pre-let' basis: the tenancy is entered into – binding both parties – but its commencement, and the payment of rent, is delayed until the works are completed. This gives security to the owner before he or she invests in the conversion scheme.

If the cost of a conversion is substantial the owner should consider two issues: what effect that additional capital investment will have on his or her finances as the investment will have an effect on his or her balance sheet and perhaps borrowings. Secondly the appraisal must take a very realistic approach to the rents that are likely to be achieved, including allowances for voids (periods when the property is empty) and bad debts. Unless there is a real prospect of a positive return and rental growth, owners should proceed with caution.

Professional advice

If a landowner wants to let to a new tenant he or she must consider what terms are appropriate for the letting including length of term, repairing obligations and rent. Where it is proposed that the letting is to be for a long term or it covers more than the odd barn or shed, it would be sensible to go to an agent or a solicitor to discuss the whole proposal. It may seem an unnecessary expense but in the context of the overall scheme and associated investment such a move may prove invaluable.

Some landowners may want to rely on their agents to provide suitable documents. It should be remembered, however, that it is an offence for a person who is not a solicitor or barrister to directly or indirectly prepare a lease for a term of over three years in return for a fee. However, no offence is committed if the document was drawn up without any fee, gain or reward being demanded.

In addition, the Agricultural Tenancies Act 1995 does allow certain accredited persons to draw up farm business tenancies in excess of three years. Such accredited persons include: a full member of the Central Association of Agricultural Valuers; an associate or Fellow of the Incorporated Society of Valuers and Auctioneers or of the Royal Institution of Chartered Surveyors.

Leases for a term less than or equal to three years do not have to be by deed to transfer the legal estate but those greater than three years do.

CODE OF PRACTICE FOR COMMERCIAL LEASES

When considering entering into a business lease, consideration should be given to the second edition of the Code of Practice for Commercial Leases in England and Wales (issued by the DTLR in 2002).

The Code sets out a number of recommendations that parties to commercial leases should consider, both at the lease negotiation stage and subsequently during the lease term itself.

THE LANDLORD AND TENANT ACT, 1954, PART II

A person who is given, or in practice takes, exclusive possession of property will have a tenancy. Furthermore, if the property is to be used for business purposes it is likely that the tenancy will be governed by the Landlord and Tenant Act 1954 (the 1954 Act). It is important to note that the 1954 Act was amended in 2004 and as such procedures that landlords and tenants previously employed in relation to business tenancies may not now be appropriate.

Business occupation

The Act 'applies to any tenancy where the property comprised in the tenancy is or includes premises which are occupied by the tenant and are so occupied for the purposes of a business carried on by him or for those and other purposes' – Section 23(1).

In the context of the Act 'business' is widely defined. It 'includes a trade, profession or employment and includes any activity carried on by – a body of persons whether corporate or unincorporate'.

The tenant does not have to occupy the whole premises to qualify for protection. Nor does he or she have to use the premises exclusively for business purposes. Premises used for mixed purposes are within the Act. So a cottage could be included with a workshop and the whole treated as business tenancy provided the occupation of the cottage is incidental to the business use and not a sham; in these circumstances the cottage would not be covered by the Housing Act 1988.

Indeed, for the purposes of the Act 'premises' can include bare land, for example gallops for training racehorses.

What is not a business tenancy?

The Act does not apply to:

- ☐ licences;
- ☐ incorporeal hereditaments (eg easements, profits);
- ☐ Agricultural Holdings Act tenancies;
- ☐ farm business tenancies governed by the Agricultural Tenancies Act 1995;
- ☐ mining leases;
- ☐ service tenancies;
- ☐ short fixed-term tenancies of less than six months provided the tenancy does not contain provisions for renewing the term or extending it beyond six months or the tenant and any predecessor in his or her business have not been in occupation for more than 12 months in total.

TERMINATION OF A BUSINESS TENANCY

Termination of the tenancy by the landlord

Under the provisions of the Act a tenant of a business lease has security of tenure so that the tenancy continues after the original fixed term has expired, unless the agreement is brought to an end in accordance with the provisions of the Act. The only exception to this is where the tenancy, or a superior tenancy, is forfeited under a provision in the tenancy agreement.

In order to bring a tenancy to an end, the landlord must give between 6 and 12 months' notice, expiring on or after the contractual term date. The landlord's notice must be given on a prescribed form stating the grounds on which he or she opposes the grant of a new tenancy. As the time limits and procedures are strict, a landlord should employ a solicitor, well versed in the law of landlord and tenant, to act for him or her.

Termination of the tenancy by the tenant

A fixed-term tenancy can be brought to an end by the tenant giving three months' notice in writing to expire at the end of the term or or by leaving the premises by the end of the lease. The tenant would then no longer have to pay rent or fulfil other obligations beyond the end of the lease. If the tenant fails to do either the tenancy will continue. Thereafter the tenant is required to give three months' notice to terminate the tenancy.

Alternatively, the tenant who wants a new tenancy to replace the existing one can serve on the landlord a request in statutory form for a new tenancy. This must specify a date for the start of the tenancy not less than 6 nor more than 12 months ahead. It must not be on a date before the existing tenancy would expire or could be determined. The right to initiate a request for a new tenancy only exists where the tenant has a fixed-term tenancy exceeding a year or where the tenancy is for a certain term and then from year to year.

A landlord wishing to oppose renewal must serve a counter-notice within two months of the tenant's request – the counter-notice must set out the grounds for opposing the tenant's application.

Grounds for opposing a new tenancy

Provided the landlord has specified one or more of the following grounds in the statutory notice to terminate the tenancy he or she can seek to prevent the grant of a new tenancy to the tenant. The grounds available to the landlord are:

- [ ] breach of the tenant's repairing obligations;
- [ ] persistent delays in paying rent;
- [ ] substantial breaches of the tenant's other obligations, or any other reason connected with the tenant's use or management of the premises;
- [ ] the provision of suitable alternative accommodation;
- [ ] where the current tenancy is a sub-letting of part only of the property comprised in a head-lease and the reversioner of that head-lease can demonstrate that the property could be let more economically as a whole;
- [ ] that the landlord intends to demolish, reconstruct or carry out substantial works of construction;
- [ ] that the landlord intends to occupy the premises for the purposes of a business carried on by himself or herself (or of a company that he or she controls) or as his or her residence. This ground is not available to a landlord who has purchased his or her interest in the property within the preceding five years.

The new tenancy

If the landlord is not successful in his or her opposition to the grant of a new tenancy, the Court can grant a tenancy for a period not exceeding 15 years. The terms of the tenancy will be those agreed by the parties or in default of agreement those imposed by the Court. The Court will have regard to the terms of the former tenancy and all the relevant circumstances.

Once the order is made the tenant has a limited time in which to refuse to take the tenancy. The Court must then revoke the order. It has, however, discretion to order that the former tenancy shall continue for a period that will allow the landlord an opportunity to re-let.

The rent

The landlord and tenant can fix a market rent for the premises. A short lease may have no rent review provision but a well-drafted longer lease should contain a rent review clause that will operate at stated times throughout the lease. Where the original fixed term has expired or where there is a periodic term, the landlord may wish to increase the rent. In order to do so he or she must serve a notice to terminate the existing tenancy. This will set in motion the statutory renewal process, which will result in the tenant being granted a new tenancy at the current market rent.

Interim rent

Once a landlord has served a notice to terminate the existing tenancy (or a tenant has served a request for a new tenancy) a landlord can apply to the Court for the payment of an interim rent.

COMPENSATION ISSUES

Compensation for disturbance of the tenant

The tenant is entitled to compensation where the Court refuses to grant a new tenancy on the grounds that the property could be let more profitably as a whole or that the landlord intends to develop the property or occupy it himself or herself. These are all situations where there has been no fault on the part of the tenant. The tenancy is terminated for the benefit of the landlord.

The tenant is also entitled to compensation where the above grounds are specified in the landlord's notice and as a consequence the tenant does not make, or withdraws, his or her application for a new tenancy.

The landlord must pay the tenant a prescribed multiple of the rateable value. For most cases the multiplier is 1, making the compensation equal to the rateable value: where the business has been carried out in the premises for the whole of the 14 years preceding the termination of the current tenancy the compensation is twice the rateable value.

Compensation for improvements

By virtue of the Landlord and Tenant Act 1927 unless there is a covenant in the lease preventing the tenant from making improvements he or she may be able to claim compensation on the termination of the lease.

However, the Landlord and Tenant Act 1927 does not lay down a list of tenant's improvements for which the landlord must pay compensation at the end of the tenancy. As such, there is nothing in it to compare with the list of agricultural improvements for which compensation is payable under the Agricultural Holdings Act 1986. However, the following points should be noted:

- ☐ an improvement must add to the letting value of the holding;
- ☐ an improvement does not include any trade or other fixture that the tenant is by law entitled to remove. Generally, what is fixed to the property becomes part of it and cannot be removed. But trade fixtures (eg petrol pumps, partitions) can be removed provided it is not forbidden by the terms of the lease;
- ☐ an improvement must be 'reasonable and suitable to the character of the premises';
- ☐ an improvement should not diminish the value of any other property belonging to the same landlord;
- ☐ a claim cannot be made for an improvement made by the tenant where he or she has entered into a contract to make the improvements and received valuable consideration.

If a tenant is to be successful in a claim for compensation he or she must serve notice on his or her landlord of the intended improvement together with specification and plan. The landlord has three months to object.

If the landlord does not object the tenant can proceed with the improvement. If the landlord does object the tenant can apply to the County Court or the Chancery Division of the High Court. The landlord can elect to do the improvement himself or herself. If the landlord does so he or she will not have to pay compensation to the tenant and will be entitled to a reasonable increase in rent by agreement, or as determined by the Court. Where the tenant carries out the improvement, it must be made within the agreed time.

A tenant who has duly completed an improvement may require his or her landlord to give him or her a certificate to that effect. If the landlord does not give a certificate, then the tenant can apply to the Court.

Sometimes improvements have to be made to fulfil statutory requirements. The procedure described above will apply in such cases, except that the landlord cannot object to the improvement. Compensation is payable at the end of the tenancy for such improvements.

The claim for compensation must be made within three months of the first action taken to determine the tenancy, which may be the service of a Notice to Quit or under the Landlord and Tenant Act 1954, or be effected by forfeiture or re-entry. Where the tenancy expires at the end of a fixed term, the claim must be made not more than six nor less than three months before the termination. The claim must be in writing and signed by the tenant, his or her solicitor or agent and must give a description of the premises, the trade or business and a statement of the nature of the claim, the particulars of the improvement and date of completion, together with the cost and amount claimed.

Generally, a tenant must quit the premises to obtain compensation. Disputed cases have to be referred to the Court for settlement.

Section 1(1) of the Landlord and Tenant Act 1927 lays down the rules for assessing compensation. They are as follows: the sum must not exceed 1) the net addition to the value of the premises directly resulting from the improvement; or 2) the reasonable cost of carrying out the improvement at the termination of the tenancy less the cost of putting the works into a reasonable state of repair except so far as it is covered by the tenant's repairing liabilities.

Under point 1 above, account must be taken of the proposed use of the premises after termination of the tenancy, and if demolition, alteration or change of use is proposed, that is to be taken into account also. In these circumstances, an improvement can be worth nothing.

Previously tenants could claim compensation from a landlord whose misrepresentation had led the court to refuse the grant of a new tenancy. The compensation provisions have been extended to enable a tenant to claim where he or she has been induced not to apply to the court or indeed withdraws his or her application due to misrepresentation.

'CONTRACTING OUT' OF THE SECURITY OF TENURE PROVISIONS OF THE 1954 ACT

Notwithstanding the previous section regarding the tenant's ability to effectively demand a new tenancy at the end of the original contractual term, it is possible for the parties to 'contract out' of such provisions. Thus, at the end of the contractual term of a 'contracted out' business tenancy the tenant neither has the right to remain in possession nor indeed to activate the statutory procedure for a new tenancy.

'Contracting out' procedure

Prior to 1 June 2004 it was necessary for the parties to submit a joint application to the court before the tenancy was granted.

Now, however, instead of the rather cumbersome and time-consuming court application, the landlord will be entitled to serve the tenant with a 'health warning' at least 14 days prior to the commencement of the lease, stating that the lease is to be excluded from the security of tenure provisions of the 1954 Act. The tenant in turns completes a simple declaration confirming receipt of the landlord's notice. Where the requisite 14 days prior notice cannot be given the tenant will be required to sign a statutory declaration stating that he has received the 'health warning' and is aware of its consequences. The new procedures are intended to ensure that the tenant is aware of the consequences of excluding security of tenure and at the same time removing the need to obtain the approval of the court.

One should always take professional advice in relation to the issue of such 'warning notices' since the ramifications of doing it incorrectly are that the tenant may gain security of tenure where otherwise it was not intended.

STAMP DUTY LAND TAX

Stamp duty land tax (SDLT), which replaced stamp duty in 2003, may be payable on the grant of a lease depending on the amount of the premium, if any, the length of the term and the rent payable. The lease, which is the document signed by the landlord and held by the tenant, should be lodged for stamping with duty at the appropriate rate within 30 days of the grant. It is for the tenant to arrange for the stamping of the lease and he should be advised of his obligation.

Leases that are liable for SDLT but have not been stamped cannot be produced in court. It is possible for documents to be stamped late on the payment of a penalty. A new penalty regime was introduced by Finance Act 1999 for instruments on or after 1 October 1999. In summary:

☐ A penalty is levied on instruments not presented for stamping within 30 days of execution.
☐ Interest on unpaid stamp duty starts to run 30 days after the date of execution.
☐ If a lease is granted for seven years or more, it falls within Finance Act 1931, Section 28 and must be produced to the Inland Revenue in accordance with the requirements of that Section.

The rules on, and rates of, stamp duty change from time to time. The current position and more detailed advice should be obtained from the Office of the Controller of Stamps, Inland Revenue, South West Wing, Bush House, Strand, London WC2B 4QN.

REGISTRATION

If a lease is granted for over 7 years the title to the lease must be registered at HM Land Registry if the lessee is to secure legal title.

It must be stressed that it is important for both landlords and prospective tenants to be professionally advised where leases of this length are being prepared.

ALTERNATIVE CONTRACTUAL ARRANGEMENTS

Tenancies at will

Where a tenant is let into occupation pending the conclusion of a formal lease he or she will have a tenancy at will. For the avoidance of doubt as to the exact arrangement the agreement should be in writing. Provided that it is clearly understood that the tenant is let in under those conditions then the tenancy can be terminated by either party if the negotiations subsequently break down. Given the inherent uncertainty of a tenancy at will, most tenants will be eager to formalize the main lease as a matter of priority.

As mentioned previously, a tenancy at will is not protected by the Landlord and Tenant Act 1954 and therefore the 'contracting out' procedure highlighted earlier is not required; however, this does not remove the need for such a procedure prior to completion of the main tenancy agreement.

Licences

The essence of a licence is that the licensee (occupier) is not granted exclusive possession of the property. This contrasts with a tenancy that requires the tenant to have exclusive occupation of the premises. Accordingly, even if a document is called a licence, or indeed the parties intended it to be a licence, it is quite possible that as a matter of law such an agreement (whether oral or in writing) will amount to a tenancy.

Typically, a licence can be used for property used for storage purposes. In such cases the licensee is granted the right to store specified goods within the building in a specified area that may vary from time to time. The owner remains in possession and control of the premises.

In order to create a licence the landowner must continue to use the property for his or her own purposes as well as giving the licensee certain rights. However, if the agreement amounts to nothing more than a 'sham', the courts will have little hesitation in declaring the agreement to be a tenancy. Clearly such a situation has far reaching ramifications for the landlord since, if the property is used for business purposes, the tenancy will benefit from the security of tenure provisions of the Landlord and Tenant Act 1954.

Alternatively, where the storage is not for business purposes, the possible existence of a tenancy should not cause too many problems. The tenancy will be governed by common law and, as such, can be terminated by giving notice equivalent to a full rental period.

However, extreme caution should be taken when considering granting a licence since potentially the agreement may ultimately be held to be a tenancy subject to the provisions of the Landlord and Tenant Act 1954.

SUMMARY

Clearly, for those landlords familiar with agricultural tenancy legislation the provisions of the Landlord and Tenant Act 1954 can appear a little daunting. However, it must be remembered that the 1954 Act is considerably more flexible than the agricultural tenancy legislation in terms of freedom of contract – thus enabling the parties to adapt their agreements more closely to their particular circumstances.

11 Business Licences and Regulations

Jonathan Reuvid

INTRODUCTION

There is no general legal requirement to apply for a licence to carry on a specific business that the purchaser of a business or property, or someone entering into the tenancy of existing business premises, must undertake. Permitted business use is attached to specific premises as a part of the planning process described in some detail in Chapter 3.

Some occupations, notably the registered professions, require that practitioners are registered members of the relevant professional body, usually involving qualification by examination. However, there are activities in the professional domain that can be carried out by unqualified people, provided, of course, that they do not claim professional accreditation to which they are not entitled. For example, the conveyancing of real estate, traditionally a lucrative part of solicitors' services, can now be carried out on behalf of others by individuals who are not members of the legal profession.

Regulation is often achieved by other means. For example, in taking on the tenancy of or buying a public house, although the premises have been licensed for that purpose, the incoming landlord is required to apply for a personal licence to serve alcoholic beverages on the premises to which other responsibilities are attached, such as the observance of authorized opening hours and the maintenance of good order. In granting a licence the Magistrates are not looking for a formal qualification but are influenced primarily by the good character of the applicant, with previous experience playing a part.

One range of service activity, which has been subjected to welcome regulation during the past 15 years, is that of financial advice. With the establishment of the Financial Services Authority, all aspects of financial services from banking to insurance, pensions, dealing in securities and including general financial advice are under permanent scrutiny. Individuals wishing to practise as intermediaries in the provision of financial services to members of the public are required to apply for registration as financial intermediaries. Applicants are required to demonstrate prescribed levels of knowledge and qualification.

Many business and commercial activities do not require qualification. Running a village shop or a garden centre does not demand formal qualification. Neither do contract gardeners, painters and decorators nor, for that matter, property developers. Second-hand car salesmen are generally unqualified, although the franchise holders of specific marques of new vehicles may be required by the manufacturer to subject their sales staff to company training programmes.

Nevertheless, there are classes of tradespeople for whom membership of a trade association is a practical necessity in order to carry on and develop their businesses. In particular, those engaged in the building trades and in the provision of maintenance services, such as electrical engineers, plumbers, timber treatment specialists and thatchers would find it difficult to operate as more than 'odd job' workers without a trade association affiliation for the reason that the providers of finance for home improvements will usually demand that the work be carried out by accredited tradespeople. Similarly, builders subcontracting their specialist work where warranties and indemnities are involved will need to satisfy their insurers' requirements. Membership of such trade associations may involve competence qualifications, but that is not invariably the case.

These occupational considerations will not be of more than passing interest to readers unless they are intending to set up their rural business in any of these fields. (Since there is a dearth of plumbers in many parts of the country, you might be tempted.)

However, there are other restrictions and regulations that apply to the use of land and buildings of which a general awareness is useful. Some regulations are of a specialist nature, such as the requirement under Section 11(6) of the Firearms Act 1968–1997 to approve a site for clay-pigeon shooting in order that a person may use a shotgun without a shotgun certificate on a designated area of land. Other regulations are of a more pervasive nature and this chapter provides overviews of employers' health and safety obligations, stemming from the Health and Safety at Work etc Act 1974, requirements under environmental law and the principles of the Data Protection Act 1984 to which all businesses are subject.

PERMISSION FOR CHANGE OF USE

Before turning to these three regulated areas, there is more to be said in respect of change of use, where an existing business with established use is purchased and the new owner wishes to extend the current use or conduct a quite different business on the premises without making any significant physical alteration to the premises themselves. The first question to resolve is whether or not you need to apply for planning permission.

Minor physical alterations

Planning permission is not always required. For example, changes to the inside of buildings or for small exterior alterations such as the installation of telephone connections and alarm boxes do not generally demand planning consent, although the listing authorities will need to approve most changes to listed buildings, particularly to Grade I and Grade II listed buildings. Other small changes, such as the erection of fences and walls below a certain height, have general planning permission for which a specific application is unnecessary. To be safe, you can check informally with the council whether your proposed 'development' needs planning permission. More formally, you can also apply for a Lawful Development Certificate on payment of a fee. If a certificate is refused, you can then either apply for planning permission, or appeal to the Secretary of State. The latter is likely to be a slower process.

Working from home

Working from home does not usually involve an application for planning permission. The key test is whether the overall character of the dwelling will change as a result of the business and permission probably will be needed if:

☐ your home will no longer be used mainly as a private residence;
☐ your business will result in a marked rise in traffic or people calling;
☐ your business will involve any activities unusual in a residential area;
☐ your business will disturb your neighbours at unreasonable hours or create other forms of nuisance such as noise or smells.

These issues involve value judgements and the first two are plainly a matter of degree. For example, at what point can it be said that the provision of bed and breakfast accommodation has changed a home into business premises? The third and fourth manifestations of carrying on a business at home are the most likely to provoke neighbours' complaints and to drive business owners into making a planning application, if they have not already done so.

Change of business use

Planning permission is not required when both the present and proposed uses fall within the same 'class' as defined in the Town and Country Planning (Use Classes) Order 1987. For example, a clothing shop may be changed to a greengrocer's without permission. It is also possible to change use between some classes without making an application. Details of the use classification system and the changes permitted by the Town and Country Planning (General Permitted Development) Order 1995 are summarized in Table 11.1.

Table 11.1 Use classes and changes not requiring a planning application

Use classes	Permitted transfers to
A1 Shops	Shops, post offices, travel agents, hair-dressers, funeral directors, dry cleaners, other A1
A2 Financial and professional services	Banks, building societies, betting offices, and other financial and professional services, A1 Sale of motor vehicles, A1
A3 Food and drink	Pubs, restaurants, cafés and food take-aways A1, A2
B1 Business	Offices, research and development, light industry appropriate in a residential area, B8 (permission limited to 235 m² of floor space in the building)
B2 General industrial	B1, B8 (permission limited to 235 m² of floor space in the building)
B8 Storage and distribution	Including open-air storage B1 (permission limited to 235 m² of floor space in the building)
C1 Hotels	Hotels, boarding and guest houses where no significant element of care is provided – none
C2 Residential institutions	Residential care homes, hospitals, nursing homes, boarding schools, residential colleges and training centres – none
C3 Dwelling houses	Family houses, or houses occupied by up to six residents living together as a single household, including a household where care is provided for residents – none

Planning applications are also not required in cases of change of use from A1 to A1 plus a single flat above; and from A2 to A2 plus a single flat above. These changes are reversible without an application only if the part that is now a flat was, respectively, in either A1 or A2 use immediately before it became a flat. Conditions for the change from A1 or A2 are conditional upon there not being any change to the outside of the building and, if there is a display window at ground floor level, no incorporation of the ground floor into the flat.

Changes of use always requiring a planning application

Material changes of use involving any of the activities listed below always require planning permission:

- ☐ amusement centres;
- ☐ theatres;
- ☐ scrap yards;
- ☐ petrol filling stations;
- ☐ car showrooms (except for changes to Class A1 uses);
- ☐ taxi and car-hire businesses;
- ☐ hostels.

HEALTH AND SAFETY

It has to be acknowledged that the Health & Safety at Work etc Act 1974 is one statute among many that imposes duties upon a company or business and its directors or owners which must be obeyed but may not be in their strict commercial interests. Enforcement of the Act is carried out by the Health and Safety Executive (HSE) working with local authorities to uniform, rigorous standards.

Employers' obligations

The Act establishes a fundamental duty of care on the employer, which extends to providing safe systems of work, equipment and a totally safe and healthy workplace environment. Specific obligations include:

- ☐ arrangements to ensure safe storage, handling and transport of all articles and substances;
- ☐ effective communication with employees, supervision and training and adequate welfare provisions;
- ☐ creation of a safety culture that prevents accident pyramids, where lack of precaution, ignorance, failure to report incidents and to react to minor accidents spirals into disasters;
- ☐ where five or more people are employed, the drawing up of a health and safety policy, preferably within a health and safety handbook for staff use, which must contain the following: general statement of the health and safety policy; name of the senior manager responsible for health and safety and how responsibilities are allocated to individuals; operation of any safety committee; safety rules; protective equipment; fire regulations,

drills and emergency procedures; reference to other specialized documents (eg regarding hazardous substances).

If this were not enough, the employer's duty of care is not confined to employees. It extends to customers in respect of product safety, subcontractors, visitors and general members of the public.

Satisfying these requirements is an onerous task and employers may choose to outsource their health and safety management to a qualified health and safety officer. However, rural business owners and directors need to be aware that neither outsourcing nor the employment of a health and safety professional will relieve them from legal responsibility.

Risk assessment

Employers are required to conduct a formal assessment of workplace health and safety conditions and to make arrangements to determine what risks there are to employees that need to be addressed by the health and safety policy. The necessary routines for the main stages in the process of assessing and controlling risks are:

- □ identifying hazards;
- □ designing, implementing and monitoring measures to eliminate or minimize risk;
- □ assessing risks (likelihood and severity) and prioritizing action.

The items covered in a typical assessment would include:

- □ physical characteristics of the workplace;
- □ arrangements for maintenance and servicing of equipment;
- □ procedures for storage, transportation, use and disposal of hazardous substances;
- □ first aid provisions and facilities;
- □ smoking prohibition or restrictions;
- □ arrangements for visitors.

Law enforcement

While HSE inspectors deal mainly with factories, service industries, such as hotels, restaurants, offices and warehouses, are dealt with by local authority officers. It follows that most rural businesses will be subject to inspection by local authority health and safety officers. Acting in that capacity, inspectors may enter premises without notice; examine books and documents; take statements, samples, measurements and photographs; and direct that work and equipment are left undisturbed.

Where contravention of a statutory provision is found, inspectors may issue either an improvement notice or a prohibition notice.

Employee obligations

Employees must cooperate in any changes relating to improving safety, must wear safety gear where required and must not be reckless. Failure to comply can result in lawful dismissal. In the event of a serious accident after wilfully ignoring safety warnings, employees may be prosecuted individually.

Criminal liability

An employer or a company and its directors may be prosecuted for corporate manslaughter, where it can be proven that a manager in charge had knowledge of the risks being taken that resulted in the death of an employee.

Occupational stress

In civil actions brought by employees, employers can be held responsible, in the context of health and safety, for failure to contain workplace stress and are obliged to take reasonable steps to relieve workplace stress arising from any of the following:

- ☐ increase in work intensity;
- ☐ aggressive management styles;
- ☐ bullying or harassment;
- ☐ lack of guidance on how to do the job;
- ☐ over-exposure to customer demands;
- ☐ over-ambitious objectives;
- ☐ excessive computer work;
- ☐ even, over-promotion.

Other key health and safety legislation

Control of Substances Hazardous to Health Regulations (COSHH) 1988

Obligations on employers using hazardous substances identified under COSHH 1988 in their businesses include:

- ☐ risk assessment at least every five years;
- ☐ introduction of systems to prevent or control risks and ensure that controls are monitored and recorded;

- ☐ staff information of hazards, training in use of controls and health surveillance;
- ☐ vigilance and reduction of risks by less hazardous materials and substances where possible.

The Reporting of Injuries, Diseases and Dangerous Occurrences Regulations (RIDDOR) 1995

Employers are required to keep records and report to the HSE instances of deaths and injuries, dangerous occurrences and violence by employees in the workplace.

Manual Handling Operations Regulations 1992

There are obligations on employers to train employees to lift loads in the correct way, provide lifting gear where applicable and consider whether automation of the lifting process is possible.

Rural business owners employing staff are also recommended to have an awareness of the following further legislation:

- ☐ The Employers' Liability (Compulsory Insurance) Act 1969;
- ☐ The Health and Safety (Display Screen Equipment) Regulations 1992;
- ☐ The Personal Protective Equipment at Work Regulations 1992;
- ☐ The Provision and Use of Work Equipment Regulations 1992.

ENVIRONMENTAL LAW

By definition environmental law applies mainly to manufacturing businesses, and rural businesses that are affected significantly will be in a minority. However, there are rural businesses, like sawmills, for which there are environmental issues, and many service industries (eg agricultural machinery repair) are not immune.

The main issues covered by UK environmental law include:

- ☐ emissions into the air (air pollution);
- ☐ water quality and effluent;
- ☐ solid waste (including toxic and radioactive waste);
- ☐ dust emissions;
- ☐ noise pollution;
- ☐ litter;
- ☐ waste disposal;
- ☐ environmental labelling.

The main provisions on these topics are contained in the four following instruments of 'green legislation':

- ☐ The Water Act 1989;
- ☐ The Town and Country Planning Act 1990;
- ☐ The Environment Protection Act 1990;
- ☐ The Environment Act 1995.

Statutory powers are vested in the Environment Agency to regulate and control pollution, inspect premises and impose bans where operating methods or controls are found to need alteration to prevent or minimize pollution.

The owners of an unincorporated business are liable in civil law for environmental damage and liable in criminal law where statutory requirements have been infringed. Directors of companies are personally liable too where they connived or consented to offences or the offence was caused by negligence.

Requirements

Businesses must be authorized before starting operations that use specified processes having an inherent risk of harm to the environment, and must operate according to the authorized conditions. They must monitor and adhere to emission limits, make adequate arrangements for the disposal of waste products and avoid causing 'statutory nuisance' from effluents. They must also be able to demonstrate that they have chosen the 'best practicable environmental option' for controlling identified pollution.

Sanctions

Where required authorization has not been obtained or the conditions of authorization are breached, the Environment Agency or a Local Environment Health Officer can issue **either** enforcement notices requiring immediate remedial action; **or** prohibition notices suspending authorization until remedial action has been taken. Breach of an enforcement or prohibition notice is subject to an unlimited fine or imprisonment of up to two years.

Finally, the business's environmental management system may be independently assessed where the owners consider there is a benefit: for example, to facilitate due diligence when seeking external funding. The business may achieve ISO 4001 certification or registration under the Eco-Management and Audit Scheme of the European Commission.

DATA PROTECTION

The Data Protection Act 1984 applied only to data held on a computer. The more recent Data Protection Act 1998, which came into effect from 1 March 2000, also applies to manual records. The latter Act gives individuals, identified as 'data subjects', the right of access to personal data and requires data holders, identified as 'data controllers' and including employers, to be open about the use of information and follow certain principles in how it is obtained, used and stored.

In particular, employers should be mindful that employees have a right to any information held about them and must have given permission for such information to be held and processed. Sensitive personal data can only be held with the express consent, ideally in writing, of the employee concerned.

Monitoring of e-mails and telephone calls

Employers have the right to monitor telephone calls and e-mails sent by their staff, provided that they notify staff that they intend to do so. An appropriate clause in contracts of employment is recommended.

Compliance and future developments

Since this is a developing area of law, there are likely to be continuing amendments to current rules and changes of interpretation. Larger employers are recommended to have a written data protection policy that is included in the staff handbook.

Caveat

In matters concerned with all legislation and regulations referred to in this chapter, readers are counselled to take professional advice before applying for permissions, licences, approvals or authorizations to avoid errors that will damage their business case or expose themselves to further regulations or sanctions.

12 Private Limited Companies

Jonathan Reuvid and Godfrey Golzen

Legislation over the years before the appointment of Gordon Brown as Chancellor of the Exchequer has made it less attractive to start out trading as a limited company unless you are in a form of business that might leave you at risk as a debtor – as might be the case, for instance, if you were a graphic designer commissioning processing on behalf of a client. The reason for this is that, in law, a limited company has an identity distinct from that of the shareholders who are its owners. Consequently, if a limited company goes bankrupt, the claims of the creditors are limited to the assets of the company. This includes any capital issued to shareholders that they have *either paid for in full or in part*. We shall return to the question of share capital in a moment, but the principle at work here is that when shares are issued, the shareholders need not necessarily pay for them in full, though they have a legal obligation to do so if the company goes bankrupt. Shareholders are not, however, liable as individuals, and their private assets outside the company may not be touched unless their company has been trading fraudulently. On the other hand, if creditors ask for personal guarantees, directors of limited companies are not protected and *personal* assets to the amount of the guarantee as well as business assets are at risk in the event of bankruptcy.

There is also another important area where the principle of limited liability does not apply. Company directors are liable, in law, for employees' national insurance contributions. This is a personal liability enforced by the Department for Work and Pensions in the same way as bank guarantees. There have even been cases of non-executive directors of insolvent companies being pursued for non-payment of national insurance contributions by companies with which they were involved, though the Social Security Act of 1975 states that the directors are only responsible in such circumstances if they 'knew or reasonably could have known' that these contributions were not being paid.

Company directors can also be held guilty of 'wrongful trading', which essentially means trading while they know their company is insolvent. In that case they may be obliged to contribute personally to the compensating of creditors.

Under EU legislation, a limited company can be formed by a single shareholder who must be a director. It must also have a company secretary, who can be an outside person, such as the director's solicitor or accountant. Apart from this, the main requirements relate to documentation. Like sole traders or part-nerships, a limited company must prepare a set of accounts annually for the inspector of taxes and it must make an annual return to the Registrar of Companies, showing all the shareholders and directors, any changes of ownership that have taken place, a profit and loss account over the year and a balance sheet.

Apart from the more exacting requirements regarding documentation, a significant disadvantage of setting up a limited company as compared to a partnership or sole trader is that sole traders and partnerships can set off any losses they incur in the first four years' trading retrospectively against the owners' income tax on earnings in the three preceding years. As the owner, this may enable you to recover tax already paid in earlier years of ordinary employment. This concession does not, however, apply to investment in your own limited company, or to investments made in such a company by those closely connected with the shareholders. If it makes losses, those losses can only be set off against the *company's* corporation tax in other years when it makes a profit. If it fails altogether, then the loss of your investment is a *capital* loss that can only be set off against other capital gains you make – not against other earned income. Therefore, if the nature of your business is a service that does not involve exposure to liabilities that you need to protect – for instance, if you are a consultant, rather than a shopkeeper or a manufacturer incurring liabilities to suppliers – there may be a distinct advantage in opting for part-nership or sole trader status rather than establishing a limited company; but see the recommendation to seek professional advice below. There may, for instance, be factors other than trading risks which need to be protected by limited liability. Highly profitable ventures can also benefit from limited company status because their profits are taxed at corporation tax rates rather than the much higher personal income tax rates. As your start-up business prospers you should review the alternative taxation status of a limited company to self-employment at regular intervals.

The cost of forming a company, including the capital duty which is based on the issued capital (we shall come to the distinction between this and nominal capital shortly), is likely to be around £250, depending on what method you use to go about it. The cheapest way is to buy a ready-made ('off the shelf') company from one of the registration agents who advertise their services in specialist financial journals. Such a company will not actually have been trading, but will be properly registered by the agents. All that has to be done is for the existing 'shareholders' (who are probably the agent's nominees) to resign and for the purchasers to become the new shareholders and to appoint directors. Full details of the procedures are available from Companies House.

Alternatively you can start your own company from scratch, but whichever course you choose, professional advice is vital at this stage. The technicalities are trickier than they sound, though simple enough to those versed in such transactions.

Ultimately, the decision on whether or not to form a limited company depends on your long-term objectives. If you are planning to become an entrepreneur, and to build a business for significant capital growth, a limited company structure and the creation of shares has to be considered at an early stage. It will, for instance, be essential if you want to raise serious amounts of money from outside investors. But if you are thinking about what is essentially a salaried income replacement venture, a sole trader or partnership structure would usually be the better and simpler option.

REGISTRATION OF BUSINESS NAMES

One problem you may encounter with an 'off the shelf' company is when it has a name that does not relate meaningfully to the activity you are proposing to carry on. In that case you can change the company name by contacting the Companies Registrations Office on 0870 33 33 636 and they will guide you through the procedure, which is straightforward and costs around £50. You can also contact the new companies section on the same number, and register a new company. This again is a straightforward procedure and costs £10. You can also write to the Registrar of Companies for information (The Registrar of Companies, Companies House, Crown Way, Cardiff CF14 3UZ). If your enquiry is about registering a new company, address it to The Registrar of Companies – New Companies Section.

The other option is to trade under a name that is different from the company's official one; for instance, your company may be called 'Period Investments Ltd', but you trade as 'Regency Antiques'. Until 1982 you had to register your business name with the Registrar of Business Names, but that office has since been abolished. Instead, if you trade under any name other than your own – in the case of a sole trader or partnership – or that of the name of the company carrying on the business in the case of a company, you have to disclose the name of the owner or owners and, for each owner, a business or other address in the UK.

The rules of disclosure are quite far-reaching and failure to comply with them is a criminal offence. You must show the information about owners and their addresses on all business letters, written orders for the supply of goods or services, invoices and receipts issued in the course of business and written demands for payment of business debts. Furthermore, you have to display this information prominently and readably in any premises where the business is carried on and to which customers and suppliers have access.

It is worth giving a good deal of thought to the choice of a business name. Clever names are all very well, but if they do not clearly establish the nature of the business you are in, prospective customers leafing through a telephone or business directory may have trouble in finding you; or, if they do find you, they may not readily match your name to their needs. For instance, if you are a furniture repairer, it is far better to describe yourself as such in your business name than to call yourself something like 'Chippendale Restorations'. However, if your name already has a big reputation in some specialized sector, stick with it.

Legislation makes it possible to protect a trading name by registering it with the Trade Marks Registry at the Patent Office. The advantage of that is that you can prevent other traders from using your name – or something very similar – and cashing in on your goodwill. You can also register a trade mark – the sign or logo that identifies your business on letterheads, packaging and so forth. The activities for which marks can be registered include service industries as well as manufacturing ones.

The rules governing the use of business names are like those for company names, except that the Registrar is less concerned about the fact that a similar trading name may already be in existence. Obviously, however, it is advisable in both cases to wait until the name you have put forward is accepted before having any stationery printed. There are, it should be said, certain words that the Registrar of Companies has proved likely to object to: those that could mislead the public by suggesting that an enterprise is larger or has a more prestigious status than circumstances indicate. Cases in point are the use of words such as Trust, University and Group. National adjectives ('British') are also unpopular. When you get to this stage the names of the proprietors (or, in the case of a limited company, the directors) have to be shown not only on letterheads, but also on catalogues and trade literature.

Limited companies, in addition, have to show their registration number and the address of their registered office on such stationery. This address may not necessarily be the same as the one at which business is normally transacted. Some firms use their accountant's or solicitor's premises as their registered office. You will probably see quite a number of registration certificates hanging in their office (they are required by law to be so displayed) when you go there. This is because it is to that address that all legal and official documents are sent. If you have placed complete responsibility for dealing with such matters in the hands of professional advisers, it is obviously convenient that the related correspondence should also be directed there. Bear in mind, though, that this does involve a certain loss of control on your part. Unless you see these documents yourself, you will have no idea, for instance, whether the important ones are being handled with due despatch.

LIMITED COMPANY DOCUMENTS

When you set up a limited company, your solicitor or accountant will be involved in drafting certain papers and documents which govern its structure and the way it is to be run. When this process has been completed you will receive copies of the company's Memorandum and Articles of Association, some blank share transfer forms (for the registration of shares transferred from one shareholder to another or to a new shareholder), a minute book, the company seal and the Certificate of Incorporation. Let us explain briefly what these mean.

The Memorandum

This document sets out the main objects for which the company is formed and what it is allowed to do. There are standard clauses for this and your professional adviser will use these in drafting the document. The main thing to watch out for is that he or she should not be too specific in setting out the limits of the proposed operation, because if you change tack somewhere along the line – for instance, if you move from mail order to making goods for the customers you have built up – you may lose the protection of your limited liability unless the Memorandum provides for this. There are, however, catch-all clauses which allow you to trade in pretty much anything or any manner you like. Furthermore, the 'objects' clauses can be changed by a special resolution, passed by 75 per cent of the shareholders.

The Memorandum also sets out the company's nominal or authorized share capital and the par value per share. This is a point about which many newcomers to this aspect of business get very confused. The thing to remember is that in this context the value of share capital is a purely *nominal* value. You can have a company operating with thousands of pounds' worth of nominal share capital. This sounds very impressive, but what counts is the *issued* share capital, because this represents what the shareholders have actually put into the business or pledged themselves so to do. It is quite possible to have a company with a nominal capital of £1,000, but with, say, only two issued shares of £1 each to the two shareholders that are required by law.

The issued share capital also determines the ownership of a company. In the case we have just quoted, the two shareholders would own the company jointly. But if they then issue a third £1 share to another person without issuing any more to themselves they would now own only two-thirds of the company. This is a vital point to remember when raising capital by means of selling shares.

Apart from determining proportions of ownership, issued share capital also signifies how much of their own money the shareholders have put into the company or are prepared to accept liability for. Therefore, in raising money from a bank or finance house, the manager there will look closely at the issued share capital. To the extent that the manager is not satisfied that the liability for the amount he is being asked to put up is adequately backed by issued share capital, he or she is likely to ask the shareholders to guarantee a loan or overdraft with their own personal assets – for instance, by depositing shares they privately hold in a public quoted company or unit trust – as security. In the case of a new company without a track record this would, in fact, be the usual procedure.

The nominal share capital of a new small-scale business is usually £100. It can be increased later, as business grows, on application to the Registrar of Companies. The point of such a move would be to increase the *issued* share capital, for instance if a new shareholder were to put money into the company. But, once again, it should be borne in mind that if the issued share capital was increased from £100 to £1,000, and a backer were to buy £900-worth of shares at par value, the original shareholders would only own one-tenth of the business; the fact that they got the whole thing going is quite beside the point.

Final questions about issued share capital that sometimes puzzle people: must you actually hand over money for the shares when you start your own company, as is the case when you buy shares on the stock market? And, if so, what happens to it? The answer is that you pay the money into the company's bank account because, remember, it has a separate legal identity from the shareholders who own it. However, you need not pay for your shares in full. You can, for instance, pay 50p per share for a hundred £1 shares. The balance of £50 represents your liability if the company goes bankrupt, and you actually have to hand over the money only if that happens or if a majority at a share-holders' meeting requires you to do so. The fact that you have not paid in full for shares issued to you does not, however, diminish your entitlement to share in the profits, these being distributed as dividends according to the proportion of share capital issued. The same applies to outside shareholders, so if you are raising money by selling shares to people outside the firm, you should normally ensure that they pay in full for any capital that is issued to them.

The Articles of Association

These are coupled together with the Memorandum, and set out the rules under which the company is run. They govern matters such as issue of the share capital, appointment and powers of directors and proceedings at general meetings. As in the case of the Memorandum, the clauses are largely standard ones, but those relating to the issue of shares should be read carefully. It is most important that there should be a proviso under which any new shares that are issued should be offered first of all to the existing shareholders in the proportion in which they already hold shares. This is particularly so when three or more shareholders are involved, or when you are buying into a company; otherwise the other shareholders can vote to water down your holding in the company whenever they see fit by issuing further shares. For the same reason, there should be a clause under which any shareholder who wants to transfer shares should offer them first of all to the existing shareholders. The Articles of

Association also state how the value of the shares is to be determined, the point here being that if the company is successful and makes large profits, the true value of the shares will be much greater than their par value of £1, 50p or whatever. It should be noted, though, that the market valuation of the shares does not increase the liability of shareholders accordingly. In other words, if your £1 par shares are actually valued at, say, £50, your liability still remains at £1.

Table A of the Companies Act of 1948, which can be purchased at any Stationery Office branch, sets out a specimen Memorandum and Articles.

The minute book

Company law requires that a record be kept of the proceedings at both share-holders' and directors' meetings. These proceedings are recorded in the minute book, which is held at the company's registered office. Decisions made at company meetings are signed by the Chair and are legally binding on the directors if they are agreed by a majority. Therefore, any points of procedure that are not covered by the Memorandum and Articles of Association can be written into the minutes and have the force of law, provided that they do not conflict with the former two documents. Thus, the various responsibilities of the directors can be defined and minuted at the first company meeting; so can important matters such as who signs the cheques. It is generally a good idea for these to carry two signatures to be valid.

The company seal

This used to be a stamp affixed with the authority of the directors, but nowadays documents can be executed by the signatures of two directors. This has the same legal effect as the seal used to have, but the seal may still be used in some special circumstances.

The Certificate of Incorporation

When the wording of the Memorandum and Articles of Association has been agreed and the names of the directors and the size of the nominal capital have been settled, your professional adviser will send the documents concerned to the Registrar of Companies. The Registrar will issue a Certificate of Incorporation which is, as it were, the birth certificate of your company.

13 Taxation Issues

John Skinner, Whitley Stimpson

This chapter considers the general taxation of business revenue profits, the interaction with 'pay as you earn' (PAYE + NIC), and VAT. Complete books have been dedicated to all these separate areas; so only a general overview is given here. General advice would be certainly to be aware of the various taxes that would affect you, but obtain professional advice, so that you can concentrate on running your business.

INCOME TAX AND CORPORATION TAX

Whether a business is run as a limited company or in some unincorporated form (sole trader or partnership), its profits will be chargeable to tax. The whole purpose of being in business is to generate income and the government imposes tax on that income to finance, in part, its spending.

Both income tax and corporation tax rates are 'banded' so there are break-points at which the rate increases, reaching a maximum of 40 per cent for income tax (currently on income over £31,400) and 30 per cent for companies (although this can increase to an 'effective rate' of 32.75 per cent).

Individuals and, more recently companies, have a band of tax-free income – £4,745 for individuals and £10,000 for companies (for the year ended 5 April 2005). The introduction of the companies' allowance was heralded by the government in 2001 as an incentive to encourage people to invest in their own limited companies.

Three years later, the Chancellor called the incentive a 'loophole' and had to block it, such had been the number of small businesses incorporated to take advantage of the scheme (it had meant that a sizeable number of people had stopped paying tax completely because of the way dividends are taxed – read on).

(While on the subject of government bashing, New Labour are very keen to point out that they have fulfilled a promise not to increase income tax. This is purely semantics – although it is true that income 'tax' rates have not increased, rates of national insurance contributions (NIC) have, and these are a tax on income by any other name!)

A limited company will pay tax on profits that will be calculated after deducting amounts drawn by the owner as salary. Once the tax has been deducted from the profits, this will leave an amount that can be distributed as a dividend (subject to the availability of cash, as profit is not the same as cash) to the owner.

An individual running an identical business as a sole trader will pay tax on higher profits, as amounts he or she has taken from the business (termed 'drawings') are not tax deductible.

To incorporate or not?

That is the question! Whether to suffer the slings and arrows of (Brown's) outrageous fortune. (Apologies to Mr Shakespeare.) As noted above, there was a fairly swift U-turn by Gordon Brown that followed the spate of business incorporations after his introduction of the £10,000 tax-free band for limited companies.

The key to understanding the attractiveness is to know how dividends are treated for income tax purposes. If you take the example of a business that generates around £15,000 of profit per year, a sole trader would be paying income tax and NIC (classes 2 and 4) of around £2,950.

The same business run as a limited company (prior to the introduction of Brown's new 'dividend surcharge') would save the owner around £2,900. This is because the owner would take a salary from the company of £4,745 (paying no PAYE or NIC on this as it is the equivalent of his or her annual personal allowance), reducing the company's profits to £10,255.

The company would pay £48 of corporation tax on £255 (the amount in excess of £10,000) and the owner would take a dividend of £10,000 from the profits remaining in the company. The owner would pay no tax on the dividend as he or she is a basic rate tax payer – he or she has personally paid no tax at all on income of £14,745!

If you multiply this equation over the number of small businesses in the country, it is hardly surprising why Gordon Brown had to address the problem.

The key is that while you remain a basic rate tax payer, dividend income is effectively tax free. Once you fall into the higher rate tax bracket, dividends are taxed at 32.5 per cent which means that you have to pay tax equivalent to 25 per cent of the dividend.

The surcharge introduced by the government means that dividends paid out by the company carry a 19 per cent levy on them, payable by the company, not the recipient of the dividend. The levy is stepped and reduces to nil by the time the company is generating profits of £50,000. Despite the new levy, it may still be beneficial for a business to be run as a limited company from a tax perspective, although you should never allow the 'tax tail to wag the business dog'.

Capital allowances

When either individuals or limited companies buy plant and machinery, equipment, cars or fixtures and fittings, the cost of these assets attract 'capital allowances' that are set against the profits that the asset has helped to generate.

For instance, a pick-up truck costing £17,000 would generate an allowance of £6,800 in the year it was purchased (40 per cent), and then 25 per cent of £10,200 (£17,000 – £6,800), being £2,550 in year 2, 25 per cent of £7,650 (£10,200 – £2,550) in year 3 and so on.

The only difference between a limited company and sole trader is that each year's allowance for the individual would be reduced by an amount to cover private use of the asset. And this forms one of the key differences between operating a business as a limited company and as an individual.

EMPLOYMENT VERSUS SELF-EMPLOYMENT

It is quite often the case that someone owning a limited company on their own may regard themselves as working for themselves, but from a tax perspective, that person is employed by the company.

Consequently, if the company provides the owner with a car, the owner is regarded as having a 'benefit in kind' supplied by the company. The above example is not particularly illustrative, as a pick-up would be classed as a van and the benefit in kind is £500 per year, but the taxable benefit on cars can easily be £6,000 and upwards.

Care should be taken when considering the provision of a company car as it may be more tax-efficient to use your own car and make a mileage claim against the company using officially approved rates of 40p per mile for the first 10,000 per annum and 25p per mile thereafter.

Another common example is the provision of health care which costs, say £900 per year. If a company were to pick up the cost of this, as long as the scheme is in the company's name, the employee would pay 22 per cent of this, as long as the employee was a basic rate taxpayer. The company would also be able to set the cost against profits.

A sole trader would pay the same rate but have no tax deduction.

A common problem with people running their own limited company is that they deem the company's money to be their own, which it is not. A consequence of this is that owners quite often owe their own company money as they spend the company's money as if it were their own.

Until the money is repaid, there are two tax consequences of this. Firstly, the company has to pay 25 per cent of the amount advanced in tax to the Inland Revenue. The tax is refunded when the loan is cleared. The second implication is personal to the beneficiary of the loan. Where, as is usually the case, no interest is charged by the company on the loan, there is a benefit in kind on interest calculated using the Inland Revenue's 'official rate'.

However, this charge is only imposed where the loan is more than £5,000.

A slightly different scenario exists for a sole trader where he or she owes the business (which is actually himself or herself) money. Where the owner is using the businesses' overdraft or loan facility to fund personal spending, he or she will not be able to claim all the interest on the overdraft/loan against profits.

There are benefits to running a business as an unincorporated entity as the regime is not quite as rigorous and there is more leeway to claim costs that would not necessarily be allowed against PAYE earnings.

Further, it is quite often cheaper for an 'employer' business to regard some of its workers as being self-employed rather than being employed. This is especially true in terms of NIC where the employer has to add employer's NIC on top of the gross salary of the employee. Also, where a worker is not an employee, they have no right to statutory sick pay, redundancy or paid holidays. Therefore, it could very well be in a business's interests to view some of its workers as self-employed. However, the government imposes a duty on the employer to decide whether a worker is employed or not and that decision is open to question when the Inland Revenue visit the business on a compliance visit.

The Inland Revenue tend to be of the opinion that their interpretation of the law is the correct one, whereas it would actually be up to a court to decide whether a worker is employed or not. This means though that the employer (or at least his or her advisers) needs to be aware of legal precedents, but there are various accepted tests applied to judge whether a worker is employed or not, including:

☐ whether work is carried out wholly or mainly for one business;
☐ who provides the tools;
☐ who bears the business risk of the work carried out;
☐ whether a substitute can be sent to carry out the work;
☐ who says when and where the work will be done.

No single factor necessarily provides conclusive evidence and the decision depends on the overall circumstances. However, the decision can be crucial as a compliance visit from the Inland Revenue could see them trying to impose tax and NIC on payments to workers whom they view as being employed.

NIC

As noted above, the total cost of employing somebody is not merely their gross salary, but also the employer's NIC, currently 12.8 per cent on earnings over £91.01 per week for the year 2005/2006. The employee also has NIC deducted from their gross pay by the employer at 11 per cent between £91.01 per week and £610, and 1 per cent thereafter (the New Labour tax increase that they claim is not a tax increase as NIC is not a tax).

Self-employed people pay two kinds of NIC – class 2, which is a fixed £2.05 per week once earnings exceed £4,745 and class 4, charged at 8 per cent on profits between £4,745 and £31,720 and 1 per cent thereafter.

RENTAL INCOME

Income tax is also payable on the profits generated from the rent of property, where the rent receivable has the running costs set against it to arrive at the taxable amount. Costs can include rates (if not paid by the tenant), repairs (also unless paid for by the tenant), agent's fees, insurance, mortgage interest and so forth.

Obtaining bad debt relief for non-payment of rent is made quite difficult to achieve, as you have to demonstrate that you have taken all steps possible to recover the unpaid rent, which normally involves using a solicitor.

If you let a property out in a furnished state, although you are unable claim a capital allowance on the cost of the furnishings, a 'wear and tear' allowance of 10 per cent of the rent less rates is available. If you let out furnished rooms in your own home, no tax is payable if the year's gross rents are less than £4,250 under 'rent a room' relief. Criteria for the relief to apply include the fact that you must live in the property as your main home for at least part of the year at the same time as the lodger, and the lodger must live as part of your family, ie not restricted to a discrete part of the property.

There are excellent benefits to be obtained by renting a property out as a furnished holiday let, as the operation is judged to be a business, such as:

- [ ] capital allowances on the furnishings;
- [ ] the fact that losses can be set off against other income in the year (whereas other rental losses can only be offset against future profits);
- [ ] capital gains tax business asset taper relief and rollover relief;
- [ ] the fact that profits qualify as 'relevant earnings' when calculating maximum pension contributions, but no class 4 NIC is due on the income.

However, there are quite strict qualifying criteria for a property to be classed as a holiday let, including the following:

- [ ] The property must be let commercially and be available for holiday accommodation for 140 days of the tax year, and actually let as such for 70 of those 140 days.
- [ ] It should not be in occupation by the same tenant for a continuous period of more than 31 days during at least 7 months of the year.

☐   Where there is private use of the property, costs must be restricted, which may affect the commerciality restrictions if income merely arises to offset costs.

VAT

When VAT was introduced in the early 1970s, it was heralded as a very simple tax. This claim has drastically changed over the last 30 years, as VAT has become a fiendishly complicated tax.

VAT is chargeable on the supply of (certain) goods and services in the UK and on certain imports. Once your sales reach £60,000 in any rolling 12-month period, you need to register with the VAT authorities and start charging VAT to your customers. You need not register for VAT if can demonstrate to HM Revenue & Customs that your turnover will not exceed £58,000 in the next 12 months.

Businesses sometimes go to extraordinary lengths to avoid registering for VAT because of the administrative hassle that it entails and the increase in their prices that their customers may not be able to recover. But there is anti-avoidance legislation in place to counter these attempts with fines and interest charged for non-compliance.

Once registered for VAT, you can reclaim (most of) the VAT charged on the expenses of running the business on a VAT return. There now exist a myriad of schemes to choose from as to how to account for the VAT that you owe that have been introduced to try and ease the burden of being an unpaid tax collector for the government. However, most businesses account for VAT on a quarterly basis.

The type of supplies that you make in your business governs the rate of VAT that you charge. For example, the vast majority of a farmer's chargeable supplies (selling crops or animals) will be zero rated for VAT purposes, but when a piece of machinery is sold, that would have to have VAT added to it.

It is quite usual for farmers to register voluntarily for VAT where the supplies that they make are less than £60,000, because they can recover the VAT that is charged to them on the expenses they incur in running their business. There are 15 other types of supplies that are zero rated including the construction (but not repair) of residential buildings, children's clothing, and food (but not as catering, or pet food, or non-essentials).

There are also a whole gamut of supplies that are exempt, ie no VAT is chargeable or recoverable. Examples include burial and cremation, finance services, health, (some) land and education.

Property renting can be a difficult area. If you rent property for residential purposes you cannot register for VAT and consequently cannot recover VAT on the running costs of the property.

If you rent property commercially, you have to 'opt to tax' which means that you charge the tenants VAT and recover the costs of running the property. It does mean however that you have to charge VAT on the eventual sale of the property, which may put off potential buyers who may not be able to recover the VAT.

If in doubt, seek advice. There is a national Helpline run by HM Revenue & Customs that can be a useful first port of call, but VAT has become so esoteric that you have to be sure you are asking the right question. The Helpline will only answer the question you actually ask, not necessarily the one you really should have asked.

DIXON WILSON
CHARTERED ACCOUNTANTS
AND REGISTERED AUDITORS

The firm offers a highly personal and professional service.
We provide partner-led advice which is creative, carefully thought out and
practical to the specific needs of our clients.

Country landowners and rural businesses operate under a variety of
more or less complex structures, including sole trades, partnerships,
trusts and companies, and we have many years of experience helping them
to maximise opportunities with all of these.

We regularly provide advice in relation to

Strategic planning
Long term capital tax planning
Property transactions
Income and capital gains taxes
Inheritance tax
VAT
Accounts for sole traders, partnerships, trusts and companies.

Areas where we are called upon to assist include agriculture based activities,
development land, woodlands, sporting, heritage property,
minerals, leisure and other diversifications.

Please contact
jameskidgell@dixonwilson.co.uk
davidnelson@dixonwilson.co.uk
davidmellor@dixonwilson.co.uk
and see www.dixonwilson.com

Rotherwick House, 3 Thomas More Street, London E1W 1YX
Telephone: +44 (0)20 7680 8100 Fax: +44 (0)20 7680 8101

19 avenue de l'Opéra, 75001 Paris
Téléphone: +33 (0)1 47 03 12 90 Fax: +33 (0)1 47 03 12 85

14 Maximizing Tax Allowances in the Rural Environment

James Kidgell, Dixon Wilson

The economic challenges that face rural businesses today inevitably direct the attention of owners and managers towards improving free cash flow and overall profitability. The introduction of new income streams and the tightening of operating margins, coupled with reducing overheads, are often the areas that receive most management time.

However, the tax bill, which for some rural businesses may represent as much as 15 per cent of turnover, is often overlooked. As agriculture becomes more intensive, and diversification continues, agricultural businesses need to review the tax allowances available to them to ensure that the maximum is being claimed to reduce the tax bill. This chapter principally considers how tax relief is given on capital expenditure on property and other assets. In most cases, relief will be given in the form of capital allowances. After reading this chapter, you should be able to identify areas where opportunities and pitfalls are to be found and need to be planned for.

It is worth emphasizing that capital allowances provide tax relief over a prolonged period of time, perhaps up to 25 years. Consequently, before claiming capital allowances, taxpayers should always ask themselves whether the expenditure is actually incurred in repairing an existing asset, rather than improving an asset or creating a new asset. If the expenditure is a repair, full relief will be available in the year in which it is incurred. This would significantly improve the cash flow position compared to claiming capital allowances.

TRADITIONAL AGRICULTURE

The starting point for capital expenditure incurred in the pursuit of agricultural activities is that almost all expenditure will qualify for some form of tax relief. The obvious limitation to this is expenditure on assets with an element of private use – for example a car used by the owner both for business and personal activities.

Tax relief will be available under one of the following provisions:

☐ Agricultural Buildings Allowances (ABAs), where relief is given at the annual rate of 4 per cent of the capital expenditure;
☐ plant and machinery capital allowances, where relief is given on a reducing balance basis at an annual rate of 25 per cent;
☐ long life assets, where relief is given at an annual rate of 6 per cent of the capital expenditure.

The most favourable relief is clearly plant and machinery capital allowances; after 10 years, tax relief has been claimed on almost 95 per cent of the expenditure incurred. When ABAs are claimed, it takes almost 24 years for the same relief to be claimed, and approximately 16 years for long life assets.

First year allowances (FYAs)

In most cases, FYAs will be available for expenditure on plant and machinery in the period in which the asset was acquired. For 2004/05, the rate for FYAs for small businesses is 50 per cent, which significantly accelerates the tax relief.

Certain types of expenditure qualify for 100 per cent relief in the first year. The most well-known example is expenditure on IT equipment, for instance replacement of the computer system in the farm office.

Careful consideration needs to be given to the ownership structure of the business to ensure that FYAs are available. Changes to tax legislation in 2001 prevented businesses operated by trustees from claiming FYAs. Whether intentionally or not, the legislation went further than this and prevented partnerships from claiming FYAs where one or more of the partners is not an individual (perhaps a trust or a company). The enhanced relief is denied to all partners, not only the corporate or trustee partner.

Restructuring the ownership of a business may arise as part of an inheritance tax planning exercise or under the terms of a will, and can often lead to part of the agricultural business being carried on in trust. It might be several years later, possibly after the completion of an Inland Revenue enquiry, before it becomes apparent that FYAs were no longer available, giving rise to an unexpected tax bill.

Agricultural buildings

The extent to which ABAs can be claimed is often underestimated; their application extends well beyond the construction of a new grain store or dairy parlour. The principal tests that need to be satisfied can be summarized as follows:

☐ The expenditure must be incurred on the construction or improvement of a building or structure.

☐ The 'building' must be used in the pursuit of agriculture; specifically in the husbandry of agricultural land.

Consequently, ABAs can be claimed on expenditure incurred on, for example, the construction of new fences or hedges; man-made reservoirs and other water installations; drainage works and farm roads.

In the case of tenanted farms, where expenditure is incurred by the landlord, he or she will be entitled to the tax allowances rather than the tenant.

Farmhouses and farm cottages

For the purposes of ABAs, farmhouses are considered to be the property from which the business is managed. Where there is a full-time farm manager, this may not always be the owner's house.

A maximum of one-third of the capital expenditure on a farmhouse will qualify for ABAs. If the scale and nature of a farmhouse is excessive for the size of the farming operations, the proportion of qualifying expenditure will fall below one-third. In these circumstances, allowances will only be available on the appropriate business proportion of the farmhouse.

Properties will qualify as farm cottages when they are occupied by farm employees. Although not defined in the legislation, it is the Inland Revenue's stated view that as a matter of fact the building has to be a cottage, ie a small house. When this requirement is met, all of the capital expenditure on the farm cottage will qualify for ABAs.

Apportionment of expenditure

The construction or conversion of agricultural buildings can require an appor-tionment of the expenditure between ABAs and plant and machinery capital allowances. For example, the construction of a new refrigerated vegetable store would give rise to significant expenditure on plant and machinery (such as fans, refrigeration units, specialist equipment to aid air circulation, etc) which need to be identified separately from the expenditure on the building itself (such as foundations and construction, insulation, etc) on which ABAs will be available.

While it might initially appear to be a simple matter to allocate expenses between these categories, in practice this is never the case. There is always an element of judgement needed to ensure that the allocation has been performed on a reasonable basis.

Where expenses have been apportioned, and the result has a significant effect on the farmer's overall tax liability, full disclosure of the basis of allo-cation should be made on the self-assessment tax return.

Long life assets

In certain circumstances, plant and machinery that has an expected useful life of 25 years or more will only qualify as a long life asset. This only applies where there is a reasonable expectation that the asset will not become economically or technologically obsolete within 25 years.

In practice, there are very few circumstances where these tests are likely to be met in an agricultural environment. However, the Inland Revenue have attempted to argue, for example, that an irrigation pipeline has a life expectancy of more than 25 years, which would result in reduced tax relief in the earlier years.

When plant and machinery is installed which might have a long life expectancy, it is advisable to retain documentary evidence from the manufacturer to protect against future enquiries.

DIVERSIFICATION

It is essential to understand that most diversified activities will not satisfy the tax definition of farming; new enterprises are therefore likely to constitute separate trading activities for tax purposes. It is easy to envisage a situation where diversified activities are supporting the farming trade, which on its own may be loss-making. It should be well known that farming losses that continue over a prolonged period cannot always be set off against other sources of income.

In an extreme case, a business as a whole could be breaking even, but paying tax on profits from non-traditional activities with farming losses being carried forward. The cash flow impact of this could quickly render the business as a whole uncommercial.

Farm shops selling a wide range of goods are becoming increasingly common. A proportion of the goods have often been produced on the farm with the remainder purchased from other local businesses. In these circumstances, running a farm shop is a separate activity from farming, and it will be necessary to allocate shared expenses between the different activities. In addition, the price at which home-produced goods are transferred to the shop needs careful consideration. If these allocations are not performed on a reasonable basis, profits could be artificially transferred between activities, and the Inland Revenue might seek to challenge the tax computations.

Agricultural contracting (as distinct from the activities undertaken by the contractor in a contract farming arrangement) does not meet the definition of farming for tax purposes. Where contracting constitutes a significant proportion of turnover, the activity should be taxed as a separate trade.

Conversion of redundant farm buildings

Many farmers have converted redundant agricultural buildings into cottages or rural offices. The associated expenditure can be significant, and it can often be difficult to claim tax relief in the short term.

A distinction can be made between buildings that have been recently used in the farm business, and may therefore be in a reasonable state of repair, and those that have not been used for many years and may be almost derelict. Provided there are no external structural alterations, work on the external fabric of a building in the first category may be a repair. In the second case, restoring the external fabric of the building is likely to be capital expenditure and will only provide relief against capital gains tax (CGT) on a future sale of the property.

In almost all cases, internal conversion works will be treated as capital as there has been a change of use of the building. The majority of this expenditure will only provide relief against CGT. Depending on the final use of the converted building, there may be some income tax relief available.

Office conversions will always include some expenditure on which plant and machinery capital allowances can be claimed. Categories of expenditure that qualify will include heating and air conditioning systems, specialist electrical work (eg for computer systems), alarms and security systems, toilets and other sanitary ware and carpets. The percentage of expenditure that will qualify will vary significantly; between 10 per cent and 20 per cent of the total project cost may not be unreasonable.

Analysis of the expenditure on developments can be time consuming and costly if it is left until after the development is completed, and is best dealt with at an early stage. This is most straightforward if a detailed specification for the work is prepared by the architect or surveyor prior to the commencement of the project.

Some properties have been converted for occupation by tenants whose business includes a light industrial process. It may be possible to claim Industrial Buildings Allowances on a proportion of this expenditure. In most cases expenditure on converting agricultural buildings into residences will not qualify for capital allowances.

Remember to consider the VAT aspects of any property conversion as there are some significant reliefs and pitfalls that should be planned for.

Sales of redundant farm buildings

Sales of separate buildings that are no longer required in the farming business can be an easy way of releasing capital for the business. However, the CGT liability can reduce the attractiveness of such sales. It is important to maximize the availability of business assets taper relief, which can reduce the effective rate of CGT from 40 per cent to 10 per cent.

When farm buildings are earmarked for sale, there can be a significant delay before the sale is completed. In the intervening period, the building should continue to be used in the farm business, if only for the storage of farm machinery, to preserve the maximum available taper relief. Evidence of the continued business use of the property should be retained.

OTHER ISSUES

For some time, there has been a requirement in the UK for the accounts on which businesses' tax computations are based to be prepared in accordance with Generally Accepted Accounting Practice (GAAP). This applies equally to a farmer with only 50 acres as to one with 5,000 acres. Conflicts between the accounting and tax treatments can easily arise and need to be planned for. To claim a repairs deduction, the expenditure should not be capitalized in the accounts.

15 Accountancy and Audit

John Skinner, Whitley Stimpson

BASIC BOOKKEEPING

Whether you run a business as a sole trader, a partnership or a limited company, you are legally obliged to maintain accounting books and records. For limited companies, the Companies Act requires that the accounting records 'shall be sufficient to show and explain the company's transactions', particularly containing 'entries from day to day of all sums of money received and expended'. For unincorporated businesses, the rules of self-assessment taxation place a similar onus on the business owners and allow the Inland Revenue to levy fines of up to £3,000 for 'inadequate records'.

On a more practical level, you should be looking to monitor your business from a financial perspective so that you know where you stand monetarily and what returns you are generating from your work. If you have no particular liking for doing your bookkeeping, ask a local bookkeeper, or farm secretary, to do it for you. Money wisely spent here should limit the amount of work your accountant needs to carry out in producing your year-end figures.

Otherwise, if you do your own bookkeeping, take a 'little and often' approach so it does not become daunting. The requirement to complete a VAT return each quarter (or monthly) should also provide enough stimulus for records to be regularly updated.

Your books and records need only be as sophisticated as the business that you run. A good stationer could provide you with a multi-column analysis book to record your income and expenditure under appropriate headings: equally this could be done on a computer spreadsheet. At the other end of the spectrum, there are various accounting packages available, again increasing in complexity depending on your needs. You may, however, need training if you are to use these effectively.

Ask for (and retain) invoices to support your expenditure wherever possible and where you have to raise an invoice, keep a copy. Look to establish a filing system for your invoices, whether alphabetical or chronological. You may even wish to cross reference invoices into your bookkeeping records to ease future locating.

At your financial year end, you are also obliged to prepare and retain a valuation of your stock (ie goods you trade with). Stock must be valued at the price you paid for it or, if lower, its 'net realizable value', that is, what you can sell it for. It can be quite difficult to establish this value unless you actually sell the particular stock item after your year end, in which case you would use that lower figure in your valuation.

It is also useful to maintain a register of your business's fixed assets (machinery, vehicles, etc), recording their purchase date and invoice cost. This would help the business safeguard its assets as well as providing a basis for the calculation of the depreciation of each asset. Also, on a practical level, a fixed asset register would prove very useful when it comes to insuring your business.

Again, this can be done manually or with computer spreadsheets, which are ideal for this sort of record keeping. Most computerized accounting packages include a fixed asset register program.

USE OF INFORMATION TECHNOLOGY (IT)

Having mentioned computer technology already, there is a range of business performance reports, not merely accounts, which can be readily generated through IT systems.

Admittedly, a reporting package can be integrated with an accounts package, or it could be a separate standalone system, but this could entail having to enter the same information twice.

Using a mixed farm business as an example, a management information system should be readily able to produce reports on:

- ☐ crop or field yield analysis;
- ☐ livestock gross margin;
- ☐ milk yields;
- ☐ cash flow management and budgeting;
- ☐ break-even analysis;
- ☐ overhead recovery analysis.

AUDIT ROUTINES

The company audit is often seen as 'the cost of incorporation'. A company is a separate legal entity from its shareholders – should the company be at fault, it is the company and not the shareholders that is sued.

The shareholders appoint a Board of Directors that is charged with the stewardship of the company's assets to provide a return on the shareholders' investment. The company's financial performance is reported in the annual accounts. With many companies, the directors are also often the controlling shareholders.

Under the Companies Act, only those limited companies with a turnover of more than £1 million, or a balance sheet with gross assets totaling more than £1.4 million, are obliged to have their accounts audited (with certain exceptions).

As an aside, if you are concerned about the financial management of a company in which you own shares, where an audit is not statutorily required, provided that you (or a group of members) hold at least 10 per cent of any class of the company's issued share capital, you can request that the company has its accounts audited.

Auditing has come under scrutiny recently with the collapse of various US-based global businesses where the auditors have appeared to be complicit in their financial mismanagement. That aside, the Companies Act places the responsibility on a company's directors to prepare accounts that show a 'true and fair view'. In basic terms, an audit is an evidence-gathering exercise that allows the auditor to form an opinion as to whether he or she agrees that the accounts do give a 'true and fair view' of a company's affairs.

An audit is not designed specifically to detect fraud or error (nor is it designed to trip up the company's accounts staff) – not every transaction in a set of accounts is considered, as this would be excessively time consuming. Given the selective nature of the items looked at during an audit, the auditor cannot say that a set of accounts is completely accurate, merely 'true and fair'.

'True and fair' has never been defined in law, as it is an ever-changing concept. Because of how the standards under which company accounts are drawn up evolve over time, what is considered 'true and fair' one year may not be 'true and fair' in subsequent years. By convention, 'true' relates to the figures in the accounts, indicating that they are as accurate as possible and relevant to the reader's need for information. 'Fair' relates to how the figures are disclosed, indicating that they are understandable by the reader and free from bias.

Alternatively, a set of accounts would be said to be 'true and fair' if they were 'materially accurate'. An item is only material if its inclusion or exclusion changes the reader's opinion of those accounts. In a multinational company's accounts £1 million could be immaterial, but £5,000 could be material if it turns a profit into a loss.

An audit can be broken down into three basic stages: planning, fieldwork and completion. Planning is crucial to the audit process as it provides the auditor with an opportunity to assess the risk involved in the audit. Work needs to be designed to minimize the ultimate risk that the auditor will draw the wrong conclusion from his or her work and give an inappropriate audit opinion.

Planning is most easily carried out with a draft set of the company's accounts to hand, or at least a trial balance. This would enable the auditor to assess the company's performance compared to previous years and in comparison to other companies of a similar size in the same business sector. This can provide valuable initial evidence as to the reasonableness of the accounts.

The auditor will develop an initial understanding of the company and the industry in which it operates during the planning stage, and should be able to identify which areas of the accounts represent the most risk (ie where errors are likely to occur) and plan his or her fieldwork accordingly. This process becomes more efficient over the course of time as the auditor becomes more and more familiar with the company and its operations.

The plan would include specific details of what work will be carried out on the different areas of the accounts. The plan can be amended as the audit progresses for any issues that arise that were not apparent at the planning stage.

Another element of planning is for the auditor to set the 'materiality level' to be applied during the audit. There are various ways of setting materiality, but quite commonly it involves taking a combination of fixed percentages of key figures from the accounts, such as sales, net profit, gross and net assets.

Even after calculating materiality on a mathematical basis, the auditor may wish to apply personal judgement given his or her own knowledge of the company and the risks involved. Materiality could be moved upwards or downwards as a result, consequently increasing or decreasing the workload. Having calculated materiality, the auditor can then carry out his or her work effectively, paying little attention to any figures that fall below this level. Again, materiality can be reconsidered as the audit progresses for any new issues that come to light.

Also, a record should be kept of errors that the auditor does come across, because although individually an error may not be material, on a cumulative basis such errors may become material. (As an aside, although an auditor may set himself or herself a materiality figure, the Inland Revenue has no concept of materiality when it comes to inquiring into a company's affairs. This can be very frustrating for the company and the auditor.)

Certain figures in the accounts are material in nature, most notably transactions with the company's directors. By law, such transactions need to be disclosed in the accounts so that shareholders can see how directors may been benefiting from their position, not merely through their remuneration.

Some of the planning work needs to be carried out 'on site', such as obtaining an understanding of a company's accounting and internal control systems. Assessing these systems will allow the auditor to gauge their reliability, which can reduce the amount of work required to substantiate figures in the accounts.

Modern auditing tends to concentrate on looking at the figures contained on the company's balance sheet and gathering sufficient evidence to support each material amount. Enough evidence needs to be accumulated to support an item's:

- ☐ physical existence;
- ☐ completeness;
- ☐ disclosure in the accounts;

☐ valuation;
☐ occurrence;
☐ measurement;
☐ rights and obligations.

Different sources of evidence have different degrees of reliability, and a certain amount of 'professional scepticism' comes into play. This is not to say that auditors will automatically believe that a company will be misleading them, just that there may be some bias involved. After all, the auditor is giving an independent opinion in his or her audit report, so the more evidence he or she can amass from unbiased sources the better.

As a brief illustration of some of the routines that may be applied, for example for fixed assets, work could include physically verifying a selection of assets to the accounting records. A fixed asset register, as mentioned above, would make this exercise relatively simple, provided that the register is updated every time an asset is bought or sold.

A sample of additions in the year may be checked against supporting purchase invoices and depreciation for the year could be checked on a 'global' basis.

For stock, the auditor would want to attend the stock take to assess the company's routines for counting its stock. As a separate exercise, a sample of stock lines could be selected to establish how they have been valued.

For debtors, the auditor would want to obtain confirmation from a selection of trade debtors acknowledging their indebtedness to the company. An alternative procedure would be to examine moneys received from debtors after the year end.

For bank balances, the auditor should write to the company's bank requesting confirmation of account balances at the year end, together with confirmation of overdraft facilities, assets held as security and so forth.

For creditors, the auditor may want to compare a selection of balances of trade creditors to supplier statements, as well as examining payments made after the year end to identify liabilities that may have existed at the year end. Auditing creditors can be more problematic than debtors, as there may be nothing in the accounts to suggest that a liability exists.

Share capital is usually quite a static figure on a company's balance sheet and can readily be confirmed by examining the company's statutory records and annual return.

The final routine in the course of an audit is the completion of the file and signing the audit report. The accounts have to be signed by the directors before the auditor can sign his or her report. Prior to signing, the accounts are re-assessed to ensure that they are in line with evidence obtained by the auditor and that all the statutory disclosure requirements have been met.

Enquiries are made to ensure that no events have occurred since the year end that would have a material effect on the accounts, and the directors are asked to give written confirmation of any issues that the auditor has not been able to substantiate by any other means. Also, the directors have to demonstrate that the company is a going concern (is able to operate for the foreseeable future) and the auditor must examine the assumptions the board has made.

Writing as an auditor, the whole audit process is eased by clients who are willing to cooperate in the process, such as by preparing schedules that substantiate the figures in their year-end balance sheet. You may regard your company audit as an expensive compliance exercise forced upon you by the Companies Act. As a firm, we use the auditing process to advise clients on how they can make their companies more efficient and how they are performing in comparison to their competitors.

16 | **Employment Practices**

Allison Grant, KSB Law

People are the most valuable asset for most businesses. The employment relationship presents employers with a minefield of legislation and procedures that, if not adhered to and respected, may damage relations between the employer and employee, increase the risk of disputes, and end in costly litigation. This chapter examines some of the risks for employers and offers guidance on how employers can mitigate the risk.

Employers who ignore our employment legislation do so at their own cost and at the cost of their employees. A mismanaged workforce is more likely to give rise to a claims culture by giving cause to grievances and employment tribunal claims, and by encouraging poor performance, low morale and absenteeism. Good employment practices understand the importance and consequence of employment legislation, recognize that there are risks for an employer arising from employee rights, and give a detailed consideration as to how these risks may be managed.

Emphasis is placed in this chapter on making employers aware of the risks and taking practical steps to manage the risks. The essential ingredients to have in managing the risks are well-drafted contracts of employment and written policies and procedures, and managers who are trained to be familiar with an employer's obligations under the law.

The main categories of individuals and issues protected by our employment legislation are listed in Table 16.1, although this is not an exhaustive list.

In addition to the protection coming from legislation are the legal rules derived from the common law, including the law of contract pursuant to which the contract of employment is enforced, and the law of torts (wrongful acts that cause damage or loss), which governs an employer's liability for the acts of its employees and civil liability for industrial accidents and for strikes and other forms of industrial action.

Table 16.1 Categories of individuals and issues protected by employment legislation

Individual/Issue	Examples of protective legislation/codee
Age	Code of Practice on Age Diversity at Work (2002)
Agency workers	Working Time Regs 1998 (WTR), National Minimum Wage Regs 1999
Carers	Maternity and Parental Leave, etc Regs 1999
Colour	Race Relations Act 1976 (RRA)
Disability	Disability Discrimination Act 1995 (DDA)
Disciplinary and Grievance	Employment Act 2002 (Dispute Resolution) Regs 2004
Employee representative status	Employment Rights Act 1996 (ERA)
Employees exercising a statutory right	ERA
Employees on fixed-term contracts	ERA, Fixed Term Employees (Prevention of Less Favourable Treatment) Regs 2002
Ethnic group	RRA
Equal pay	Equal Pay Act 1970, Code of Practice on Equal Pay 2003
Gender	Sex Discrimination Act 1975 (SDA)
Health and safety representative	ERA
Maternity	ERA and Maternity and Parental Leave, etc Regs 1999
Nationality	RRA
Parental status	Maternity and Parental Leave, etc Regs 1999
Part-time employees	Part-Time Workers (Prevention of Less Favourable Treatment) Regs 2000
Pregnancy	ERA and SDA
Race	RRA
Redundancy	ERA
Religion	Employment Equality (Religion or Belief) Regs 2003
Rest periods	WTR
Sexual orientation	Employment Equality (Sexual Orientation) Regs 2003
Shop workers who refuse to work on Sundays	ERA
Trade union membership	Trade Union and Labour Relations (consolidation) Act 1992
Unfair dismissal	ERA
Victimization	ERA, DDA, SDA, and RRA
Whistle-blowing	Public Interest Disclosure Act 1998, ERA
Written statement of particulars	ERA
Young persons	WTR, Children (Protection at Work) Regs 1998

The employment relationship in chronological order has three distinct phases: recruitment, employment and termination of employment.

RECRUITMENT AND ENGAGEMENT

There are a number of legal considerations that the employer will need to take into account when recruiting and engaging an employee. These include the following:

☐ When advertising for prospective employees, the employer must be careful not to infringe the provisions of the anti-discrimination legislation. It is unlawful to discriminate on the grounds of sex, race, disability, sexual orientation and religion/belief.

☐ An employer may use any interviewing and selection procedures he or she wishes, provided they are not discriminatory. For instance, in arranging an interview for a disabled person, it may be necessary for an employer to make reasonable adjustments to enable that person to attend.

☐ Special rules apply to the employment of children and young persons under the age of 18 years.

☐ It is an offence under immigration law to employ a foreign employee who is not entitled to work in the UK.

☐ Frequently, employees when leaving a job nowadays are subject to giving proper notice of termination and to post-termination non-competition and non-solicitation restrictions, which may affect an individual's ability to take up another job.

☐ Criminal offences can, under the Rehabilitation Offenders Act 1974, become 'spent', which means the offence may not have to be disclosed.

☐ An employer should inform a new employee of the terms and conditions under which he or she is to work and the commencement date and is obliged by law to give the employee written particulars of employment within two months of the employment starting.

To address the legal considerations properly, there are a number of practical steps that an employer can take:

☐ Give careful consideration to the advertisement and the job description. Think carefully about the language used in the advertisement and avoid using phrases that imply age or gender restrictions, such as 'young graduates' or 'mature person', or 'the right man for the job'.

☐ Have those people within the organization who are familiar with the complexities of the anti-discrimination legislation attend to the interviewing and selection of candidates.

- ☐ Keep a written record of the selection, as this will prove more than useful if you are required to explain the decision not to offer employment.
- ☐ Have the application form require the candidate to provide comprehensive information to include employment history, health, qualifications and criminal records.
- ☐ Carry out basic checks before the employment commences, such as taking up references and asking the individual to provide appropriate documents to evidence the right to work (eg a P45, passport and other formal document with the national insurance number).

Having selected an applicant, the offer letter and the employment contract will be instrumental in minimizing any potential issues that might arise during and at the end of the employment.

A job offer is an expression of a willingness to be legally bound. In preparing an offer letter the employer should spell out the main terms on which the employment is offered. The key terms include the job title, remuneration and benefits, place of work, holiday entitlement, hours, notice period, and restrictions that will apply post-termination. In carrying out checks on an applicant, key considerations are to have the offer of employment made conditional on satisfactory references, evidence of qualifications, satisfactory medical, the applicant being free to start the employment by a certain date, acceptance by a specified date, and securing sight of the individual's post-termination restrictions from his or her existing or previous employment to ensure that these will not impede that person's ability to work.

The legal position is unclear if the applicant commences work before all of the checks have been made. Therefore, to avoid a difficult position should a reference prove unsatisfactory, it would be better for the employer to provide that the offer 'and any subsequent employment' are subject to the supply of satisfactory checks.

It is essential the employer puts in place a well-drafted employment contract and has this signed by the employee. There is no hard and fast rule as to when the employment contract should be sent to the applicant, although the contract should be delivered at the same time as the offer letter. This way, the offer of employment can be conditional on the candidate agreeing to sign the contract. If it is left until the employment commences, the employee may refuse to sign the contract and look to negotiate some of its provisions.

Be aware that the employment contract is the legal foundation of the employment relationship. The contract assumes great importance when the parties are in dispute. It must be clear and unambiguous to avoid disagreements about the terms and conditions of employment and without recourse to litigation. Oral terms can lead to dispute when there is nothing to hand to clarify the terms.

In drafting the contract, there are a number of important provisions and considerations to be aware of:

☐ Consider including a specific period of probation to have the employee's performance and suitability for the job monitored and carefully evaluated during the initial months of employment. This would enable the employer to give a shorter period of notice before, say, 12 months' service has been completed.

☐ Have the job title include a job description to spell out the main duties and requirements of the role. Widely drafted duties ensure a degree of flexibility, and where overseas travel is required, this will need to be spelt out.

☐ Include a payment in lieu of notice provision to give the employer the option of summarily terminating the employment upon the payment of a sum in lieu of notice.

☐ Include a 'garden leave' provision to give the employer the option of removing the employee from the workplace once notice to terminate the employment relationship has been given or received by the employer. This will protect the employer's business by preventing the employee from continuing to have access to clients and employees of the business, during what could be a crucial time when the employee is either setting up his or her own business or joining a competitor.

☐ It may be sensible to include a clause in the contract to allow a change of hours to meet future business needs.

☐ An express right to make deductions from the employee's salary in relation to any outstanding debts (eg season ticket loan) or other sums due (eg holiday overpayments) is advisable.

☐ Bonuses should be expressed to be non-contractual and payable at the unfettered discretion of the employer. In the absence of this provision, an employee may become entitled to a bonus.

☐ An express right to suspend an employee on full pay, in circumstances when it is deemed necessary to investigate the employee's conduct, is advisable.

☐ Be aware that there is no automatic power to change contract terms, so provision for this must be built into the contract.

☐ Ensure that the contract is sufficiently detailed to avoid unnecessary implied terms.

☐ Include specific provisions to protect the employer's business activities, trade secrets, pricing policy, product development plans, marketing strategy and other such confidential information during and after the employment has ended. Subject to the nature of the business, this may involve a separate document to the employment contract, called a 'non-disclosure and confidentiality' agreement.

☐ Consider post-termination, non-solicitation and non-compete covenants to protect the business after the employment has ended. Care is needed in drafting the covenants to ensure that they are enforceable through the courts.

☐ Any reference to written policies and procedures of the type usually found within a handbook should make it clear that they do not have contractual status (if that is the case).

MANAGING THE EMPLOYMENT RELATIONSHIP

At the commencement of employment, employees will often be provided with a substantial amount of documentation. These documents may be presented under a variety of titles such as 'employer policies' and 'company handbooks'. Well-drafted policies and procedures are essential to managing employment risks. Without these it is difficult to see how an employer can manage the employment relationship.

It is advisable to have the policies and procedures kept together in a handbook, which must be made available to all employees by providing every employee with a full copy of the handbook and/or delivering a communication informing employees of the handbook's existence, for example on the intranet. A written record should then be placed on the personnel file to demonstrate that the employee has been made aware of the handbook and has access to it. It is advisable to ask all employees to sign a declaration that they have read and understood the policies and procedures contained within the handbook.

It is of vital practical importance that the handbook states which parts are contractual and which are non-contractual. This question may arise, for example, when the employer seeks to vary the provisions of a policy or of the handbook. If a policy is contractual, it may not be unilaterally varied without the consent of the employee, as in the absence of the employee's consent a breach of contract is likely to occur. By classifying a policy as non-contractual from the outset, it can be unilaterally amended, and will remove the risk of a breach of contract claim.

The policies and procedures that should appear in a handbook

☐ Disciplinary and grievance procedures – a written procedure is going to reduce the risk that basic rules of fairness will be ignored or overlooked, important legal rights (such as the right to be accompanied to a disciplinary hearing) are not complied with and that there will be inconsistency of treatment in relation to disciplinary and grievance issues. A key change introduced by the Employment Act 2002 on 1 October 2004 is an obligation on all employers to have an internal dispute resolution mechanism.

Employers need to remember that the new procedures are a minimum requirement. Employers should check that their grievance and disciplinary procedures are compliant with the new rules.

☐ E-mail/internet use policies – these will make clear that the employer owns the system, notify employees that they do not have an individual right to privacy when using the system, notify them that e-mails are likely to be monitored, set out permissible uses and those that are prohibited, and notify employees that they must report any inappropriate use of the system. Having such policies will reduce the misuse of e-mails and the internet, and inform employees that any misuse of the system will be subject to disciplinary action.

☐ Maternity policy – this will make managers, supervisors and employees aware of the legal rights of mothers-to-be and new mothers, both in the workplace and while on maternity leave, and will reduce the risk of the maternity laws not being complied with and reduce the potential for discrimination claims.

☐ Equal opportunities policy – this will help the employer to avoid unlawful discrimination, improve employment recruitment and retention practices, and take action against those who infringe equal opportunities principles. The policy should take into account staff awareness and training, job advertisements, application forms, interviews, terms and conditions, harassment and bullying, employees with a disability, disciplinary and grievance procedures, flexible working practices, family-friendly rights, and third parties.

☐ Harassment and bullying policy – this will make employees aware that harassment and bullying are subject to the employer's disciplinary process and possibly dismissal, and so are not tolerated. Having such a policy will ensure that harassment claims are fully investigated and disciplinary action is taken where claims have been substantiated.

☐ Whistle-blowing policy – this will give a clear statement that malpractice will be taken seriously in the organization, give examples of the type of matters regarded as malpractice, and provide a worker with the opportunity to raise concerns outside the line management structure. Employees who 'blow the whistle' on their employer by making a 'protected disclosure' have the legal right not to be dismissed, selected for redundancy or subjected to any other detriment (demotion, forfeiture of opportunities for promotion or training, etc) for having done so.

☐ Disability policy – this will confirm the employer's commitment to employ disabled workers, to comply with the requirements of equal treatment and to make reasonable adjustments, and raises awareness among managers and the workforce. It is a major step in mitigating the risk of disability discrimination from the workplace.

Other issues and aspects of the employment relationship that an employer should consider as prudent to cover in the handbook include an alcohol and drugs policy, stress policy, data protection policy, flexible working policy, parental policy, travel/company car policy, health and safety policy, a policy on relationships at work, smoking policy, and a paternity and adoption leave policy.

BRINGING THE EMPLOYMENT RELATIONSHIP TO AN END

Termination by the employer, with or without notice, may give rise to claims in respect of:

- [ ] unfair dismissal and/or wrongful dismissal;
- [ ] a discrimination or victimization claim;
- [ ] a statutory or contractual redundancy payment.

Occasionally, an employee will terminate the relationship in circumstances where the employee regards himself or herself as 'constructively dismissed'. This type of dismissal may give rise to the claim that the employee was forced to leave by reason of the employer's conduct.

The main legal considerations that an employer should have regard to when contemplating a dismissal are:

- [ ] the employee's right to not be unfairly dismissed;
- [ ] the procedure to be followed in terminating the employment;
- [ ] whether the dismissal runs a risk of raising a discrimination-based claim;
- [ ] the employment contract, in particular those provisions in respect of termination and notice or payment in lieu of notice.

On completion of 12 months' employment, and in some cases from day one, an employee has the right to not be unfairly dismissed. An employer who dismisses an employee without good reason or without following a fair procedure lays itself open to a claim for unfair dismissal.

The following are potentially fair reasons for a dismissal:

- [ ] capability;
- [ ] conduct;
- [ ] redundancy;
- [ ] statutory rules that require the employee to stop working;
- [ ] 'some other substantial reason'.

It is imperative that an employer makes sure the grounds for dismissing an employee fall within one of the five potentially fair reasons. When dismissing an employee, always confirm the fact and reasons for the dismissal in writing.

It is vital that there are clear procedures in place for dismissal to be clearly communicated in writing.

Even if a reason for dismissal is self-evident, such a dismissal will be unfair if the employer does not act reasonably in carrying it out by following a fair procedure. The new statutory obligation to have an internal dispute resolution mechanism applies in nearly all cases, and particular attention must be paid to the statutory procedures. Regardless of its size, an employer must, as a minimum, have followed a three-stage statutory disciplinary procedure before it dismisses an employee or imposes a sanction, such as demotion, loss of seniority or loss of pay. The guidance below is subject to adhering to the new procedures:

☐ When dismissing for misconduct, employers must carry out an investigation, give the employee notice of the charges, allow the employee to state his or her case at a disciplinary hearing and provide a right of appeal.

☐ In the context of a capability dismissal on performance grounds, investigate the reasons for underperformance, consider offering training, set reasonable targets and time periods for improvement and warn of dismissal in the event of insufficient improvement.

☐ In dismissing on the grounds of ill health, consult with the employee, give warning of the possibility of dismissal, fully investigate the underlying medical problem and prognosis and give consideration to alternative employment before moving on to dismiss.

☐ For redundancy dismissals, warn and consult at all stages with the employees, select an appropriate pool, select objective criteria, apply them fairly and consider alternative employment.

In the case of dismissals for any of the above reasons, there is a risk of a finding of unfair dismissal if the employer fails to act reasonably and fails to follow the minimum requirements imposed by the three-stage statutory dismissal and disciplinary procedure.

CONCLUSION

The risks inherent in an employment relationship are many but, with the right approach, employers can manage the risks and the relationship can be rewarding.

17 Insurance for Rural Businesses

Tim Price, NFU Mutual

BEFORE YOU START

In the rush to establish and consolidate a new business insurance is one of the last things on your mind. But without the right insurance – and the right level of cover – an incident such as a fire could put paid to your business ever getting off the ground.

So how do new and growing businesses work out what sort of cover they need? Many insurers offer policies to suit different types of small firm – ranging from those run from owners' homes, through shops and workshops to businesses whose owners tend to work in other people's premises, such as plumbers.

The first step is to find insurance advisers with an understanding of your needs. Adverts in magazines covering your sort of business and local newspapers can help you build up a list. Trade bodies are also a good source of information, but personal recommendations from people running similar enterprises are invaluable.

Using an insurer whose advisers are prepared to make visits to business customers should make this process easier. If your insurer's staff come to your premises they are more likely to understand what you are doing and what you need than if your only contact with them is by telephone – which means that you can focus on running your business knowing that they are looking after your insurance.

COVER FOR HOMEWORKING

Many new rural enterprises begin life in a spare bedroom or converted outbuilding. Even for a modest business insurance is an important issue for the rising number of people who run a business from home. That is because cover for homeworking is not provided by standard home and contents insurance policies, putting the business at risk if there is a break-in, fire, or a claim against the business from a member of the public.

To meet the insurance needs of people who work from home, a number of insurers offer cover as an extension to home and contents policies. These policies usually provide cover for liability to the public, together with increased cost of working, loss of business money, and book debts insurance. Optional add-ons like cover for personal possessions used for business purposes outside the home, liability to employees, and computer breakdown, including reinstatement of data and increased cost of working are useful for some businesses.

YOUR OWN PREMISES

If you are starting out with your own dedicated premises then you have responsibilities whether you are the owner of the building or you are renting it.

Commercial policies usually offer a range of optional covers rather than the 'all inclusive' approach of modern home policies. This means that it is up to you and your insurance adviser to put together the right cover package.

Typical perils that can be covered include fire, explosion, storm, flood and malicious damage. Whether you take the 'safety at all costs' approach and take out cover for every contingency, or opt for the insurance required by law and the major perils that could affect your business depends on your attitude to risk and the state of your bank balance.

AVOIDING UNDERINSURANCE

Underinsurance means that the sums insured in the policy are not enough to cover the full replacement cost of the buildings and their contents. If this figure is not correctly set when the policy is taken out, or is not amended when subsequent alterations or extensions are made to the buildings, there is a serious risk that the policyholder will be left with a bill to pay in the event of a claim.

Some policyholders assume that if they are underinsured, they will only lose out in the unlikely event of their buildings being totally destroyed. In fact, insurance companies can proportionally reduce claim payouts if the business turns out to be underinsured when a claim is made. This means that following a fire in a building insured for £20,000, but with a replacement cost of £24,000, the insurer will only settle five-sixths of the claim.

To get the sums insured accurate from the outset, it is best to get a professional valuation of your buildings. Then – provided that the sum insured is linked to the appropriate building cost index, and details of any new buildings or extensions are passed on to the insurer – another professional valuation should not be needed for five years or so.

Turning to equipment and stock inside the buildings, it is equally important to keep the sums insured accurate. Regular reviews should be made of stock levels so that different amounts or new types of produce being stored are covered, along with any new equipment.

It is especially important for businesses working under tight margins to take out loss of income insurance in addition to covers for their premises, stock, and tools of their trade. This is because when fire or some other disaster strikes it is often not the damage to the buildings, stock, and equipment, that causes the business the most serious problems, but the income lost while the unit is out of production and overheads like rent, wages and interest charges still have to be paid.

This strain can place an impossible financial burden on a business, particularly as a serious incident can mean that it will be out of production for months. Often in the aftermath of a disaster, loss of income insurance can keep a sufficient income flowing into the business to enable it to survive the period while it is out of action waiting for buildings to be repaired, or new plant installed.

EMPLOYERS' LIABILITY INSURANCE

Quite a few people starting out in business are surprised to find out that in the UK employers' liability insurance cover is required by law not only for staff employed full- or part-time but also for anyone who helps out with a business: casual staff, odd job workers – whether or not they have a formal contract of employment. Insurance is required if friends help out, even if they receive no payment. This means that employers' liability insurance must be held by every UK business that has a regular employee or uses any casual or seasonal labour.

This is an important issue for small businesses to consider because courts may rule that anyone undertaking specific direction is, at that time, an employee. Genuine contractors, with their own insurance arrangements, who are carrying out work for you in the course of their business, will not usually need to be regarded as employees.

PUBLIC AND PRODUCT LIABILITY

If members of the public are invited on to your premises or land, then you are at increased risk of claims following accidents or damage to property. Product liability insurance will also be needed if you produce goods for either wholesale or retail operations.

Liability claims can be very expensive, particularly if one or more people are seriously injured and require ongoing care. For this reason even a small business would be wise to have public and product liability cover.

THEFT INSURANCE AND SECURITY

While the majority of rural thefts are still small-scale and opportunist, rural crime has increased significantly in recent years although with the exception of a few areas, crime levels in the countryside are below those in urban areas, and insurance premiums tend to reflect this. This means that anyone setting up a country-based business should take security seriously and make sure they have theft insurance in place.

When deciding on a location for a new business, and evaluating appropriate security measures, it is worth considering the following questions:

☐ Is the site deserted at night, enabling thieves to break in undetected?
☐ Is it so remote that police will be half an hour or more away?
☐ Can the building be effectively secured to an appropriate level for the type of stock and equipment you are concerned with?

These are important considerations because the high levels of security that are now commonplace in urban businesses and homes have led professional thieves to target rural areas, which have traditionally needed less elaborate security measures.

MONEY

Money insurance should also be considered if the enterprise involves cash transactions being made on a regular basis and/or money kept at your premises. This is an especially important issue for remote locations where daily visits to the bank are impractical, or most business is done at weekends.

PREMISES

Insurance for new construction or change of use of existing buildings should be arranged as early as possible. Involving insurers at the planning stage is prudent as it enables safety measures to be incorporated into the initial plans. In some situations, a project's overall viability may be lost if an enterprise is set up only to find that expensive safety precautions need to be taken.

HOTELS AND BED AND BREAKFAST BUSINESSES

It is estimated that one in six farms now offers accommodation to the public, either using the farmhouse or converted barns or outbuildings, and many more people are converting large houses into holiday accommodation. Commercial insurers offer polices specially designed for these sorts of businesses including a range of cover options, which you can mix and match to meet the requirements of your business.

Both the buildings and contents can be covered against fire, lightning, storm, water damage, subsidence and other major risks. The policies also typically provide cover for employers' liability, business property, money, and theft by guests. Policyholders can opt for an extension of cover to make up lost income following damage by an insured event, such as fire, or even food poisoning. Cancellation cover, which makes up lost income if guests fail to arrive following a number of specified causes, is also available.

INFORMATION TECHNOLOGY (IT)

Insurance for business computer systems is becoming increasingly important as IT becomes a key management tool.

Theft and fire are the main causes of claims reported to insurers and replacing a hard drive is the most common computer claim. Professional IT thieves generally will not bother to take the whole computer – it is the expensive hard drive they are after, and they can remove this in minutes.

While PCs used solely for domestic purposes can normally be covered under a household contents policy, computers used for business purposes require insurance under a commercial policy. These policies usually cover the cost of replacing the computer hardware and software, including printers and other peripheral equipment. Recovery of data stored on the computer's hard drive can also be covered. This pays for experts to try to access damaged hard drives, or preferably re-install data backed up in a remote location. Other cover options typically include consequential loss insurance, which pays the increased cost of working while the system is out of use.

Premiums tend to be higher for laptops as they suffer many more claims than desk computers. It is important to note that extra covers may be required for networked IT systems or computers used to control manufacturing processes.

RISK MANAGEMENT

As people are becoming more wealth oriented the UK is becoming a more litigious country. Increasingly, an accident or mishap, often resulting from an oversight or simple mistake, can result in litigation and end up incurring considerable cost to a business. Whereas in the past unintentional damage or inconvenience would have been settled amicably, many incidents are now finding their way to court.

There is an increasing danger that, unless you have effective public liability cover, an incident beyond your control could result in the loss of your livelihood. It could be something as simple as someone tripping over a stone you had put on a footpath while building a wall.

Every year several hundred people are killed while at work in the UK and many thousands suffer injuries. At the same time many millions of pounds' worth of equipment and buildings are destroyed or damaged unnecessarily, resulting in claims that could have been avoided.

With a little forethought and planning many accidents that occur on business premises could be prevented. This is why insurers are increasingly working with their commercial business customers to help them reduce the risks in their business. To help keep your business safe, it is well worth insuring with a company with experience of dealing with claims in businesses similar to yours.

PROTECTION FROM BAD LOSSES

Every month hundreds of businesses in the UK become bankrupt or insolvent. This usually results in their suppliers being left with non-recoverable debts for goods or services provided, which can have drastic consequences for those suppliers. Credit insurance enables businesses to claim for money owed to them by companies that have ceased trading.

INSURING VEHICLES

Whether you are using your existing vehicle or investing in a van or other form of transport for your business, there will be insurance implications. Insurers should be informed if you are starting to use your car for business use. A vehicle like a van or lorry should be insured on a commercial vehicle policy.

GOODS IN TRANSIT

Your produce is probably more at risk of loss or damage while in transit than when it is stored in your warehouse or on display in a shop. Insurance for goods in transit covers the risk of loss from perils such as fire, theft and even accidental damage while goods are being moved.

FINALLY...

It is important to keep your insurance company up to date with changing circumstances in your business. If your staffing levels have fallen you may qualify for a reduction on your premiums, or if you are expanding or moving into a new area you may need extra cover to protect your growing enterprise fully.

18 Marketing and Sales Promotion

Roderick Millar and Jonathan Reuvid

There is much confusion about marketing. This stems from two sources. Firstly, the definition of 'marketing' requires clarification. And secondly, the amount of resources a small business should allocate to it needs to be addressed.

The definition is simple to deal with. To marketing professionals and academics marketing can be summed up as 'offering what you can sell'. To the public it is more usually thought of as 'selling what you can offer'. If you are to run a successful business, the first definition is the better one to be guided by, and so a more holistic approach is necessary, involving what those in the trade refer to as 'the four Ps': product, price, place and promotion. To this the PR industry also adds a fifth 'P': perception.

The amount of resources you can and should allocate to marketing is much more subjective. There is no empirical test to tell you what you must spend in both time and money in order to achieve any specific level of return. The marketing industry in all its many forms, from advertising sales people and trade show organizers to copywriters and PR agents, will all make cogent arguments why you should use their services. And being sales-people they will often make you worry that you will be left behind if you do not use them. The bottom line should never be 'Can you afford not to?' but always 'Will the marketing return justify the costs?'. No doubt everyone would like to take full-page colour spreads in the weekend supplements backed up by TV and billboard campaigns – but clearly that is not an option to those on a limited budget and inappropriate to most country businesses. This chapter will try to indicate some of the options available to those on a small business budget.

MARKET RESEARCH

The beginning of your marketing process should be in place long before you start trading your new product or service. This applies as much to Microsoft's latest software as to the new hairdressing salon on the high street. They must both establish whether there is a market demand for a new product and what exactly the demand is for; they must conduct market research. The difference is that Microsoft has rather larger marketing resources than the hairdresser does.

Established businesses have a huge advantage over start-up businesses in carrying out market research. They have exposure to market sentiment and everyday reactions through their current business activities. Added to this is their database of past and present customers that they ought to be able to analyse and, should they wish, contact for views and opinions. This information can also form the basis for extrapolating their current data to build up likely market information for different geographic areas or market sectors.

The brand-new start-up business is unlikely to have any of these resources readily available to it, and while discussion among like-minded competitors is often a lot more open than you may expect, you will not be handed databases and customer views by your future competition. Therefore, the prospective businessperson must try to build a picture of what the market for his or her product or service is currently like and whether there is sufficient demand for the concept and its benefits. Gathering this information can be done either by collecting brand-new data direct from the marketplace specifically for your own purposes (primary data) or from data already gathered by others that you can shape for your own use (secondary data). Obviously, primary data will be more relevant and more up to date; you can assess how reliable it will be because you know how it was collected and collated. Secondary data may well require you to make some assumptions as to how and where it was gathered and how reliable it is; it may be slightly out of date and also is likely to be only partially relevant to your product or service. However, it will be very much cheaper to acquire than primary data.

In today's economy there is no shortage of available information. The trick is to sift out the wheat from the chaff. Identifying the correct questions to ask is important. You must think carefully about what factors you need in order to sell your product or service successfully. This will include the profile of your potential customers (age, spending power, where they live, family status, sex) a profile of the market (Is it growing or shrinking? Which sectors of the market are doing best and why? What is the long-term trend?), and some marketing research (What are your competitors doing to sell their products? What is working and what is not?).

If you have a rural business selling locally, then your market research can be done more on a primary than on a secondary basis. You can go out and speak to potential customers; you can observe the competition. The more disparate your potential customer base the more difficult it will be for you to track them down and have a useful dialogue with them. In this case secondary data collection will become more important and, for tracking sector trends, will be your only option. The following are possible sources of information:

- □ Trade magazines and financial press will offer some information but probably unsystematically – it will be pot luck what you find.
- □ The background information you seek will most likely be somewhere on the internet, but sourcing can be tiresome and assessing its reliability and how up to date it may be is often a problem.
- □ Larger libraries will have a range of market research books that can give you useful information.
- □ In addition to these sources you may find that your local authority business advice unit will have current information available to you about local business and markets, as will the local Chamber of Commerce and Business Link office.

Most of these sources of information will be either free or inexpensive to access. If you still require more information and have the money to spend, then you can purchase market information from market research and business information companies. The British Market Research Association will be able to provide a list (www.bmra.org.uk).

SEGMENTATION AND STRATEGY

Having gathered the relevant market information for your business concept's sector, your next marketing task is to identify where exactly your product or service fits within the sector. The most basic segmentation is to know if you want to sell to business or consumers. Consumers are more numerous and normally will pay higher prices, but they are more difficult to reach (they do not list themselves like companies do in trade directories and magazines, or in the *Yellow Pages* with contact names and numbers), more fickle (most companies will not change their suppliers just because a new one comes along), and purchase in smaller quantities less regularly.

As a small business you will need to focus on specific segments of the market since you will be unable to offer all things to all comers. Are you going for high-end users willing to pay for quality and/or uniqueness, or are you trying to provide a service locally where none currently exists? What is your 'unique selling point' – or 'USP' in marketing jargon – the feature that sets you apart from the competition?

With your sector knowledge and your segment identified you must now design your marketing strategy and thence plan. The information gained will indicate what is the best way to reach your potential customers. This could be by using:

- □ trade magazines;
- □ local press;
- □ national press;

☐ local radio;
☐ bus advertising;
☐ promotions;
☐ trade shows;
☐ leafleting;
☐ direct mail;
☐ inserts.

And there is one other channel to market for businesses in the countryside seeking to attract consumers to their rural outlets: roadside advertising. It costs nothing but, as Chapter 30 illustrates, it can be a highly effective direct marketing tool.

You will have an idea of how generous or frugal your marketing budget can be so you will have a feel for how much advertising and PR you will be able to afford. The research you have carried out to this point in identifying your gap in the market, who you should be selling to and what in particular it is they want will provide a clear indication as to what type of media you should be using.

If your target market is well-paid young individuals who purchase goods for their image and lifestyle associations rather than pure value-for-money, then your advertising must be in media that projects image and lifestyle. While this is obvious from the unpressurized standpoint of writing the business plan, when you are in the thick of trying to get some media exposure you can easily start to lose control of the original plan. Even the smallest business will be approached occasionally by sales departments wanting you to spend your business's money on promoting yourself in their publications, on their products or at their shows. It is for this reason that it is very important to design a clear marketing strategy that you can refer to and keep as a controlling influence over the media offers that will come your way. Amend and update the strategy as an ongoing project certainly, but in your own time – not because someone else tells you to!

The strategy you build is like a road map – it will show you where you are and where you want to get to. It will also show the preferred route for getting there and the most comprehensive strategic plans will also show you how to get back on track if you lose your way or are detoured by events beyond your control. The first task is to set your targets – where you want to go – whether that is to increase sales of an existing business by 15 per cent or generate sales for a new business to a minimum level. Then plan a timetable of marketing events; these can be any marketing action such as a press release, placing of adverts, leafleting your local area, trade show or whatever you choose – all of them will be chosen because they reach out specifically to your target market and you believe they will bring in more added sales value than they cost.

Critical to all these events is the evaluation process that you must go through after each one of them. Especially for a new business where the response to any event is fairly unpredictable, it is vital to know which marketing tactics produce results and then work out why. The simplest way to track the success of events is to note down all responses you get from potential customers from the event and how many positive sales this leads to. It is very easy not to ask customers enquiring about your product where they heard about you, but it is also very foolish. Nobody will mind being asked, it gives an impression of a well-organized company and, vitally, it provides you with critical information on which to base future marketing events.

IMAGE

Part of the marketing function is to build the image of your business and your products. As a small business you will have very limited resources to address to this area of marketing. You should be focusing your product trading on a homogenous sector of the market and your goal should be to present as coherent an image for your business as possible across all its aspects. Essentially, all companies do this. If we look at the Ford Motor Company, their Ford branded cars are placed so as to be attractive and affordable to the mass market, but Ford also owns Jaguar and Aston Martin, producing executive and super-luxury cars, which they keep very distinct from the Ford name in their marketing, although it is well known that many components are shared between the different cars in the group range.

It is therefore important to consider the impact that every marketing event you undertake will have on your entire range of products or services, not just the single item you are promoting. The quality of the material used in your advertising or promotion will underscore the message you want to get across. That your business's reputation takes years to build but can be destroyed in moments is no less true for being a well-worn cliché.

DIRECT MARKETING

Direct mail is often considered to be the black sheep of the marketing toolbox. However, it is really a victim of its own success. If the response rate to direct mail was not so high, in terms of cost in relation to increased sales, then it would not be as prevalent as it is currently. It is this prevalence that leads to the problem of 'junk mail' piling up behind your door every morning.

The advantage of direct mail to the marketer is that it is very flexible. You can choose your recipients' geographic area, their income level, their leisure preferences and so on. You can also choose how much you wish to spend on any given mailout with great flexibility. The drawbacks are in choosing to whom the mailout should be sent, the expense and the legal implications. For the start-up business, purchasing a list can be relatively expensive, and also requires a degree of specialist knowledge in selecting your list broker and the criteria by which the particular list is built up. It is worth researching the use of direct marketing carefully if you intend to spend a significant percentage of your marketing budget on it. The British Direct Marketing Association (DMA) (www.dma.org.uk; tel: (020) 7291 3300) can provide much useful information. For overseas information, Kogan Page annually publishes *The Directory of International Direct and E-Marketing*.

If your business is well established you are likely to have built up a database of past customers' details. Several of the case studies in Part Five emphasize how the building of a potential customer database was to their success.

If your business is not of the type where you collect your customers' details as a matter of course, it is worth considering methods by which you might be able to gather such information through a loyalty card, notification of sales offers or similar schemes. When you have a list of customers you are in a position where not only can you re-contact them but you may be able to trade your list with other companies in your area. However, there are increasingly strict data protection laws governing notification of customers (at the time of taking their details) if you wish to share their details, in any way, with other bodies. Again the DMA can guide you with this.

ADVERTISING AND PR

It should be so simple to get your message across. You know your product or service inside out, you understand the benefits and you recognize the quality. What is more frustrating is that you also know that people will enjoy using your product – all you have to do is persuade them to try it. And that is the problem.

The situation is difficult because all your competitors are trying to gain the consumer's attention as well. There is a lot of 'noise' out there in the marketplace and your job is to make sure you are heard above everyone else. Advertising and PR are your routes to doing this, but be aware that markets in the UK are very sophisticated and it will take a fair amount of expertise to make your business stand out. This chapter is not able to cover the vast range of skills and advice needed to ensure that your advertisement or press release is eye-catching. The basic principles are simple enough, although the details are where the difference is made. For most rural businesses, PR activity that leads to customer awareness through local press editorial is more likely to be effective than advertising. The following are key points:

- [ ] ABC – accuracy, brevity, clarity – make good copy.
- [ ] Avoid jargon and formality.
- [ ] Never bend the truth (this includes phrases like 'once in a lifetime chance' if it is not); it cheapens the message and damages your reputation.
- [ ] Keep it interesting and relevant (if you are writing a press release, open with an idea that will work as a headline).

The ability to write good advertisements and press releases owes more to experience than natural skill. If you have the time to learn about it then it will be time well spent; if not it may well pay to find an expert to help you out. If you have any contacts in the media they may well be able to help draft the copy for you and show you what makes the difference. If this route is not available and you feel your attempts with only a book to help you are uninspiring, then it may be time to use professional help – the PR agent.

The problem with PR agencies is that you have to pay them! That in itself is not surprising, but quantifying their success is awkward. Most agencies will be keen to get you on a monthly retainer. If your marketing budget can afford this, then it will probably serve you to sign up to a limited-term contract as you will then be able to set out exactly what you expect them to provide over what time period and discuss with them what they hope to achieve in this period in terms of copy placed or extra sales achieved.

The advantages of PR agencies, beyond their ability to write compelling copy, is that they should have a good selection of media contacts through which they can get your message heard. Your business is to produce and sell a successful product; often this will not give you much space to build relationships with the media, and your PR agent is there to overcome this barrier. Their business is based on their ability to get their client's messages into the media, be it local press, national press, radio or any other medium you feel would work, through an established network of contacts.

In choosing a PR agent or agency you must therefore make sure of a number of key points:

- [ ] The most important is that you trust them; this means that you should get hold of references from their existing clients and see what they have done for them.
- [ ] You should also feel completely comfortable working with them. Do you have a rapport? Do they understand your business implicitly? Do they have time for your business? How quickly do they return your initial calls?
- [ ] Beyond your relationship with them you need to know how effective they are. What are their copywriting skills like? Agencies are not all as good as each other by any means. What are their media contacts like – especially in the area of the media you are interested in?

☐ Get a limited-term contract written up, which sets out your requirements and budget.
☐ Keep a very tight rein on costs – often the retainer fee will be small while the 'extras' can mount up quickly.

Towards the end of the limited-term contract, and you may need six months before any real progress can be judged, evaluate what difference to your profit margins the PR agency has made. If you feel that it is negligible then discuss this with them and, if needs be, be prepared to leave them.

DAMAGE LIMITATION

An area often overlooked in small businesses is a damage limitation or crisis management plan. PR agents should be good at helping to develop these plans, but they are essentially straightforward and you should be able to create a plan yourself.

No business wants a crisis but, inevitably, they will appear from time to time, in varying degrees of severity. If you have taken time to consider what you should best do in various disaster scenarios before they occur you will be very much better placed to deal with them should the scenario become reality. Not only will the plan give you a clear idea of how to progress, but its very existence should reassure you and give a sense of calm. Crisis management falls into two parts. The first is how to deal with the practical side of the problem, whether it may be power or machine failure that stops production, transport problems that prevent distribution to customers, accident or injury to personnel or, perhaps the most business critical, a problem with the product or service that causes illness, injury or significant financial problems to the customer. Your plan will identify each different scenario and then follow it through certain stages: action to stop further damage and action to restore service. The second element is the communications side. There should be clear procedures to inform your customers what the problem is, how long it will continue, what measures are being taken to rectify the problem and what measures are being taken to ensure that it does not occur again. With health and safety issues you will also need procedures to notify relatives of injury or even fatality. You will also need to have a plan for dealing with the press. This is, from a marketing point of view, where the plan comes into its own. The reputation of your business will rely on a single, coherent message being put out about the crisis. A single senior person, essentially the owner or chairman, should be the spokesperson. They should unambiguously give out all the known facts, avoid any conjecture, indicate how the problem is being contained and ensure that any essential safety information is clearly provided. The silver lining to crises is that the media attention can be turned to the business's advantage if it is correctly handled. The eradication of panic and chaotic reaction will go a long way to doing this.

THE INTERNET

The limitations of the internet as a transforming marketing tool have been clearly seen in the last three years. The reality that the internet will not instantly create an endless stream of cheap sales has been clearly, if belatedly, understood. With hindsight, it is becoming clearer that the internet is good as a very effective means of providing information about businesses. It is not so good at directly selling products or services. In a way this is good news for the small business. It is relatively cheap to establish a simple website for your business, but expensive to set up a transactional site. A simple website should provide as much information as possible, without running the risk of becoming quickly out of date. So give a brief description of what your business does as a necessary opening requirement, and take the opportunity to show where the business originated from and why, as this draws the reader in. Include a clear list of what products or services you offer, with greater detail available if possible. Given that your website is primarily an information rather than a dialogue portal, it is important to provide a postal address and telephone contact numbers. It is also useful to provide a guide to 'who is who' in the business so that the appropriate person can be contacted.

The expensive element of the internet arises if you wish to conduct sales over the net. This requires a much greater investment in computer hardware and software, which will need a substantial volume of transactions to make it profitable. Many companies are now realizing that the consumer primarily wants information from the website and is happier to make purchases by traditional means. Clearly this does not apply to all products and businesses and there will be many successful internet sales businesses in the future, but unless you intend to be an internet specialist you must cost carefully the investment required (and time involved developing and maintaining the software and equipment) against your expected return.

Fortunately, there is an enormous amount of detailed information on internet marketing, both freely available on the internet itself and in printed form. With the ever-growing use of PCs direct contact by e-mails to your customer database is a cheap and useful approach to direct marketing.

TRADE SHOWS AND EXHIBITIONS

Trade shows or fairs and exhibitions may offer great opportunities to showcase your business and increase your sales, but like all other parts of the marketing equation you have to know why you are there and what you want to get out of it. Just turning up and 'being there' will be an unrewarding experience. Therefore you must go through the familiar routine of asking yourself what your objectives are – in this case from being at a trade fair; are they to launch a new product or service; heighten your profile in a particular geographic area; or increase sales to a specialist sector? Evaluate a realistic target for the exhibition: get 200 new potential customer names; sell £10,000 of product; get a profile in the local press and so on.

Having identified your specific objectives it will be much easier to decide whether or not the trade fair is appropriate. Ask for the media pack from the organizers to see who goes, where they are from and what you can expect them to spend. Time and money invested in an unsuccessful trade show can be easily avoided by a little research at this point. For rural businesses, trade shows and exhibitions that draw in potential customers and are focused on your catchment area may be few and far between. Many do not provide an effective channel to market.

Once at the exhibition hall, as with other advertising, you must make yourself stand out from the crowd. A little money invested in bright and clear display materials will pay dividends quickly if the alternative is an amateurish look. Probably the most important task is to make sure that your staff is enthusiastic and knowledgeable. An upbeat and animated person on the stand will be more successful than a bored and embarrassed person regardless of the product or quality of display materials.

Finally, the post-exhibition follow-up is vital. Throughout your marketing process any lead that is not followed up is a lost lead, and is therefore money wasted. With trade shows you should plan your follow-up procedure before you go to the show so that you can get it dealt with swiftly afterwards. This avoids the risk that you delay it too long so that it never happens, or happens too late, and also ensures that your follow up, whether it be an enquiry form or telephone call, gets to the customer before anyone else's.

SUMMARY

A checklist for marketing

- ☐ Do you 'offer what you can sell' or try to 'sell what you can offer'?
- ☐ How carefully do you collect your sales data and analyse it?
- ☐ What are the key research objectives you need to answer? Have you carried out any primary research? How objective have you made it?
- ☐ What is your ideal customer profile? Does it exist in your area?
- ☐ Have you clearly identified your USP? What sort of potential market does this direct you to? Does it exist in your area?
- ☐ Have you considered all potential markets in your area? Are you going for the most accessible and/or lucrative? If not, are you happy why this is the case?

- ☐ How can you best reach your customers? Do you have any experience with this form of media? Do you know how best to use it?
- ☐ Are you confident your cost of marketing for any 'event' is less than its minimum likely return? If not, do you know why you are spending money on it?
- ☐ Does your product or service lend itself to direct marketing? If not, are you sure there is not an angle you are missing?
- ☐ Have you considered investing in a PR agent? If so, do you have a mutually agreed list of targets and a timetable for achieving them?
- ☐ Are you maximizing your profitable exposure to the internet? This can mean are you spending too much on it as well as not enough.
- ☐ Consider the use of e-mails as a direct marketing tool.

Part Four:

Financial Management and Funding

19 | Finance and Funding

Philip Coysh, Farming & Agricultural Finance Ltd

Developing your new rural enterprise will undoubtedly require a full review of your finances. Even during periods of agricultural recession many farming and agricultural businesses have managed to survive simply on a long-term mortgage secured on the land plus a working capital overdraft. While financial restructuring has always taken place in the industry during and following each period of agricultural recession, the main clearing banks have always seen farms and agricultural property as 'a good bet'. The reasons for this are two-fold: firstly, land values have traditionally remained high even during times of low farming income; and, secondly, bad debts in agriculture have historically been minimal due to a very strong asset base. The rural sector has been categorized as being asset rich and cash poor!

However, lenders will not necessarily view a new diversified business in the same light. There may be less security available, the business will not have a track record and the owners are likely to be inexperienced in this new area of business. It is therefore essential that a detailed business plan be produced, that will cover such areas as overall business strategy, research undertaken and demand for the product, local competition and the effect that the new enterprise will have on your existing business. The business plan will need to include two to three years' cash flows or projections and should be drawn up with the assistance of professional consultants who know the sector well.

Only when you have clearly thought out your strategy and are armed with your professional business plan should you approach lending institutions. It is probably best to talk initially to your own bank; you will have a track record with them and, it is hoped, a good existing relationship. But you should also approach other lenders, perhaps a specialist in the sector or a competitor bank. For while you may consider your existing bank manager to be the best in the agricultural sector, for instance, he or she may not be as knowledgeable or understanding of your new venture. Likewise your existing bank may be keen to lend in one sector but, at the moment in time when you approach them, they may feel overexposed in your new sector or their model may, for whatever reason, have a problem with some aspect of your business plan.

But what sort of finance facilities should you be seeking and what are the options and sources of finance available for a new rural development project? Traditionally, the rural sector has been financed by long-term mortgages of up to 40 years combined with working capital overdrafts. Often capital development and purchases of land have been placed on overdrafts and consolidated onto long-term loans at a later date. But it is undoubtedly more sensible to structure your debt according to the anticipated life expectancy of the capital item being purchased.

LONG-TERM MORTGAGES

Long-term mortgages are available from banks and specialist commercial and residential lenders, usually for periods of between 10 and 25 years. The lender will normally insist on a first charge security on property – and perhaps a first or second charge on the proprietor's home for a new start-up business.

In most business sectors there is a clear distinction between the commercial premises from which the business trades and the family home where the proprietor lives. In the agricultural and rural sector this distinction becomes somewhat blurred. A farmhouse, for example, forms part of the farm and may be extremely close to the buildings that are being developed for the new enterprise. Likewise, a successful businessperson may own a fine home in the country with farmland and buildings that are used for equestrian purposes. He or she is clearly not a farmer but may run his or her own non-rural business from the 'farm' or a rural enterprise from the buildings adjoining the 'country home'. In these circumstances it becomes extremely difficult to segment such properties into 'business' or 'residential' categories.

It is therefore beneficial to talk to various lenders to see whether a residential or commercial mortgage is the best 'fit'. Residential mortgages tend to be cheaper and more flexible than commercial mortgages although it may be more difficult to justify allocating the loan interest as a business expense. High street residential lenders will also wish to split off the house from the commercial aspects of the property and this could result in increased legal fees. They also will normally wish to see evidence of historic income and may not be so willing to lend against a business plan. However, if there is sufficient equity in your own domestic property to fund the new enterprise a residential mortgage may be your cheapest option.

Commercial mortgages are available from most high street banks – although some may wish to limit the loan period to a maximum of 20 years – and specialist commercial mortgage lenders, some of who will be operating exclusively in the agricultural or rural markets.

The main clearing banks will undoubtedly wish for you to transfer all your banking to them, rather than simply operating a transactional mortgage facility. For new limited company start-ups they are likely also to require directors' guarantees, supported by first or second mortgages on the family homes. These guarantees are designed to ensure that the founders of the company have a tangible incentive to ensure the success of the business.

On the plus side, the banks will be able to offer you all your borrowing requirements – both long term and short term – as well as other services too. Most banks will provide you with a business manager with whom you can develop an ongoing relationship. Ideally you should find out how long the business manager has been in the role and how long he or she is likely to remain there.

While it is often convenient to have one financial source who can provide all your financial needs, it is not always the best option. For one thing it limits your options if there is a change of credit policy on the bank's part. It also means that you do not necessarily always obtain the most competitive rates and terms. Increasingly, businesses in the rural sector are allocating their financial facilities across a number of different lenders; this enables them to obtain competitive quotes as well as ensuring that not all their eggs are in one basket.

Agriculture has traditionally been served by a small number of specialist long-term lenders, mostly owned by major financial institutions but operating under specific sector brandings. Some of these have branched out to provide facilities for diversified and non-farm rural enterprises while others have stuck primarily to farming. It is worth seeking out these lenders as they do offer competitive standalone long-term facilities and can be very flexible. One of their advantages is that they understand the rural economy; another is that, after an initial setting-up fee, they do not charge ongoing fees or seek annual reviews. A third advantage is that they will often structure repayments on a seasonal basis, especially if the income stream for the business is seasonal. This not only applies to farming but also to such enterprises as holiday lets or tourist activities where the main income is likely to be in the summer months.

Interest rate margins for long-term loans to agriculture have traditionally been much lower than in other business sectors, largely due to the low risk of loss and the relatively high and stable value of farmland. Margins of between 1 per cent and 2 per cent over base rate have been standard, with rates sometimes falling below 1 per cent for quality businesses. However, farmers who are diversifying into other enterprises should not expect rates as fine as they have been used to for commercial farming. Risks will be higher, the business will be unproven and the business premises may not be as attractive as farmland to potential purchasers. Mark Twain famously said of land, 'They ain't making it anymore!' For this reason, if no other, farmland is always likely to be attractive to buyers at the right price whereas a purchaser for the converted farm building may be more difficult to find. This means that lenders will be looking for an interest rate premium for mortgages where the security is other than bare land. For this reason you are likely to be able to negotiate a finer interest rate margin if the main security offered is a mixture of land and residential property, rather than, for example, a former barn being converted into office accommodation.

Usually both variable and fixed rates are available, although some lenders are reluctant to lend on a long-term fixed-rate basis and will offer variable-rate lending as a matter of course. The mortgage can usually be fixed for any period from 1 to 25 years, with appropriate breaks if required when a decision can be made to either stick with the new fixed rate or transfer to a variable rate.

It is also important to structure the term of the mortgage to the life of the property. It is not appropriate, for example, to fund a poultry shed over 25 years when its useful life may only be 15 years. As a rule of thumb the loan period should be no longer than the expected useful life of the property before it needs refurbishing.

Some people simply take the longest loan term available – usually 25 years – because this reduces monthly payments and eases cash flow but they may fail to remember that the longer the term the more interest is paid to the lender as the balance of the mortgage remains higher for longer. The same, of course, applies to interest-only loans. Most commercial lenders will agree to a one or two year capital repayment holiday while the new enterprise is being established; some may even agree to roll the interest up for 12 months. But, while interest-only mortgages have become commonplace in the residential mortgage market – and some would argue that this is a worrying trend as it simply stokes up trouble for the future – it is certainly unwise to take out a long-term interest-only mortgage for a commercial venture. The whole point of a long-term mortgage is to discipline oneself to structure regular repayments over a longer period in order to clear the loan within the chosen time frame.

PRIVATE LOANS

Medium- to long-term private loans are commonplace in the rural sector, especially with parents assisting children to continue working in the countryside and maintain the family farm. Private funding, however, has its downsides as well as benefits and all parties should be aware of the risks. For the recipient a private loan is usually a cheap and easy way of raising capital but many family frictions have occurred because of misunderstandings about the terms of the loan, often because no documentation has ever been drawn up.

The best plan is to get a solicitor or accountant to draw up an agreement that should cover the terms of the loan – the rate of interest, repayment terms and the circumstances in which it can be withdrawn. It is also beneficial to all parties to make it clear in the document whether the lender is to have any control in the running or management of the business or any entitlement to share in the profits.

A private loan may well be a real boon for someone starting a new business enterprise but the fact that family funds are available should not detract from the hard work of preparing a professional business plan and undertaking the necessary market research and competitor analysis that is required to help secure the success of the new venture.

BANK LOANS

A variable-rate flexible business loan from the local bank is the favourite means of business funding in both Germany and Spain; 70 per cent of German businesses are funded through variable-rate business loans and in Spain the figure is as high as 80 per cent. However, in the UK it is fixed-rate business development loans that have proved popular.

Both variable- and fixed-rate bank loans tend to be for medium-term requirements, usually between 5 and 20 years, and can be for a wide range of business requirements, such as the purchase of machinery, property or vehicles. Again, the term of the loan will reflect the value and expected life of the asset. Repayments will usually be made monthly or quarterly on a capital and interest repayment basis, although capital repayment holidays of up to two years may be available.

These loans may be offered on a secured or unsecured basis depending upon the strength of the proposition. However, rates for unsecured lending will be significantly higher than secured loans – typically 1.5 per cent to 2 per cent higher – but even secured business loans will be tend to be higher than long-term secured commercial mortgages. Again, a bank will require you to maintain a current account if you take up a business loan with them.

ASSET-BASED FINANCE

Leasing and lease purchase schemes are a popular way of financing machinery and vehicles. The major feature of asset finance is that the finance company looks to the value of the asset as security rather than to the strength of the balance sheet of the business. This means that it is extremely useful for new start-ups and also means that any available deed security is used to fund long-term capital requirements rather than machinery and vehicles.

Lease purchase is a flexible hire purchase scheme that enables you to own the asset at the end of the repayment term. Usually you would need to put down a deposit of approximately 20 per cent of the cost price and then repay the capital and interest over a term of between two and seven years, depending upon the life of the asset. At the end of the term the asset becomes your property.

Finance leasing is similar to lease purchase except that it is a rental scheme rather than a purchasing scheme and therefore enables you to claim higher tax allowances. It is particularly useful where there is no requirement to own the asset at the end of the agreement, for example, a car or computer that may well be out of date in a few years' time. Depending on your tax and VAT position, certain leasing structures may be more advantageous than bank loans but you will need to consult your accountant for advice on this.

All the major banks have their own in-house leasing and HP companies but there are also specialists working in the agricultural and rural sectors who may be able to fund specialist equipment that a standard leasing company would not be attracted to.

FACTORING

For many businesses unpaid invoices are one of the largest assets. Factoring used to be the preserve of the struggling business but today it is another finance option, particularly useful for smaller companies undergoing fairly rapid growth, typically with a turnover of between £50,000 and £300,000 per year.

Factoring immediately releases a percentage of outstanding invoices (usually around 80 per cent) and frees you up from the job of chasing debt so you can concentrate on managing the rest of the business. The funding is more flexible than bank debt and is available more quickly than an overdraft facility as factoring companies will look forward to the strength of the balance sheet, rather than back to past trading performance.

Many start-up businesses are restricted in their growth by the lack of working capital and factoring can often be the solution, although it is important to guard against over-trading or growing too rapidly. Factoring is usually more expensive than bank borrowing, but the advantages of providing cover against bad debts and reducing administration may outweigh this extra cost.

BANK OVERDRAFT

During the early 1990s nearly 60 per cent of lending to small businesses in the UK took the form of an overdraft facility. Since that time banks have sought to reduce dependence on overdrafts and this percentage has fallen fast.

In the agricultural sector overdrafts have historically been used to fund everything from a whole farm purchase to a new combine. Fortunately, the use of the overdraft as the sole means of borrowing money is a thing of the past but small business owners in the rural economy still naturally veer towards the overdraft when considering new investment for their business.

Sticking with an overdraft through thick and thin is a bit like using only the first gear in a car – great for going up steep hills but not such a good idea once you hit the motorway. But, having said that, the overdraft remains a useful tool especially for new start-ups and for getting to grips with cash flow problems.

An overdraft is beautifully elastic – as small or as big as you want – and you only pay for what you use. The problems start when you get into the habit of using your overdraft to make large capital purchases or to fund growth. An overdraft facility should simply fund your normal trading fluctuations and no more. Of course, to know what level of overdraft you actually need requires careful financial planning and the use of cash flows to see where your peaks and troughs are.

Remember that the bank will constantly monitor the level of the overdraft and will expect it to fluctuate, including the account going into credit periodically. If this does not happen and a 'hard core' of borrowing is identified, then the bank will wish to convert part of the overdraft into a short-term loan with a structured repayment programme. One important aspect for you to remember is that overdraft facilities are usually granted 'on demand' which means that the bank can demand instant repayment at any time, although some banks now have agreed to a 12-month guaranteed overdraft facility which does give some security for the borrower.

Interest rates for overdrafts will vary depending upon the perceived strength of the business and whether the facility is secured or unsecured. Of course, all overdrafts are granted on a variable-rate basis. Again, as with other facilities, rates as low as 1 per cent over base rate for secured overdrafts, which have historically been available to good agricultural businesses, will not be available to businesses diversifying away from commercial farming. You should expect your bank to quote margins of between 1.5 per cent and 3 per cent for fully secured overdrafts and over 4 per cent for a start-up company with no track record.

GOVERNMENT GRANTS

Finally, we must look at the cheapest of all forms of funding – cheapest but certainly not the easiest or simplest. There are a large number of government grants available to rural businesses. However, the schemes are becoming more complex as funding now comes from a variety of different sources and more government agencies are involved. Further, whereas subsidy payments to farmers used to be given as of right, modern-day grants are usually project-based, collaborative and competitive – and there are different schemes for different parts of the country.

If you are about to embark on a new rural diversification, it is imperative that you take professional advice as to whether any grants can be applied for. You will need to undertake research, obtain planning consent, provide quotations, consider both environmental and health and safety aspects, be prepared for a mass of paperwork (including a business plan) and compete with other applicants – and there will be no guarantee of success.

20 | Equity Alternatives

Jonathan Reuvid

INTRODUCTION

The various forms of debt finance available to individuals seeking funds to start up rural businesses, either as sole traders, in partnership or through a limited company were identified and discussed in Chapter 19. The alternative to debt finance is equity funding; selling a proportion of the share capital in the company established to run the business to outside investors. By definition, equity finance is only applicable to businesses that are incorporated. However, a sole trader or partnership can always reform the business into a limited company in order to attract investors, although this will necessarily affect the taxation of the business and the personal taxation status of the owners.

Debt and equity finance are not mutually exclusive alternatives and, for every company, a number of funding solutions are possible involving different combinations of debt and equity. At the upper end of the scale, companies that are considering public flotation are likely to adopt a funding package in which equity is the main element. For readers of this book public flotation is unlikely to be more than a remote future possibility and, in the present depressed state of equity markets, as unlikely as winning the National Lottery. This chapter focuses, therefore, on the forms of equity finance that are realistic for the owners of rural businesses and ignores or makes passing reference only to those that are not.

PRIVATE PLACING

A company can raise finance from outside investors without any commitment to an ultimate independent public offering (IPO). Generally, professional investors and investment funds will have little interest in buying shares in a company unless there is a clear exit route, for example, the possibility of selling the company in the future to another company in the same trade or another group of investors. One exception to this rule is biotech and other high technology businesses, which can raise money from investors knowledgeable in their sector. They may be confident that if the technology proves successful, the rewards will be substantial whichever exit route is chosen. Of the case histories included in Part Five of this book only the energy renewal business described in Chapter 26 would qualify.

For rural businesses generally, the most likely private investors are relatives, friends and wealthy individuals living locally, who have an interest in supporting the original owners personally or a business of which they approve 'on the doorstep' where they hope to enjoy contributing to the creation of a flourishing enterprise. Even if the new investors are a small group of family or friends, it is important that they are treated as investors at arm's length and that some form of investment memorandum is prepared that gives full details of the company and an accurate description of the business, its history and the directors' aims and objectives for its future development. If the business is established, audited accounts should be included in an appendix. If the business is a start-up, that will not be possible. No formal profit forecast is necessary in either case, but an outline business plan for a new business should be included.

It is important that investors should have clear expectations; if you do not intend to pay dividends, you should say so. All too often private investors are persuaded, or persuade themselves, to buy shares in a company of which the directors are known to them with expectations that are totally unrealistic. Inevitably, disillusionment follows and in the consequent bickering family feuds are born and friendships falter.

In the case of one or two private investors taking a substantial stake in the company, perhaps as much as 25 per cent or more, a more hard-headed approach is usually taken by the investor. Often a seat on the board of the company is demanded and it is normal for the original and new shareholders to enter into a shareholders' agreement that defines how the affairs of the company shall be conducted. For example, the shareholders' agreement may specify that decisions to increase the borrowings of the company, to issue more shares or to purchase or sell significant assets above a certain value may only be taken with the unanimous consent of the shareholders. Such agreements supplement the provisions of the company's Articles of Association, which may also be strengthened, typically in respect of the pre-emptive rights of shareholders to purchase each other's shares in the event of sale.

The law provides that a small group of investors (in simple terms less than 50 persons) can invest on the basis of a private placing memorandum. This is classified as an investment advertisement and, as such, must be approved by a person authorized under the Financial Service and Markets Act 2000. The person approving the document must ensure that the document is correct in all material respects and does not mislead the reader in any way whatever. For this purpose, the directors of the company inviting investment should appoint an authorized Financial Services Intermediary – most likely a local chartered accountant or solicitor.

At the next level of investment, an offer to the public (which, in simple terms, is to more than 50 persons) must be made in the form of a prospectus. The prospectus must conform to The Public Offer of Securities Regulations 1995 (the POS Regs), a statutory instrument that defines an offer of securities to the public and specifies the form and content of the document that must be published when it has been decided to make such an offer. The POS Regs contains most of the information found in an AiM admission document or listing particulars.

PRIVATE EQUITY AND VENTURE CAPITAL (VC)

The VC industry in the UK thrived until the 2002 investment slump. According to the British Venture Capital Association (BVCA), the UK private equity or VC industry, was the largest in Europe, accounting for 38 per cent of private equity investment in Europe in 2000 and second in size only to that of the United States. The UK private equity industry had invested over £43 billion (£35 billion in the UK) in close to 20,500 companies since 1983. Of this, 50 per cent is used for expansion or development, the rest for management buy-outs and other transactions.

Colin Aaronson of Grant Thornton points out in *Going Public* (Reuvid, 2002), that VC is something of a misnomer.

> Although around one hundred firms are listed by the BVCA as being interested in funding early stage businesses, most VC money is used to provide development capital of MBO finance. VCs will provide a mixture of debt and equity, calculated to earn them the desired rate of return, which will usually fall between 30 per cent and 40 per cent per annum on an investment. This level of return can only be achieved through growth, and is required to compensate the VC firm for the high degree of risk and the high level of resources it must commit to each investment. The greatest risk in any investment is that the VC will not be able to find a suitable exit route.

For this reason, only a limited number of rural businesses are likely to attract VC funds. Of the businesses profiled in Part Five, probably only the York Auction Centre, the Barn Brasserie and A Day in the Country (featured in Chapters 31–33) would be eligible, and then only in relation to aggressive development plans. Smaller rural businesses should look to the alternative source of private equity, described as business angels, in the next section of this chapter.

Companies looking for private equity can contact the BVCA to identify potential investors. All VC firms have stated sets of investment criteria, based principally on industry sector, geographical location and the stage of a company's development. Colin Aaronson of Grant Thornton identifies as an alternative route the appointment of a financial adviser, possibly your local firm of accountants, to introduce a suitable VC firm. The adviser will know which VC firms are investing in a particular sector at any one time, and which are likely to be interested in funding your company. 'Using an adviser can save time, and should avoid the company unnecessarily hawking its business around the market. Indeed there are many VC firms who either prefer or expect to deal with an intermediary.'

On first contact, the VC firm will require a business plan including thorough information on the company and detailed financial forecasts. The VC will review the business plan and meet with management on several occasions before it decides to proceed with verification (the 'due diligence' process) as a pre-condition to investment in a business. Rather depressingly, Colin Aaronson quotes estimates that no more than 2 per cent of business plans gain funding.

After a VC decides, in principle, to make an investment in a business there is normally an interval of three to four months before funds are received by the company. During this period, extensive due diligence is undertaken (at the expense of the company), involving accountants reporting on the operations of the business and on the integrity of the financial forecasts, industry experts reporting on the commercial operations of the business and on the assumptions underlying the financial forecasts, and lawyers reviewing contracts, questions of title to tangible assets and intellectual property and various other legal matters.

Most VCs will insist on a non-executive being appointed to the board and some become more involved in the management issues of the companies in which they have invested. There is a cost to this involvement, but many companies welcome the experience and advice that these non-executive directors bring to the company.

BUSINESS ANGELS

Business angels are successful and experienced businesspeople who want to become involved with a young growing business and have funds to invest. Some of the potential local investors described earlier in this chapter for private placings may be classified as business angels. However, business angels generally become actively involved in the companies they invest in; so being able to work with one is crucial to the success of the relationship, and you need to be sure that you are comfortable with such an investor before making a commitment. Research indicates that angels place greater emphasis on location rather than industry sector, with most looking to invest in businesses located within an hour's drive from home.

Because of the confidential nature of the investment, it is only possible to approximate the size of the business angel market. Research suggests that there are approximately 20,000 business angels in the UK, investing around £500 million a year in 3,500 businesses in amounts from £25,000 to £1 million, and occasionally more. Individually, angels rarely commit more than £50,000 to a single investment; amounts greater than that are usually provided by syndicates of angels.

Being a business angel is a high-risk, high-reward activity. It is estimated that one-third of all investee companies fail; at the other end of the spectrum, around 20 per cent generate returns of greater than 50 per cent per annum for their angel investors.

The most common outcome for business angel investments, at around 40 per cent, is some form of insolvency. However, about half of all investments are sold either to other shareholders, management, a third party or to another business through a trade sale, and around 10 per cent through some form of flotation.

Business angels will require much the same information during negotiations as VCs but are more likely to carry out parts of the due diligence themselves, particularly the reviews of commercial operations and the underlying business plan assumptions.

EQUITY VS DEBT FINANCE

There is a natural inclination on the part of most business owners to avoid introducing outside shareholders. On the one hand, the idea of having to satisfy shareholders' expectations and answer to them at meetings seems likely to be an irritation; on the other hand sharing the capital value of a growing business with investors who are not family may be deeply distasteful.

For rural businesses, asset-backed by substantial farmland and buildings, the ability to raise long-term finance through secured loans may be greater than for other small businesses, so that there is no compulsion to look for equity funding. The argument for debt finance is strengthened further by the current low rates of interest. Nevertheless, business owners should be mindful of the impact of increasing interest rates on cash flow and profits wherever the interest payable on loans is related to base rate.

There is a general expectation that interest rates will stabilize in 2005 at not more than 5 per cent before slackening again, and for those starting up or expanding businesses now it may be wise to be prudent about their levels of borrowing. The risk that accompanies heavy debt, even when the asset cover is strong, is often forgotten, and there is sufficient risk for private companies now in the current business environment without further hostages to fortune. If additional debt also entails the giving of personal guarantees, the risk is greatly heightened.

In this climate, provided that commitments to incoming investors to provide an exit from the business within a specified time can be avoided – particularly where the location of the business premises and your living accommodation are inseparable – equity investment, if on offer, should not be turned down lightly.

21 Buying and Selling the Business

Jonathan Reuvid

BUYING VS SELLING

This chapter is intended primarily for readers who are considering buying into country living by purchasing an established business that someone else has developed. It is also relevant for those at the other end of the investment continuum who have built up a rural business, probably over a period of many years, and have reached a point or time in life when they are contemplating a sale.

At first sight, it would be tempting to think that entrance is the converse of exit and that the criteria which an astute, well-advised purchaser will apply to buying a business will be matched by a seller who recognizes prospective purchasers' requirements and structures his or her offering accordingly. However, there is one essential difference between buyer and seller which overrides all other factors and imposes its own logic on their mindsets and on the pattern of most negotiations: whereas the prospective purchaser can walk away from the transaction up to the point that contracts are signed, the prospective seller cannot abdicate from the business he or she is trying to sell.

The purchaser can abort in the negotiations stage at any time if he or she decides the terms of purchase are not suitable, changes his or her mind about the attractiveness of the business, or loses confidence in the post-completion business plan. No doubt, there are many alternative business propositions that the purchaser can evaluate – plenty more 'fish in the sea' for the frustrated suitor. The vendor's situation is quite different: he or she too can abort the transaction up to the moment of signature, but cannot walk away from the business he or she is trying to sell. The vendor can look for another purchaser but that may not be too easy in a buyer's market when investment opportunities are plentiful but private investors are thin on the ground. To adopt a racing analogy, the seller can change riders but he or she cannot change horses. The purchaser, in the role of the rider, can always look for another mount.

For this reason alone, the vendor of a business needs to prepare for sale carefully by presenting the business clearly and intelligibly in an attractive light, but without misrepresentation. The owner will be well advised to take professional advice before putting his or her business on the market. The role of advisers is discussed in some detail towards the end of the chapter.

Certainly, the vendor needs to understand in advance the information that the prospective purchaser will demand, the concerns to which he or she is likely to attach the most importance and, not least, the purchaser's mindset. In order to examine these issues and how to manage them, this chapter addresses the elements of buying and selling a business, first from the standpoint of a well-prepared and well-advised purchaser; and then from the standpoint of a vendor, selling a business for the first time.

THE PURCHASER'S POSITION

Before investigating any specific opportunity to purchase, the prospective investor is advised to define his or her business objectives and to establish the ground rules that he or she will follow in review and negotiation. This will save considerable time and self-questioning later and help to avoid the temptation of adapting principles to circumstances in the face of an attractive but over-priced or otherwise unsuitable opportunity. The following are some of the fundamentals on which a prospective purchaser should take a firm up front view.

Location

Be absolutely clear which alternative locations for the business are acceptable. To be certain, you may need to research quite widely. For example, if you are looking for a tourist-based business in a coastal area, you may rule out Scotland, and the north-east and south-east of England before you start, but that still leaves large areas of Wales, East Anglia, the south coast and all of the south-west. As your research proceeds you will be able to zero-in on one or two more closely defined locations, such as within 20 miles of Truro. The scope of your research will encompass the environment, living conditions, a preliminary survey of the local market for the kinds of business that you have in mind and going market values.

Role of the investor

The primary differentiator in your approach as a purchaser will be whether you want to purchase a rural business solely as an investor, or whether you and your family intend to play an active part in running the business. In the first instance, your priorities will be the estimated return on investment (ROI) and likely appreciation in capital value. Since the business you buy will require management, you will also be taking a view on the availability of suitable tenants or managers. A poor tenant or, worse still, an incompetent manager, will damage your investment and may ruin your ROI.

The second instance demands total confidence that you and your family really want to run a business of the kind you have chosen, and whether you have the capability to do so. For example, before setting out to acquire a village shop on the north coast of Cornwall, are you sure that you can accept the long hours and monotonous work involved in high season, let alone all the year round? If you have that confidence, then the ROI which you demand from such a business may be tempered by the benefits 'in kind' which you can expect from the business and the ability to draw earned income for yourself and family members who work in the shop.

Price

Earnings-based valuations

There are a number of alternative formulae in common usage for pricing a private business, but invariably they are earnings-based or asset-based. Earnings-based formulae are usually a simple multiple of pre- or post-tax net profits based on recent years' financial results, current year performance or both. Remembering that profit multiples are the reciprocal of investment returns, it follows that a purchase price representing, say, four times pre-tax profits will deliver a return on the purchaser's total investment of 25 per cent before the tax payable on the business's profits and the investor's own income tax.

However, there are two issues that can be confusing and about which purchasers should be especially wary: the valuation of future earnings; and credit for owners' remuneration in kind.

Either issue or both may be put forward by the vendor of a business or his or her advisers as a means of raising the price. In the case of a village shop, for example, where planning consent has just been granted for the construction of 200 new holiday homes (a 10 per cent increase on the total number of homes within the shop's catchment area) the vendor might argue that sales are likely to increase accordingly and that an allowance should be made in the purchase price for the future increase in profits. The purchaser's response should be that the projection is not relevant to the present value of the business. He or she might also suggest that the additional population may justify a new regular bus service to the local town where residents will be able to shop at a nationally branded supermarket instead of the village shop. Realistically, it may be reasonable to give some credit in the purchase price for an improvement which the vendor has generated but which has not yet come into effect, such as an off-licence to sell beer, wines and spirits, where the benefit to the business is assured. On the other hand, the purchaser should never factor into his or her valuation the benefits of any improvements that he or she will make post-acquisition.

The second issue of 'benefits in kind' that the owner has received from the business is more insidious. Salary paid to family members is readily identifiable and it is not too difficult to decide whether such payments were a substitute for profit distribution or whether they represent genuine remuneration for services rendered, which would have to be hired externally at an equivalent cost if not provided by members of the owner's family. However, other expenses against the business that were wholly of benefit to the owner and his or her family and not essential to the operation of the business, such as motoring expenses, building repairs and decoration or kitchen equipment, may be harder to substantiate and may be ignored by the purchaser in pricing the business. It may be argued that the reward is sufficient if the vendor has received such benefits tax-free during his or her ownership of the business, and that he or she has no logical entitlement to their value being written back to arrive at an estimate of maintainable future profits.

Asset-based valuations

Asset-based valuations relate to the net assets of the business, evidenced preferably by its audited balance sheet. They are applied in preference to earnings-based valuations where losses have been incurred, the profit stream has been erratic, or where the business is highly personalized and its future is dependent on the owner-manager's personal relationships with providers of work. If the business is incorporated, the provision of a current balance sheet should present no problem, although small companies are not compelled to file balance sheets with their annual report and accounts. The company's accountants can be tasked to prepare a balance sheet which, if unaudited, can be warranted by the directors. In valuing the business on the basis of its asset value, the purchaser and his or her advisers will look at the net shareholders' funds equivalent to tangible assets net of any balance sheet goodwill, with the addition of any surplus in market value of the fixed assets over their balance sheet value.

If the business is not incorporated but is run as a sole trader business or partnership and there is no balance sheet, a statement of the business's net tangible assets should be constructed from the accounting records.

There used to be a convention among some advisers that valuation could be based on net tangible assets plus a provision for goodwill calculated as a multiple of several years' post-tax profits. This approach is now generally regarded as too generous to the vendor, except where there are assets included in the sale which are separate from and unused by the business. For example, in the case of the sale of a farm and its business consisting of the farmhouse plus redundant agricultural businesses converted into a restaurant, it would be valid to value the whole as the sum of the farmhouse at residential market value plus the restaurant on the basis of a multiple of earnings.

Cash flow considerations

Remember that the cash that you have to provide as owner of the business for its operation may be significantly more than the balance sheet indicates. As a prospective purchaser, you should examine closely the cash flow of the business, particularly in cases where the level of business is highly seasonal. The balance sheet numbers may be deceptive depending on whether the accounting year end is in or out of high season. The cash demands of the business should be factored into the total investment that you are prepared to make.

INVESTIGATION AND NEGOTIATION

Market research

In valuing a business, the task of carrying out market research in developing the parameters for a post-acquisition business plan cannot be avoided. To rely on any projections submitted by the vendor or his or her advisers would be unwise.

Financial due diligence

As purchaser you may wish to use your own accountants to examine the accounts of the business and to ensure that the information with which you have been provided is accurate. If there are no audited accounts, a more detailed examination of actual accounting records will be necessary. Your accountant will pay particular attention to stock valuation methods, the adequacy of provisions for bad and doubtful debts, depreciation of assets and for periodic expenses such as rent and utilities in forward projections. The terms of bank borrowings will be examined and the tax affairs of the business will come under scrutiny. If you are intending to purchase a company you will need to be sure that there are no unprovided liabilities to corporation tax and that PAYE and national insurance payments in respect of past and present employees are up to date, as are all statutory filings. Finally, your accountant will form a view as to whether the business you are buying is adequately funded.

Legal due diligence

At some stage you will need to engage a solicitor to prepare the purchase contract but, before that, there is work to be done in examining all material contracts relating to the business which you are evaluating. If you are purchasing the shares of a company, the contracts to which it is a party will normally remain in force when the shares are transferred. However, as in the case of a sole trader or partnership business, there may be some contracts in the name of the owner(s) that will need to be assigned to the new owner. A lease of premises, for example, may be in the name of an individual rather than the company and assignment to the new owner is likely to require the consent of the landlord. In any case, you will want your lawyer to check the terms of all leases and to verify that there is a clean title to any freehold property offered. Equally, equipment leases and hire purchase or lease purchase agreements should be scrutinized.

External consents of one sort or another may also be required in relation to particular types of business such as licensed premises, as described in Chapter 11. Even contracts with some customers or suppliers where performance has been guaranteed by the owner of the business may require consent to ensure continuity.

Your solicitor should also check that all planning consents are in order and that the current business, with any additions or variations which you intend, does not infringe any by-laws, or any health and safety and environmental law requirements. You should also check that adequate insurance cover is in place to meet statutory requirements and third party liabilities as well as the protection and replacement of assets.

Warranties and indemnities

It is normal for the purchaser to seek protection from the vendors of a business in the form of warranties against the integrity of information supplied, including statements of account, asset and liability values, pensions and other employee matters, and environmental and planning issues. The time limit for making a warranty claim is generally two to three years. Protection against future unprovided tax liabilities may be covered by a separate tax deed which may run for up to six or seven years. Usually, a limit will be set to the amount of any one or the total of all warranty claims often expressed as a percentage of the purchase consideration. Indemnities are similar and refer to undertakings made by the vendors to reimburse the purchaser for the cost of specific contingencies that may arise after the transaction.

Vendors can provide relief for themselves against warranty and indemnity claims by declaring specific circumstances or events that may affect the business adversely, known as 'disclosures', against which they will not warrant or indemnify. From the purchaser's point of view the demand for protection serves the purpose of flushing any skeletons out of the cupboard in the form of disclosures which can be taken into account when agreeing the final purchase price.

Restrictive covenants

Assuming that the vendor is leaving the business upon completion, the purchaser needs to be protected against the vendor setting up in competition and enticing existing employees and customers or clients away. Therefore, it is normal practice to include a restrictive covenant in the purchase agreement. Be aware in drafting such covenants that they may not be legally enforceable if too restrictive in terms of geographical area or duration.

THE SELLER'S STANCE

Taking on board the likely requirements of a well-briefed purchaser, it is clear that the seller of a business should be equally prepared and there are a number of key issues to be addressed well in advance of offering the business for sale.

Accounts and accounting records

If your business is operated through a limited liability company, ensure that full audited accounts for the most recent financial year are available and monthly trading accounts since the year end. The same applies if you operate as a partnership and, in this case, be sure that a balance sheet is included.

If you operate as a sole trader, it is important to distinguish clearly between the business and your personal finances. Although there may be disadvantages to you in terms of personal taxation, you should consider, for at least 12 months and preferably several years before the intended sale, maintaining separate bank accounts and completely separate accounting records. As already discussed, no prudent purchaser will allow you credit for those items of expenditure not strictly necessary for the progress of the business which have been debited against pre-tax income. Expenditure that is partly attributable to the business and partly for the benefit of the owners should be allocated reasonably. Again, regular balance sheets should be drawn up in which all the assets and liabilities of the business are correctly entered.

Taxation

Be sure that past year's taxation has been fully assessed and that current tax liabilities of the business are correctly declared.

Property

If the business owns freehold or long leasehold property to be included in the sale which is included in the balance sheet at less than current market value, consider having a formal professional valuation made which can be included in the documents made available to purchasers. If the business is to occupy premises of which you will be the freeholder or superior tenant after sale, instruct your solicitor to draft a lease on terms that are acceptable to you. The lease does not have to be signed until completion of the sale.

Contracts

Make sure that all material contracts to which the business is a party or from which the business benefits remain in force after transfer of the business or are assignable to a new owner.

Warranties and indemnities

Before entering into negotiations decide the limit of warranties and indemnities that you are prepared to provide and list the disclosures that you intend to make. There is merit in declaring disclosures early on in negotiations so that they do not become a bargaining chip in later discussions about price.

Pricing the business

Take advice on what is a fair valuation for the business and measure that against the 'drop dead' price at which you are prepared to sell and walk away. Then develop an asking price which can be supported by the evidence and which is stiff but not unrealistically exorbitant. Unless there is heavy competition to buy your business or you are an exceptionally talented negotiator, the probability is that you will not achieve the asking price. Therefore, you should set a price that is at least 15 per cent above the 'drop dead' price, after allowing for the professional fees you will have to pay to your advisers.

Memorandum of particulars

In preparation for the selling process you and your advisers should prepare a memorandum for prospective purchasers, rather like an estate agent's particulars of sale, which provides a short history of the business and its management, any relevant local information and circumstances of interest to buyers and identifies the supporting documentation, such as audited accounts and property valuation which will be made available to interested parties. Do not include an asking price in the memorandum. Your views on asking price may change and you should wait until prospective purchasers ask you.

Confidentiality letter

You will not want the details of your private business affairs circulated widely and discussed by all and sundry. Therefore, you are recommended to have your solicitor draft a standard form of confidentiality letter, to be signed by any interested party who wishes to be recognized as a prospective purchaser and who wants to examine the details of the business beyond the original memorandum. The letter will commit signatories to treating all information received in confidence and to returning documents at the termination of negotiations. Confidentiality letters help to sort the wheat from the chaff by identifying those with serious intent.

USING PROFESSIONAL ADVISERS

Both purchaser and vendor will need to use solicitors at the contract stage in the sale of a business. In this chapter we have also identified tasks which are best carried our by lawyers in the preparatory phases. The vendor will probably be taking advice from accountants in the preparation of accounting information about the business and very possibly in setting pricing expectations. A purchaser may decide to rely on the audited and warranted financial information provided by the vendor without employing his or her own accountants; alternatively, he or she may require more detailed investigation under the heading of financial due diligence.

In choosing these advisers, there are two main considerations: quality and cost. In some respects, buying or selling a smaller business involves a more exacting advisory role. There will be a strong subjective element in the whole negotiation process and in arriving at a final decision. It is of the utmost importance, whether you wear the purchaser's or vendor's hat, that you have a high level of confidence in your advisers' judgements. If you do not feel comfortable with the solicitor or accountant you first approach, look for an alternative adviser and go on looking until you are satisfied.

The cost of professional advice only becomes a contentious issue if you shirk addressing it up front. Lawyers and accountants should be asked to quote like any other service provider. This involves a discussion to specify the work that may be carried out on your behalf and to price each element. In this way you will know the fees to which you are committed throughout the progress of the preliminaries and the later stages of the transaction. This approach is greatly preferable to agreeing an hour or day rate without a definition of time to be spent, which will leave you vulnerable to a 'taxi fare' system of charging.

There is a third category of professional adviser to be considered: the business broker specializing in the sale and purchase of small- and medium-sized businesses. The advantages to the vendor of employing a business broker are threefold. First, the broker acts as a medium of exchange. Through his or her network of business contacts and associates the broker will have an awareness of prospective purchasers for your kind of business whom he or she can approach in confidence. Second, if he or she is a successful broker he or she will have knowledge of the current marketplace in terms of prices realized and will be able to advise you on asking price and pricing expectations. His or her knowledge of purchasers' requirements and attitudes will also be useful in drafting the memorandum of particulars. Third, the business broker will act as your intermediary, negotiating on your behalf, and acting as a buffer between purchaser and vendor. At the very least, this will help to take the pressure off you to react instantly to points and proposals that the purchaser may throw at you. The advantages to a purchaser of using a business broker are less obvious, other than the value of being on business broker mailing lists.

As with accountants and lawyers, the need for trust and confidence is paramount in selecting a business broker. Before choosing, you should check that the firm he or she works for is properly registered as a financial intermediary and ask for references from previous clients. It is not essential that you like your business adviser, but affinity is helpful as you go through the sale process together.

The cost of the consultant's services will be related to the sale price achieved and is normally paid by the vendor on completion as a percentage of the consideration paid. Most business brokers will also ask for a retainer at the beginning of the assignment to cover their preparatory work and expenses, which may be deductible from the finder's fee when the business is sold. When negotiating fees you should not expect that the business broker's involvement will reduce the chargeable work by your accountant or solicitor. The consultant's value resides in his or her ability to generate bona fide purchasers and to help you to negotiate a satisfactory price.

22 | Insolvency – Management and Mitigation

Matt Howard, Larking Gowen

Insolvency can affect individuals with or without a business and also corporate entities.

Many people consider themselves or their interests to be immune from insolvency. However, circumstances change over time and sometimes insolvency problems do occur. This may be as a result of things out of the individual's control, and sometimes through no fault of that person.

The keys to avoiding these problems are:

☐ to understand the basic principles of the insolvency legislation and terminology so that we understand what we are trying to avoid;
☐ to recognize the warning signs of a potential insolvency problem, if and when they occur;
☐ to act on the warning signs and seek professional help at an early stage.

UNDERSTANDING THE BASICS OF INSOLVENCY LEGISLATION

Broadly there are four tests of insolvency:

☐ the balance sheet test – where liabilities exceed assets;
☐ the commercial insolvency test – where debts cannot be paid when they fall due;
☐ unsatisfied statutory demand – where a written demand has been served for a sum of £750 or more and remains unsatisfied after 21 days;
☐ unsatisfied judgement – where an execution or other process issued on judgement is returned unsatisfied in whole or in part.

The insolvency terminology used will depend on the entity that is insolvent. Administration, receivership and liquidation relate to companies. Bankruptcy is the procedure related to individuals. This is irrespective of whether or not the individual traded as a business. Contrary to popular belief, companies do not go bankrupt; nor do individuals, sole trader businesses or partnerships go into liquidation.

In appropriate circumstances it may be possible for companies and individuals to enter into informal arrangements or formal voluntary arrangements with their creditors, as an alternative to, say, liquidation or bankruptcy, respectively. This may allow time for payments to creditors to be organized and may in some circumstances mean that creditors do not receive payment in full. Generally, however, the payment will provide a better likely outcome than would liquidation or bankruptcy. Creditors must agree to these proposals and, in the case of a formal voluntary arrangement, have the opportunity to vote on and potentially modify the proposals at a specially called creditors' meeting.

Generally, the primary objective of an insolvency procedure is to maximize the return to creditors. However, some procedures work specifically for one particular class of creditor; for example, in an administrative receivership, where the insolvency practitioner is appointed by the holder of a floating charge for the purpose of realizing funds for that chargeholder (subject to payment first of preferential creditors – see below).

Maximizing the return to creditors may mean rescuing a company or business and allowing it to continue to trade either with the existing management or by achieving a going concern sale. In other circumstances it can mean the break up and sale of the company's or individual's assets.

In any insolvency, a strict order of payment is applied, as follows:

1. any individual or organization holding a fixed charge security over an insolvent individual's or company's assets;
2. preferential creditors (such as employees' wages arrears and holiday pay entitlements);
3. holders of floating charges over assets;
4. unsecured, non-preferential creditors (including HM Revenue & Customs);
5. shareholders or, in bankruptcy, the debtor themselves (after payment of statutory interest on the above debts).

RECOGNIZING THE WARNING SIGNS

The warning signs, as with the terminology addressed above, vary depending on the entity involved.

Personal debt problems

If individuals can identify with any of the following problems they may need help with personal debt problems:

☐ They owe more money on credit cards or store cards than can comfortably be afforded each month.

☐ Changes in personal circumstances (such as divorce, long-term illness or unemployment) are having a negative effect on the financial position.

☐ The bank is threatening to dishonour cheques and/or withdraw overdraft facilities.

☐ The bank is stating that it is unable to offer further advice.

☐ Creditors are starting to exert pressure and possibly threatening to commence court proceedings.

☐ Mortgage arrears are growing.

Business debt problems

If individuals trading an unincorporated business as a sole trader or in partnership with others can identify with any of the following problems they may need help with business debt problems:

☐ Suppliers are insisting on cash terms or threatening legal action.

☐ Creditors are threatening to commence court proceedings.

☐ The bailiff and/or sheriff is attempting to seize assets.

☐ VAT and PAYE arrears are growing.

☐ The bank is threatening to dishonour cheques and/or withdraw overdraft facilities.

☐ The bank is stating that it is unable to offer further advice.

☐ There is danger of personal credit ratings being negatively affected.

☐ Changes in personal circumstances (such as divorce, long-term illness or unemployment) are having a negative effect on the financial position.

☐ Mortgage arrears are growing.

☐ The balance between personal and business financial commitments is becoming a struggle.

Problems with company affairs

If directors trading a company can identify with any of the following problems they may need help with company affairs:

☐ Suppliers are insisting on cash terms or threatening legal action.

☐ Creditors are threatening to commence court proceedings.

☐ The bailiff and/or sheriff is attempting to seize assets.

☐ VAT and PAYE arrears are growing.
☐ There is danger of the company's credit rating being negatively affected.
☐ The bank is threatening to dishonour cheques and/or reduce or withdraw the overdraft facility.
☐ The bank is requesting further security over company's assets.
☐ The bank is stating that it is unable to offer further advice.
☐ Directors are concerned over their potential personal liability for the company's debt.

ACTING ON THE WARNING SIGNS

In every situation, early action will greatly increase the chance of you or the company being able to avoid formal bankruptcy or liquidation proceedings, respectively. There are a number of options available to you or the company if action is taken early enough. Each scenario is unique and therefore it is necessary to identify the situation and adopt a solution to the specific circumstances of the case.

Personal debt

For individuals with personal debt problems, it may be possible to:

☐ Negotiate an informal arrangement with your creditors, whereby you pay all or part of your debts based upon what you can realistically afford to contribute.
☐ Restructure your debts or re-mortgage your property to help you avoid formal insolvency procedures.
☐ Prepare and implement an 'individual voluntary arrangement' – a court-backed procedure whereby you pay all or part of your debts and receive protection to prevent your creditors from taking further action against you.
☐ If there is no viable alternative, seek advice on your rights and responsibilities in the event of bankruptcy and obtain guidance regarding your home and other assets.

Business debt

For individuals with business debt problems, it may be possible to:

☐ Ease your cash flow problems by obtaining help in chasing your problem debts.
☐ Change the way that your business manages its cash flow to help ease your financial problems.

☐ Obtain help to liaise with your creditors to offer you breathing space, giving you time to consider your options.

☐ Negotiate an informal arrangement with your creditors, whereby you pay all or part of your debts based upon what you can realistically afford to contribute.

☐ Restructure your debts or re-mortgage your property to help you avoid formal insolvency procedures.

☐ Prepare and implement an 'individual voluntary arrangement' – a court-backed procedure whereby you pay all or part of your personal and business debts and receive protection to prevent your creditors from taking further action against you, while allowing you the option to continue trading.

☐ If there is no viable alternative, seek advice on your rights and responsibilities in the event of bankruptcy and obtain guidance regarding your home and other assets.

Individuals with or without businesses need to avoid getting themselves and the business, if applicable, further into debt. However, this is sometimes easier said than done and the prospect of losing your business and facing bankruptcy is a very daunting one. A common misconception for individuals trading an unincorporated business is that the business financial affairs are separate from their personal financial affairs. However, this is not true as business and personal assets are available to all creditors, and all business and non-business non-preferential unsecured creditors rank equally.

Company's affairs

For directors with concerns over the company's affairs and viability, it may be possible to:

☐ Change the way that you manage the company cash flow and obtain help to chase problem debts, which will help to ease its financial problems.

☐ Obtain help to liaise with creditors to offer breathing space, giving you time to consider the company's options.

☐ Obtain help to make better-informed decisions on the company's behalf by allowing an Insolvency Practitioner to attend creditors' meetings for you.

☐ Negotiate on the company's behalf an informal arrangement with its creditors, whereby the company pays all or part of its debts based upon what it can realistically afford to contribute.

☐ Prepare and implement a 'company voluntary arrangement' – a court-backed procedure whereby the company pays all or part of its debts and receives protection to prevent its creditors from taking further legal action, while allowing it to continue trading.

☐ If there is no viable alternative but to cease trading, obtain assistance to wind the company down in a controlled way and receive advice on the disposal of assets. This may include obtaining advice to help the company to enter into voluntary liquidation.

In many circumstances, directors will have some personal liability for the company's liabilities, which in turn may lead to financial concerns for their personal affairs. Furthermore, a director's conduct is reviewed on the insolvency of a company and a report is made by the office-holder (eg liquidator) on this conduct and may in due course result in director's disqualification proceedings being brought against the individual concerned.

In addition, some transactions may be overturned in an insolvency, or a civil recovery action may be brought personally against the director. This may result in the director being asked to contribute financially to the insolvent's assets from personal funds or may lead to bankruptcy proceedings being brought if the individual is unable to pay.

A further concern for a director should be the potential criminal charges that can be brought in relation to conduct. The nature of the charges may result in fines or imprisonment or both.

Obviously, the potential seriousness of the above demonstrates that directors should seek professional advice if there is any possibility that the company may enter into insolvency.

This advice should include:

☐ ascertaining your responsibilities and potential personal liabilities as a director;

☐ obtaining assistance to minimize the risk to your personal financial situation, for example, if you have given personal guarantees;

☐ obtaining assistance with the completion of director's conduct questionnaires;

☐ obtaining legal representation in the event of director's disqualification proceedings being commenced.

Transactions that may be overturned

A common mistake made by individuals and directors under financial pressure is to panic and to try to hide things from creditors and from the authorities. Trying to 'hide things' may include transactions such as selling assets at less than their true market value (often cars sold for negligible value to relatives or friends) or transferring the company's interest in property or a personal interest in a house to an associate or a connected party.

These transactions may be legal while the individual or company is solvent, but can be overturned at a later date in formal insolvency proceedings, when they are known as voidable transactions. It is also possible that paying one creditor in favour of another can also be unravelled. The insolvency practitioner may in this scenario seek to have the position restored to how it was before the payment was made. This could include asking the courts to request the return of assets or cash transferred.

The insolvency practitioner or official receiver will look back at the transactions that have taken place in a given time frame. The length of this time frame will depend on the parties involved. If the parties are deemed to be connected or associated then the time frame is longer. For example, in bankruptcy the transfer of a matrimonial home to a spouse might be looked at if it took place in the five years prior to the date of the bankruptcy order.

Attempting to hide cash from creditors is often something else discovered by insolvency practitioners. The motivation for this is understandable, as people are naturally anxious to put money aside to re-establish their business or company, since it is their future livelihood. Again, these transactions may be unravelled and overturned.

Accordingly, to prevent any problems at a later date, the directors of a company, the partners or a sole trader should engage advisers to get debtors in order and attempt to improve cash flow or perhaps restructure loans. Seeking and acting on professional advice at an early stage serves by taking the stress off the person or people who are being burdened by financial pressure. It also provides time for the options to be discussed and considered and may prevent individuals or directors being forced into a corner where there will probably be only one option.

Seeking professional help

Taking the plunge to ask for assistance is a very difficult step for some people to take. Many people are frightened to seek advice or genuinely believe that circumstances will improve next week, next month or next year… There is also a huge pride issue; people who have traded the business or company for many years do not want to face up to a potential failure.

Sadly, however, the national survey undertaken by R3, the Association of Business Recovery Professionals, shows that poor management is the biggest cause of business failure today. The research shows that throughout the 1990s, almost 70,000 businesses failed because of incompetent managers. R3 also comments that many insolvencies could have been avoided if professional advice had been sought earlier and state that: 'the longer a company waits before seeking help, the more likely it becomes that the company or its business will not be rescued. Likewise, the longer an individual waits before seeking advice, the greater that individual's debts are likely to be'.

Most insolvency practitioners offer a free initial consultation. That meeting provides an opportunity for the insolvency practitioner to gain an understanding of the present problem, together with the history that has led up to this point. Up to a point, the history is relevant, as is who is to blame and why it has all gone wrong; however, the most relevant point is where the business is today and what can be done to improve the situation. The potential clients of an insolvency practitioner need solutions to their problems and guidance as to the best way forward.

The role of an insolvency practitioner often has similarities to the role of a counsellor; the adviser will be leading people through one of the lowest times in their lives. Taking the initial leap to discuss financial affairs is a big step, but at least when the step has been taken the first hurdle is down because the individual or director has begun to face up to the fact that he or she has a problem.

Part Five:

Rural Business Case Histories

23 | Farmhouse Renovation and Barn Conversions

Geoffrey Fitchew, Newfell Properties, Cumbria

LOOKING NORTH

As the price of land in the South-East continued its inexorable rise in the early 2000s, the small firm of developers, Newfell Properties Limited began to look further afield for development opportunities. Having built new homes and converted some old municipal buildings, including a fire station and derelict council property, a more affordable challenge away from the London commuter belt was needed. Although more common in the Home Counties, barn conversions have been a feature of many disused farms or redundant farm buildings since the early 1970s. We looked to rural Cumbria for our first venture, a previously tenanted farm near Appleby-in-Westmorland, now in complete disrepair but with planning approval and up for auction.

We became the proud owners of one 18th-century farmhouse, a number of ramshackle stone barns with various lean-to and add-on buildings, a new build development site (or so we thought) and the remaining 2 or 3 acres of the now defunct farm in November 2000; just two months before foot and mouth disease struck. The first year of our new investment was wiped out, we were in the epicentre of the outbreak and although we could access the site, tradespeople could not and the planning officer was confined to his desk.

Although the slaughter of livestock continued, we were eventually able to begin work on site in the late summer of 2001. Initially employing a local quantity surveyor, who in turn contracted local trades, we began the renovation of the farmhouse. As intimated earlier, the farm and buildings had been poorly maintained by the absentee landlord and although originally built for a gentleman farmer, the farmhouse was now damp and uncomfortable. Renovation of old buildings is not an exact science, and certainly the budgeting is subject to massive, upward only, variations. So it was that some £140,000 was spent (three times over budget) and two years' work. Only the improving sales market allowed us to walk away with some dignity.

During this period we refined the plans for the barns to make two three-bedroom, two-bathroom dwellings and applied for planning approval for a parcel of land on the opposite side of the road, eminently suitable for a small bungalow. By this stage we had identified that we needed a single main contractor who would have his or her own workforce and machinery, rather than working in the ad-hoc way we had to date. With great good fortune, over a pint, we were introduced to Mike; young, energetic and most importantly, experienced in barn conversions. He also brought a good deal of hard facts and common sense. Our vision had been of an old-worldly pair of houses with uneven walls and floors and the ubiquitous oak beams at every turn, Mike saw straight lines and a constant battle with building control officials.

RAINFALL AND BULGES

Those who know Cumbria will be familiar with the region's prodigious rainfall and our area seemed to receive more than its fair share. The site was running wet at all times; numerous land drains and becks criss-crossed the ground which sloped towards the buildings, defunct and broken drains then ran under the barns. Each movement with the mechanical digger disturbed yet more natural and man-made drains, our first priority must be to reroute the drainage so that we could exert a measure of control. The retaining wall which was designed to hold back the sloping access road and parking from the gardens and hard-standing areas around the properties became a major excavation necessitating the removal and redistribution of thousands of tons of sodden earth, clay and, boulders, at one point to a depth of 4 metres. New high-capacity drains were laid on the uphill side of the retaining wall and further drains dug to redirect water away from the buildings. Eventually we achieved some control and work could begin in earnest on the barns.

From the beginning we had been concerned over a bulge in the front wall of the main barn where in some distant time a first floor hay loft door had been inserted, over an existing ground floor doorway. We had installed steel ties earlier on and now awaited the results of the engineer's report and the building inspector's views. Once again our worst fears were realized, either we had to underpin, a very slow process and one which had very real possibilities of collapsing the whole building, or we must systematically drop the front wall of some 20 metres long and two storeys high.

I haven't yet mentioned that these are all listed buildings, meaning that planning approval is also subject to listed building approval. Often this situation caused conflict between the building control department and conservation department at Town Hall, but as both departments had equal validity in planning law it was in our interest to persuade the two parties to compromise. Specifically in this case, building control required the demolition of the front wall, the conservation department would not accept this on a 'building of special architectural or historic interest', to use the jargon. Only after considerable wrangling were we able to persuade the conservation department to allow this 'alteration of listed building' and then only with detailed drawn and photographic record to which we could refer in the rebuilding stage; such that all windows and door openings, dressed stone and slits were all replaced in the exact same position. I referred earlier to Mike's straight-wall policy, and the main visible feature of this was the dry-lining system used internally, which greatly improves insulation properties and creates flat surfaces. Similarly the rebuilt front wall would be of modern block work construction with the dressed stone replaced on the face. Simple enough until I explain that much of the original stone was the full depth of the old wall, particularly around openings, and up to 800 millimetres wide in parts. This meant the cutting of many substantial stones to create uniform depths, while still keeping the original face in the same place on the rebuilt wall. We were very fortunate to have the services of an excellent stone mason during this period, without his enthusiasm and attention to detail we would have had far greater difficulty with the conservation officer, as it is there is actually one series of stone blocks around a doorway where you can still trace the line of ancient ivy meandering upwards.

THE PLANNING GAME

The planning authority for our region, like all others in the UK, are constrained by their individual local plans. A detailed list of policies reflecting the views of many, both at district, county and parish level, as well as the highway authority, local interest groups and others. One common feature of most such policies is that they are out of date before they are enacted; so it is with ours and the parcels of land earmarked for development during the life of the local plan take little account of changing needs and demographics. Specifically in our case, many farmers took the opportunity after the foot and mouth epidemic to apply for planning approval on land and buildings, should they be unable to continue farming. This weight of approvals has effectively used up the allocation in the region, although very few of the granted permissions have been, or are likely to be, started. The net result of this is an almost blanket ban on future development in this area, at least until a change in policy in 2006 when the existing plan ceases. The Office of the Deputy Prime Minister (ODPM) is responsible for housing planning overall and is currently expected to scrap local plans in favour of regional planning.

With this background, we somewhat naively applied for planning permission on land opposite the current site, for a single bungalow. This was turned down and we appointed a local firm of property consultants to consider our application and advise whether an appeal to the Secretary of State would be successful. Their advice was not encouraging and so we retain this parcel of land and hope for changes in the new plan, whatever and whenever that may be. This episode has reconfirmed our belief, at least in the North-West, that only land with existing permission or land already allocated for development is worth applying for planning permission.

THE RIGHT WAY UP?

Meanwhile we are progressing on the two barns; once the new front wall is up we are able to bring the roof trusses in. This is quite a complex roof as there are two main levels as well as a long slope over one of the original lean-to additions, but eventually we can felt and baton and we are dry at last. Roofing materials are always an issue in conservation areas and on listed buildings. Here the preferred material is natural Westmorland slate, an extremely costly and rare beast. After some discussion we are able to agree with the conservation officer that our planning approval states only 'natural slate' and we are permitted to use one of the imported slates, in this case from India, I believe. These have the additional benefit of being a roughly uniform shape, unlike their local predecessors which are laid in a diminishing course, large at the ridge and progressively smaller towards the eaves, a very time-consuming job demanding roughly twice the material and labour cost. In the 'middle' barn we applied for an amendment to plans to include a full height ceiling, quite common in barn conversions, which gives a wonderful airy feel. This in turn gave an opportunity to install a 'warm-roof system' whereby all the insulation is fixed directly under the roof and not in the ceiling joists as normal, an expensive option but one which gives greater flexibility and is effective in meeting current insulation requirements.

The preceding paragraph will suggest another common feature of barn conversions, upside-down living. This feature is normally brought about by the large first floor hay loft and the low ceilinged ground floor animal byres. The first floor will typically have large double doors, suitable for replacement with glass screens. In the past this storage space would have been accessed by an earth mound gradually brought up to height (a wonderful source of damp on the lower floor wall and one that should be removed at the first opportunity, wherever possible). The first floor sitting room will normally benefit from panoramic views as well, although it should be noted that most working farm buildings tend to have any openings or windows on the south or south-west side and experience suggests the view is on the north! This style of living is not to everyone's taste, but does have the added benefit of allowing access to bedrooms and other facilities on the ground floor to the elderly or infirm. Quite rightly, the Disability Discrimination Act 1995 requires that equal access for all is designed into new buildings, including wheelchair users, although there are common-sense exclusions in respect of some conversions where it would be impracticable.

SELLING AT THE RIGHT TIME

Work is now progressing smoothly and a local estate agent is appointed to market the still unfinished middle barn in December 2003. Immediately we attract interest and are able to agree a sale at asking price within a matter of weeks. We are doubly fortunate in having every builder's dream, a happy and helpful client; between us we agree on a number of changes to suit both parties and the buyer is able to choose kitchen, bathrooms and finishes. In April 2004 we complete on the sale and given the ease in which we sold, decide not to instruct estate agents for the second barn, indeed there had already been considerable interest shown. At this point it became clear that the two-acre paddock to the rear that we had been trying to sell to all three properties in turn was actually a disincentive to most potential buyers, that which we had assumed to be a selling feature became a white elephant that we eventually sold to the local farmer for a song. It really is true that people do not want land anymore!

In due course the second unit sold and except for some final landscaping and tarmac to the drive, by August 2004 we were able to look back and do some final arithmetic.

FANCY A GO?

In conclusion, the old adage 'location, location, location' holds true but without the rising market of the past few years we would have struggled to show any return. Let there be no doubt, barn conversions are very costly undertakings with budget overruns that would make the large housebuilders wince. We will do more, in the same area, but with eyes open a little wider. The selling market is still strong despite the downturn in 2004 but if you are tempted I offer the following provisos: the right building in the right location, a good steady and trustworthy builder, but most importantly I suggest you ensure that the land and buildings belong to you in the first place! That way there is a profit to be made.

24 Diversification into Natural Fibres: Wool for Fashion and Interiors

Myra Mortlock, Natural Fibre News

The return to farmers for wool sold through the British Wool Marketing Board (BWMB) is governed by the price achieved at auction. The return to the farmer pays for little more than the shearing. Grumble as one may, there is no better system for dealing with the annual wool clip. There are, however, ways of making wool profitable and in recognition of this, the BWMB allows farms to purchase back their wool after it is graded. The Board pays the farm for the wool and charges the farm a set fee for the buy-back; recently it has been the average price for that grade in the last three auctions.

Processing the fleece into yarn adds some value. Making knitwear, fabric, fashion clothing or soft furnishings increases that value. Provided, that is, you have a start-up finance, at least one sales outlet, some creative or design skill, entrepreneurial flair and a basic understanding of marketing. Few will start with these useful assets. Yet, a growing number of people take up a second career in farm-based textiles. Some have opted for a change of lifestyle, perhaps leaving a stressful city job. Others are already farming and see the possibility of a second (or third) income.

How to start, how to avoid some obvious pitfalls, how to make the business grow and where to look for help are what I hope you will learn a bit about from this chapter. A contact list of useful addresses is given in Appendix 2.

PRELIMINARIES

The altitude of your farm and harshness of the climate govern what wool you can profitably produce. The worst weather for sheep is cold and wet. To survive they need a heavy coat of mixed soft and harsh fibre. Sheep of this type are classed as mountain and hill breed. Herdwick is an example. Every upland region has its own type. These fleeces are ideal carpet and upholstery wool as they spring back when compressed and are hard wearing. Only the most robust knitwear can be made from them, but in that narrow category there is scope in big Arans in naturally coloured fleece such as Steel or Black Welsh, and the shaded colours of Herdwick. If this is your scene you need access to tourists and hill walkers for the (brief) season, with mail-order and internet sales in the winter. In most economically bleak areas there are business support organizations and various grant structures.

Wool fineness improves as the altitude and rainfall decrease. Fineness is traditionally measured by the Bradford count. The lower the number, the coarser the wool. Most hill breeds have a count in the 40s, the best reaching 54. Shortwool and down breeds such as Southdown, Ryeland, etc mostly provide fleeces with a count of 56 to 58, the best reaching 60. The fine wool types such as Merino and its various derivatives go up into the 70s. Primitive breeds such as Hebridean, Shetland and Jacob are difficult to place as they can vary a lot both over the body of one animal and across the breed. For this reason the return as yarn from farm produced fleece varies from about 45 to 63 per cent of the fleece weight. It is best to buy stock from a breeder who has specialized in producing good wool. Advice is available from The British Coloured Sheep Breeders' Association, most of whose longstanding members are experienced in the designing, making and selling of wool clothing.

A useful rule of thumb is that 58 is the lowest count of wool wearable next to the skin by ordinary people. Sensitive adults and children will not tolerate much lower than 70. At 56 (approximately 30 microns), a filament, when its (possibly pointed) tip is pressing into human skin will not bend aside but continue to press into the skin. If there are a few such pressures in a small area, a reaction may occur such as an outbreak of rash, as if the brain has sensed brushing against nettles. In a very small number of people the reaction is alarming. It is important to breed wool as fine as practicable and to breed out kemp (a stiff hollow fibre). The BWMB, with whom all commercial sheep breeders must be registered, will visit your farm by arrangement to assess your ram fleece on the hoof, an easy route to flock improvement.

A further category of longwool sheep requires some specialist knowledge. They are slower to 'finish' as butchers' lamb, and in some cases are best kept on as mutton. Beginners can receive advice from individual breed societies. The finest fleece in this category is Bluefaced Leicester, Teeswater and Wensleydale are larger and stronger fleeces, Leicester Longwool is a similar medium type in this group, and Lincoln Longwool is coarser. Although generally less fine than the shortwools, these sheep have a very sleek and lustrous fleece which resembles Angora Goat (mohair) fibre. It drapes well and dyes very beautifully. These sheep are usually cream or white but other coloured animals do occur and in some cases can be registered. An imported breed, the Gotland, has natural colours ranging from pale silver to dark steel grey.

How to make the choice? Talk to local farmers to see what breeds do well locally. Visit smallholders' and regional agricultural shows to see what you like the look of, subscribe to one of the smallholding interest magazines and to *Natural Fibre News*. Get the publication *British Sheep and their Wool* published by the British Wool Marketing Board. If time allows visit the important breeders' show at the Three Counties Showground, Malvern, Worcestershire. This happens on alternate (even-numbered) years and is called Sheep 2006, etc. A publication called *The Sheep Farmer* can be had on subscription to the National Sheep Association (NSA).

Novices should start in a small way, perhaps with no more than three ewes plus followers to an acre, if the sheep are big. The incidence of lameness and other disease increases with the density of the flock. Devise a chart or plan for the year and mark on it when you hope to shear, introduce rams, start lambing, etc. Take care not to treat sheep with chemical dips in the last three months before shearing. (Some processors will send your fleece back to you if it smells of chemicals: they will not take the risk of contaminating the water course.) Limit the use of colour markers. Use only reputable antiseptic and colour sprays and follow the instructions on the can. Take care to be present at shearing, roll the fleece yourself, remove coarse or contaminated or colour marked areas, and set aside poorer fleeces for further sorting. Angora goat breeders often bag each fleece separately with weight and scores for various qualities marked on the bags. The information is then recorded for breeding purposes. The improvement in the British Angora goat flock over the last few decades may owe much to this practice.

Choosing a processor is a serious part of the learning experience. Ask around. The grapevine is a good indicator. Mini-mills exist which can take very small quantities, even single fleeces. The market leader in small contract commercial spinning is the Natural Fibre Company Ltd, in Lampeter, Wales, which has a minimum entry of 20 kilograms (10 to 12 average fleeces) per processing run. Small contract weaving is mostly done by three firms which belong to the Gwlan Teifi rural cooperative, also in Wales.

REGIONAL INITIATIVES

'Disadvantaged' farming areas are eligible for European funding such as the Objective and Leader programmes. These have encouraged vigorous new enterprises. Information will be available from your local county council or business centre, but here are some examples of rural initiatives.

In Cumbria, The Wool Clip Ltd is a cooperative of 15 women. Some farm and produce wool and mohair: others are fibre artists or creative weavers, knitters, spinners and dyers. The company was formed three years ago to help farmers add value to the fleece they produce, to upgrade the image of natural fibre and to increase its use by the public. The group operate a thriving shop and visit schools on an education programme.

From June 2005 they will hold an annual Woolfest to celebrate all aspects of natural fibres: sources, use and products. The festival in 2005 will be at the new livestock mart in Cockermouth in the Lake District, some 25 miles from the M6. The festival layout will incorporate trade stands, demonstration areas and workshops related to natural fibre production and processing – no other crafts unless directly related – and the special emphasis will be on wool – British wool. A warm welcome is extended to all in the trade and to the general public. Exhibitors will be from all over the British Isles and northern Europe. This will be the first UK event to mirror the huge sheep, wool and craft and educational festivals in the United States. Dates for 2005 are June 24–25. The web page will advise of further activities.

In Powys, Wales, an ecologically based project called Glasu began with a major conference at the Royal Welsh Showground in 2003. It was attended by the British Wool Marketing Board, the Macaulay Land Research Institute from Scotland, and representatives of the Atelier movement in France, the Welsh Assembly Government and primary producers from Cumbria, the English borders and most of Wales. The conference addressed the need to add value to wool by innovation, sustainability, process development and marketing.

As a direct result of the conference, Glasu published an *All Sheep Directory* of producers, suppliers and related services which is a useful resource for anyone starting a wool-related business. An example of an active participant is Joyce Pitts, who helped to administer the conference and teaches machine knitting to farmers' wives and visits them with contract work, supplies of yarn and to give advanced training. Garment pieces are collected and assembled by Joyce who also receives and despatches the orders. Contact details for Joyce Pitts are in the *All Sheep Directory*.

Currently, Glasu is investigating the provision of a wool-scouring facility for the several small- to medium-sized processors for whom the initial cleaning of the wool is a huge problem. At the other end of the process, Glasu is concerned with better product branding. The future of Glasu lies in collaborative ventures. A festival is planned to link the Powys initiative to other groups in Cumbria, and County Antrim, Northern Ireland. The intention is to share best practice.

An all-Ireland group called the Irish Fashion Industry Federation (IFIF) undertakes marketing and training programmes of all sorts for new and expanding businesses. This scheme is a decade ahead of the two above. A flourishing relationship exists between Irish producers and retailers in the United States. While the market has been more difficult recently, the IFIF is still a huge benefit to the new businesses under its wing. It fits into the European Interreg programme which fosters cross-border cooperation. Residential courses and guided visits to main European trade shows over a period of two years prepare participants for a product launch, with sophisticated marketing support, at an international trade venue. A second transnational fashion project in which IFIF joined Coleg Sir Gar in Carmarthenshire, Wales, has just been completed. Information is available from Lynne Abbott at Coleg Sir Gar.

In Cornwall a major wool-processing initiative is in the planning stage.

A regional advice service can be contacted through Business Link on the internet.

Contact details for these organizations are given in Appendix 2. Further and updated information will be given in *Natural Fibre News*.

PRODUCT

So, you have your farm, and your flock. Your first fleece is with the processors. Now for the wait. Small contracts have to be sequenced for colour and type or the cost of processing would be astronomic. Certainly expect to wait three months, more if your product is both spun and woven. While waiting, you can hone your skills, learn hand spinning, weaving, machine knitting, natural dyeing. This is the time to attend classes, learn IT skills and perhaps web page design. You will of course be designing your product. Be aware of fashion trend and colour predictions. Various regions offer subsidized conferences at which world-class trend prediction experts outline the moods, styles, colours, etc for 12–18 months. If unable to attend, refer to fashion TV, and key magazines such as *Vogue*, *Elle*, *Marie Claire* and their interiors counterparts. The magazine *Country Living* is required reading at certain design colleges. *Homes and Gardens* carries a trend prediction supplement in January each year. Follow its ideas as they appear in soft furnishings such as throws, cushions, fabric bags. Look at its advertisements section for contact addresses of colleges offering distance learning and qualifications in interior design.

You will need to work out you own 'signature' labelling and packaging. During this time also research your postage options. Contact Royal Mail on 08457 950950, explain your project and you will be referred to a New Business Adviser in your postcode area who will look after you zealously. Use the Royal Mail website for marketing information.

Presumably your start-up will be funded at least in part by yourself. The best time to source grant aid is while you still have your own cash to invest as there will be some sort of match funding requirement. Local business advice will be available in your nearest big town. Research the goody bags offered by high street banks. You may want to contact your county council finance and tourism departments.

KEEPING OUT OF TROUBLE

For free legal advice and much more, join the Federation of Small Businesses.

Avoid polluting your local river or your neighbour's land with dye or scouring effluent (not likely if a small operation) and make sure that used water is discharged into the appropriate type of drain. Make sure that your premises are safe and that your have the necessary insurance cover.

You must have good, clean storage with shelving so that you can stack everything accessibly, and your windows, especially roof lights, should be covered with yellow filter film even if the room is not very sunny. Protect your goods from rain, flood, fire, moth, mouse and family cat. Woven polypropylene bags have multiple uses. The 60 x 24" size will cover and conceal garments on hangers during transport and line your car boot but will not prevent fading as light filters through the fabric. Cheap garment bags in a darker but still breathable fibre are available in supermarkets.

It is important to avoid returns of knitwear that you have made to order. 'Ease' is a vexed question. It is the currently fashionable difference between body size and garment size. Using a calculator and the size chart in a fashion catalogue, work out the ease percentage for women's, men's and children's clothing. It might be 20 per cent. Repeat this exercise with another catalogue and do it ahead of each season. Too little ease makes a jumper look old fashioned. Bear in mind that old knitwear patterns will definitely have too little ease, maybe 5 per cent only. If clients send you a pattern for making to measure, phone them to discuss the ease. A hand-knit in thick wool can measure correctly across the surface of each section but when sewn up, the bulk of the fabric will take up the ease. Washing a big garment and drying to a slight stretch can be a correction. It is worth making simple, adjustable wooden frames for drying. It is best to wash all natural wool garments after knitting, whether by hand or machine will depend on the wool type and programmes offered by your machine.

If you limit your styles, you will be able to tolerate returns of 'don't fit' jumpers and send out replacements promptly. You can add variety to your range by buying in good quality textile accessories such as cashmere or alpaca socks, woven scarves and gloves. Hand-made soap is a pleasant complementary line and will help to keep moths away.

There are trading standard regulations about the sale of wool as single items of yarn. Weights allowed are 50, 100 and 200 grams. The tolerance is small: only 3 grams either way. Packed kits are simpler to manage.

Your first snap of cold weather may bring a quick succession of orders and you run out of product. Christmas looms. Your sheep are unreasonably hanging on to their fleeces until next spring. The Natural Fibre Company and its related design firm, Naturals, can supply you with products comparable to your own on good wholesale terms. Naturals has an annual mail-order March Hare Sale, and a small shop at the Craft Centre in the Georgian harbour town of Aberaeron, Wales. A visit to the Naturals shop will help you to design your products, or send for their small catalogue. Fashion trend and supplier or service information appears in *Natural Fibre News*.

THE PLACE TO SELL

You must target your market correctly. If selling knitting yarn, forget the public at large: half are of an inappropriate sex, and most of the rest are too old, too young or too busy. At a national Knitting and Stitching show you will have close to a 100 per cent accurate target. It is worth paying more to be in the right place.

Consider these different strategies:

- ☐ Take a stand at key shows at regular intervals say twice monthly from Easter to Christmas.
- ☐ Establish a regular presence in your nearest leisure shopping town either by joining a cooperative, taking a franchise at a retail outlet or hiring a stall at a farmers' market.
- ☐ Sell from home. Send out regular welcome messages, via advertisements, newsletters, website updates, etc in order to disperse inhibition about entering your property. Try to avoid registering part of your home as retail premises: swingeing taxes may result and additions such as disabled facilities can be costly. Find out what the law allows. Seek advice on how to operate within your farm business.

The main thing is regularity. Publish the times when you will be available in your shop, and when you will be away. Invite special customers to your show stands. Consider simple hospitality wherever you are. Nice coffee and a friendly chat go a long way.

In rural areas, craft trails are popular with tourists. Knitting is an ancient and reputable craft but integrity requires your patterns should be yours, and there should be a perceptible ' signature' on your work – if, that is, you are a self-declared craftsperson.

Integrity in the rural woollen industry does not have to mean 'craft'. There are specific markets in most big towns for regionally sourced produce: an association of farmers' markets has its headquarters in Bath. Local authorities and regional administrative bodies also administer markets.

If you are designing for a country lifestyle, visit the Country Living shows and the Royal Show at Stoneleigh. Assess the suitability of various game fairs, horse trials, yacht races, etc for selling your jumpers. Always have enough of your product in hand when you book a show stand. Never rely on mills being able to produce in time. They may close for their annual holiday at just the wrong moment. At shows, encourage people to join your database and be sure to mail them within two weeks of the show. Don't expect to sell much at the event. Use shows to assess the success of a product, make contacts, get orders and view the competition. An important thing is to enjoy yourself at shows. It helps if you like camping and have a roomy van to sleep in when unloaded.

If selling from home, can you offer any hands-on activity, some tuition or a residential course? Are you a gifted cook? There is serious money to be made from creative residential courses in lovely old farmhouses. Your holiday tuition schemes may lead the way to teaching a local group maybe at an evening class during the winter. There are City and Guilds qualifications you can work for.

Farm outbuildings can be converted to self-catering cottages, furnished with your Jacob blankets and sheepskin rugs, etc. You will sell blankets, throws and sheepskins to guests who want to re-live their holiday at home. The sale from a guesthouse base is probably the most reliable.

A 'sales' shop in town is a further step. This type of shop sells off your proto-types, returns, ends of line, seconds, etc at low prices. Location is not so crucial because your regular customers will travel for a bargain. You may be able to hire temporary premises in a community hall or hotel, but again it pays to make the sales regular, predictable and well publicized.

FINDING A NICHE

Organic textiles

In the UK, organic (Soil Association Licensed) processing of wool so far exists only in Wales. Market research indicates that ecological issues are becoming more important all the time, though apart from the food industry these issues are not yet the primary reasons for purchase. If your farm is organic, it's a small matter to get your wool included in the licence, and there might be a benefit in the future from doing that. A move by the United States to limit the import of organically processed wool could have a damaging effect on British organic wool farming. This is a situation to watch.

The British Wool Marketing Board buys organic wool and sells it separately from other wool. As yet, the demand from merchants is not strong. The management of traditional farms where animals can be moved from pasture onto arable land to clean up the leftover crop is compatible with organic farming but the loose soil can get into the fleece. There is probably a bit to be learnt about the management of organic sheep for wool.

Rare breed textiles

The BWMB has agreed with the Rare Breeds Survival Trust an exemption for 12 named breeds annually. These fleeces may be sold direct from the farm to private buyers who have a supportive attitude towards preservation and will pay a premium. However, that market is not assured as private plans change from one year to the next.

Much rare breed wool is interesting, in some cases beautiful, and has a following. The North Ronaldsay breed has an extraordinary story (= selling point) and a helpful society. There is an annual Rare Breeds Survival Trust (RBST) show and sale at Melton Mowbray in September. Minority breeds are also worth considering. The most notable is the Jacob, now widely popular as a fleece breed, and possibly the only sheep easily identified by the public. The breed society is active and helps its members to market their products at well-designed stands in many regional shows.

Alternatives to wool are mohair, cashmere, alpaca, angora rabbit and vegetable fibres like linen, cotton, silk, hemp and bamboo.

Mohair

Mohair has a small but well-established following in the UK, and some of the products of Angora goat fleece, such as socks, are in much demand due to the fibre's natural inhibition of bacteria. The marketing of mohair socks by small businesses has been exemplary. A cooperative called British Mohair Marketing operates on similar lines to the BWMB. The quality of mohair in the British flock is high. The goats need careful management and are shorn twice yearly. They have great charm and make a farm an attractive visitor centre. The fleece is excellent for dyeing and is promoted by several outstandingly talented and creative teachers and craftspeople.

Alpaca

Alpaca is a more recent introduction to the UK. Stock is still expensive to purchase. Fleece quality has not yet settled down but grading techniques have improved among breeders, and that is just a matter of time. Alpaca is classed as a 'noble fibre'. At best it rivals cashmere and has a greater variety of natural colours. It does not need de-hairing which is what makes cashmere so expensive. Management of animals is relatively easy and the owners clearly find them very rewarding indeed to keep. More processing facilities are needed in the UK. Look out for a significant development in Cornwall. Given fast and reliable processing there should be a bright future for British Alpaca. In its absence, the return on the fleece does not yet match the cost of the stock. The meat is not commonly eaten in this country. A marketing cooperative arranges the export of fleece to Australia in return for high quality alpaca products: this is a worldwide scheme.

Alpaca and mohair are compatible with wool for blending in all proportions and enhance the beauty and prestige of woollen clothes.

The design niche

Be receptive to new (even outrageous) ideas which come your way at shows. Joyce Pitts, who trains farmers' wives in machine knitting as explained, runs a small firm called Woollies which uses top quality wool from local farms to make designer garments exhibited at shows. An enquiry from Universal Studios led to her making a knitted striped cloth for a sequel to the 'Chucky' series of horror films. The cloth would be made into jumpers to fit several animatrons and four dwarves. The original order for 10 metres of knitting grew to 60 metres. After the jumpers were made they were slashed and frayed and put into a cement mixer with gravel and dirt to be distressed. Not the usual fate of Woollies' carefully made garments but a good introduction to a very promising client. One sequel leads to another...

PRICE

Diffidence can lead to setting the price too low. The public takes the price as an indication of the quality. By all means have sales but set the normal prices as high as they will go. View the competition to judge that.

Business centres give advice on how to calculate your costs, add in your required profit and work out how many items must sell, first to break even, then to reach the target profit. Make systematic costings with proper reference to your fixed and variable costs. If a product refuses to sell, withdraw it, re-brand and repackage it and **increase the price**.

Never sell below cost. That may seem obvious but is easily done if costing has omitted to calculate the percentage of waste (fabric used for prototypes and samples; flawed cloth, offcuts and your manufacturing rejects). This could be 14 per cent in year 1 and will probably never be less than 4 per cent since your farm wool is a variable raw material.

It is not advisable to compete on low price. The abolition of textile tariffs means that clothing from China will be impossible to beat on price. Offbeat elegance, signature design, inspirational branding, quirky slogans and fast production of new ideas and clothes will keep your customers coming back. Build up a client base for whom you can design personally. If you feel diffident about this, seek a design graduate as an assisted 'placement' for three months or so. Repeat as necessary.

PROMOTION

As your business grows you will need capital to expand, get more stock, perhaps rent a shop or form a marketing cooperative. Your local Business

Management of alpacas in the United Kingdom

By Nick Weber, Westways Alpacas. May 2005

My background before alpacas was in livestock farming. In1996 after 20 years of pig farming, riding all the ups and downs of the volatile pig market, and facing a significant re-investment, which could not be justified on the past performance, the decision was made to leave pig farming and look at something else. That something else was the alpaca. Our foundation stock came from Chile, part of the mid 90's importation into Britain. Most of this stock was of sound conformation but as we discovered later lacked good fibre characteristics. In taking our herd forward we decide to utilise the high quality stud males in the Bozedown Herd, which had started with similar quality animals but was now making huge improvements through the importation of Peruvian blood. Our second and third generation animals are now significantly improved and reflect the recent gains made in the Bozedown Herd. As a result we can now confidently enter the show ring and win rosettes and classes. Rapid improvement can be made through careful selection and the challenge to breed quality alpacas is most rewarding. The UK herd now reflects the best of the worlds breeding and is catching up fast with the best in the world. Yet again Britain's livestock breeders are showing their flair for the development of bloodstock.

Our first contact with alpacas had captivated us. They were totally engaging, displaying an intelligence and awareness that we had not met with other classes of stock. Today, seven years later our enthusiasm is undiminished and we have begun to feel something of the passion, which the Incas held for these animals. We have found them to be so biddable and easy to manage that they are a positive pleasure to work with. I have seen herds of alpacas on the open alto-plano in Peru that are controlled by two people with short lengths of rope to throw out, thereby extending their arm length, and utilising the strong herd instinct to reform as a group. It is the same for us and intelligent use of this knowledge makes it easy to gather in the animals and manage them in yards or even in an open field. Once penned selecting out an individual is largely a matter of cornering the animal with outstretched arms. Once it feels that there is no escape it will turn away from you and face the corner. It then becomes a matter of reaching forward to encircle their neck with one arm and firmly pull them towards your chest. A quiet and confident manner in these situations reduces anxiety and stress, leading to more compliant animals. Tasks such as toenail trimming, drenching, injections can all be carried out in this manner.

Beware the potential for injury to yourself. They are strong but not unduly heavy; an adult weights 70-80 kg so wear well made boots that will withstand the weight. They can kick, usually hitting you on the leg where you already have a tender spot, but the bone is not heavy and the impact is therefore not severe. Perhaps the most painful injury occurs to the unsuspecting when restraining an animal with its head held down and which when it rapidly lifts it collides with your own. Ouch that hurts! Young stock is often the most difficult to control safely. Being inexperienced they can thrash about and whilst they are light but strong they are more likely to hurt themselves than you. Straddling the animal gives you more control. For greater security, such as when shearing or dental work we restrain by tying out on the floor with ropes on spreaders.

Alpacas lend themselves to being head collar and lead rein trained. They learn quickly and respond to being simply walked or lead in the show ring.

Alpacas don't generally challenge fences. Provided that they have food available and are not threatened they will remain together and if one is separated from the others it tends to try to return to the group rather than wander off. The exception to this is the Stud Males whom we restrain behind strained fences or else accept the consequences of a roaming male amongst our females! We provide fencing made up of square mesh stock netting topped by two strands of plain wire up to four feet high. Mating pens are reinforced by wooden rails because of the proximity of working males to each other. Away from the presence of females entire males may be safely kept in large groups, which are generally quiet and without undue problems, keeping an eye out for the occasional bout of bullying. More often than not disputes within the group are settled quickly, bullies are tolerated for a while then turned upon by their victims. Sufficient space to out run one another is important though.

I recall a vet saying that if their water isn't fit for you to drink then it isn't fit for them either. Clean water is important, as alpacas are very selective about what they eat and drink. We use small storage tanks and clean them out weekly. They can then be usefully used to supplement vitamins and minerals. Selective grazers are also fussy eaters out of hayracks and will quickly remove the best bits leaving a rack full of straw. We change our hayracks' contents every three days maximum and give plenty of space at the feed face to allow the more timid feeders access. Left to eat last at a rack that has had its best bits removed before you get there is close to being on a starvation diet.

Alpacas are very hardy. They can tolerate very cold dry conditions but being heavily fleeced are susceptible to hot humid conditions.
We regularly winter out in the fields utilising what natural shelter is available. In the south west of England we enjoy relatively mild winters but it can be very wet. Prolonged wet weather is potentially dangerous when it is also cold as in January and February. With a fleece that is dry, unlike sheep it has no lanolin, it is possible in a prolonged period of rain for the fleece's resistance to wet to be overcome and for it to become saturated. In these conditions chilling will very quickly occur. We have made sure that we can house all our animals should the need arise, albeit for only 24-48 hours to dry off, before they are released outside again. A portable field shelter can be provided in the field but in my experience it is seldom used. Some owners train their animals to use them by feeding in the.
The provision of a simple shade net or a windbreak in an L shape is often sufficient and allows the animal to select its requirements without entering a building. Alpacas transport readily, being flown, trucked and trailed around the world. In the main they sit when in transit, so given adequate space they become quite settled. As with all stock they need a regular break on long journeys, but can be reluctant to urinate or defaecate unless the right smell is present, so carrying a sample to encourage them is sensible.

The alpaca's digestive tract has developed down a different evolutionary route from that of other ruminants. Whilst it has developed a similar multi-stomached system of digestion to ruminants, using a fermentation sac to enable microorganisms to assist with the break down of roughages, it has only three compartments to the ruminants four.

Alpacas are highly adaptable browsers and grazers with opportunistic selective feeding habits. With narrow mouths and prehensile lips they are able to take advantage of a range of plants selecting them with great accuracy. This makes them adaptable to a greater variety of habitats than other ruminants. In addition the primary fermentation sac has secretory glands that offer a beneficial buffering of the pH in the compartment by releasing bicarbonate and phosphate. This stabilises the microbial environment enhancing their activity and results in up to 25% greater efficiency of digestion of roughages. There is also evidence of a greater ability to absorb the products of digestion from the first compartment, which also contributes to their enhanced utilisation efficiency.

However they have a reduced capacity from other ruminants. It has been measured at 1-1.5% of body weight as dry matter. This compares to cows and sheep at 1.5-2.0% of body weight. Overall that is some 30% less. An alpaca on poor quality forage does not have the capacity to make up for the deficit in quality and will lose weight despite its undoubted digestive efficiency. Whatever feeding system is used, from 100% maintained on hay to 100% pasture, supplementation may well be needed to meet dietary needs dependant upon condition, pregnancy, lactation and fibre production. Good quality fodders are much more desirable than concentrate feeds as replacements for poor pasture, and grains should only be used sparingly and preferably whole to reduce the rate at which they will ferment. Mineral requirements in alpacas are not yet fully understood but it is certain that they are not the same as cattle and sheep. Proprietary feeds for camelids are now manufactured with mineral levels that are elevated from normal levels for other species but care should be taken not to rely heavily upon these to make up for deficiencies in pasture. Dried alfalfa (Lucerne) is an example of a replacement fodder that is both palatable to alpacas and offers extra protein and energy in a suitable form when required.

Evaluation and monitoring of dietary status is essential with alpacas. As with the monitoring of health, observation and handling is key to success. Obviously an alert appearance with bright eyes and shiny fibre would indicate a healthy animal. But given the complexity of dietary programmes evaluation of its effectiveness is desirable. Alpacas are stoic and can hide changes under their abundant coats to the point of collapse. Fixing problems at this stage is not to be recommended and usually ineffective. Too much too late! Equally it doesn't pay to be changing things when it is working well. The answer is to carry out regular body condition scoring. This method subjectively grades animals into categories of 'fatness' by assessing the amount of subcutaneous fat stored at different parts of the body. Assessment is made by palpation over the ribs, loin and pelvis. A scoring system that grades animals from 1 to 10 or 1 to 5 can be used depending upon preference. A score of 1 is emaciated and 5 or 10 is obese. The key factor is that the same person should make the assessment each time in order to be consistent. This "hands on" approach has the double benefit of evaluating the effectiveness of the dietary regime for the herd at the same time as checking for signs of individuals falling behind for other reasons such as poor health. It keeps you 'in touch' with your animals to boot!!

Advice agency will help you to learn and set up e-commerce. You may not be able to look after so many sheep and need to buy fleece of the same type from other producers. You will need to advertise in order to expand. This could be the time to register as a licensee of the BWMB. It costs £250 per year but you get concentrated and sophisticated advice, provided you ask for it, with visits to your premises, referred enquiries and potential sales, help to design your corporate image, a presence on the Board's extremely prestigious website, and if you are a big enough producer, representation in the magazine adverts placed by the Board, and on their exhibition stands. And of course, you can use the shepherd's crook logo on your catalogues and packaging. It is a sign that you have arrived.

So far, say in years 1 to 3, you may have been a small producer and the shows you have gone to are direct selling events. Now you will look at trade shows. Attend several as a 'buyer' . Take your business card, collect catalogues and ask all the questions about supply level and turnaround time that your customers will ask you. A step up requires finance. Business banking managers come into their own at this point. Do you need to change your business set up, move on from being a sole trader? To enlarge your product range or increase supply you may need a more substantial loan. Be cautious about what you will guarantee against it. Apply for grants. You can attend trade fairs abroad with organized groups, and then go on solo speculative trade visits. Although English is a universal business language, you must become fluent in the import conditions, sizing and labelling rules for each country, and the implications of exchange rates.

PLANNING AHEAD

Have your business plan always in mind, and work out an ambitious five-year target that really excites you. A catalogue need not be large but must be supported with enough warehoused stock to meet predicted orders. You will need a sales shop for end of runs, out of season goods, returns, etc. This could be an internet shop to start with. It is worth sending for both the Boden and Toast catalogues and studying their websites. While you work out how they have been so successful you can cheer yourself up by wearing their lovely clothes.

You may well sell enough to open a factory on the farm, initially employing 5 to 15 people. Don't offer to do anything more than short runs, say, six of each item in each size. You will probably cut out wholesalers but your customer must have an absolute assurance that you can supply on time. To do this you may carry the minimum in completed items provided you have adequate stocks of yarn, cloth, trims, labels and fastenings so that you can rush through short runs. If you don't carry a lot of stock you may have to work 24/7, as they say, from time to time.

At this stage you will not need any more advice from people like me. The contact list in Appendix 2 may however be perennially useful.

The Development of Alpaca Breeding in the UK

by Joy Whitehead, founder of Bozedown Alpacas

Breeding alpacas is both challenging and rewarding. The ancient indiginous peoples of Peru had developed their breeding programmes to a very high standard. We know this through the evidence of thousand-year-old mummified alpacas excavated in southern Peru. My challenge is to produce the same evenness, fineness and uniformity of fleece that I witnessed while working on those ancient mummies. My reward is that every succeeding generation of alpacas I have produced is nudging closer to that goal.

Fleece samples were taken from one of the ancient mummies, taken from 16 sites from high in the neck, across the blanket, and down the legs, to give an average across the whole body. That average was 17.9 microns (μ), with a standard deviation of 1.1. Breeders today take one fibre sample only from each alpaca and although a few alpacas may have fineness of 17.9μ or lower, standard deviations of 4 to 6 are very common, with very few going down to 3 or lower. And bear in mind this is only on the very best part of the fleece – not taking any account of the coarser legs, neck or belly. We have a long way to go.

Many alpaca breeders in the UK are taking up the challenge, and breeding their females to the very finest, densest Stud males they can find. Finding those outstanding stud males is not an easy task. A few have been imported from Australia, where Peruvian alpacas have been bred for about 10 years longer than in the UK. Some have been selected in Peru itself, from breeders who take pride in their long association with the alpaca – the alpaca which legend says was given to them by the Earth goddess Pacha Mama, created out of the very earth of the Andes mountains.

A world famous breeder Don Julio Barredo, now in his late 80's, has been line breeding his alpacas all his life, with the aim of producing 20 pounds weight of 20 micron fleece for 20 years of the alpaca's life. Some of the 'Accoyo' alpacas he bred are now found as far apart as North America, Australasia and Europe.

Many Peruvian breeders concentrate primarily on volume of fleece (the Peruvian fibre industry buys fibre by weight), and some of these have succeeded in producing very fine fibre with plenty of crimp, character and lustre, over the major part of the alpaca's body – right up the neck and into the top knot, down under the belly, and down the legs. These are the Stud males and females we look for when we select in Peru. Peru has the largest resource of alpaca genetics in the world, with 3 million alpacas, although they are spread over the vast Andean mountain range, and finding the best animals involves crossing the Andes on rough dirt roads several times.

Bozedown Alpacas has made a 5th Peruvian selection in 2005, having made our first in 1998. Each time, as we have built on our experience, we have been able to locate finer, denser alpacas than the previous time. Each time we have been able to sell a number of the selected alpacas to other breeders in the UK to enable them to go forward with their own breeding programmes, for the benefit of the entire UK industry. The 4th 'Dream' Selection, made in 2004, arrived in the UK in January 2005. The interest this selection aroused was soon very evident, with breeders buzzing around like bees around a honey pot in the ensuing weeks after their arrival.

Bozedown Alpacas has proved its ability to select and breed alpacas. The Show Ring is a tough place to parade your pride and joy. But many different judges awarded Bozedown Alpacas animals Supreme Champion awards in 2004 alone – 9 different judges in fact, on 9 different occasions. This is no reason for complacency. It means we have to stay on our breeding toes! We have established our own bloodlines. But there are plenty more good alpacas out there.

In 1989, when I bought my first alpacas as a hobby, there were only about 150 alpacas in the country, and they were mostly in zoos. So there was not much choice, and I bought the only alpacas I could find - 4 females and a male; I was assured this was a really excellent male. I found out the hard way that this male was not all he was cracked up to be. I knew nothing about fibre, and in the early days nobody tested their fibre samples. My first male turned out to have 44 micron fleece. But, on the other hand, he had excellent conformation, and good bone. I noticed that he passed this on to all his progeny, who showed great uniformity, and I realised that this was what breeding was about - this ability of a Sire to pass on his strong genetic traits. He always improved on the conformation of my females, giving me even progeny, called 'crias'; these crias provided me with a good basis for improving the fibre quality in the next generation. And so the hunt was on for Stud males with better genetics. This was hard going, with the limited number of alpacas in Europe at that time.

In 1994 the first small importation of alpacas into Europe arrived from Chile – bringing a few more alpacas with a bit of colour variety, i.e. white alpacas, which had hardly been seen in the UK previously. Then in 1995 came a larger shipment into UK directly from Chile. But the big breakthrough came when Switzerland and Peru approved a Health Protocol between their 2 countries, enabling Peruvian alpacas to enter Switzerland and, after a period of 12 months, those alpacas were allowed to complete their journey to the UK. At last I had the Stud males I had been longing for. Strong proven genetics from some of the biggest co-operative alpaca farms in Peru - mainly Alianza stock; Alianza, with its herds of 10,000 to 40,000 alpacas. Also the females worthy of these males. The progeny from those first Peruvians I selected in 1998 are still winning shows despite alpacas from many later importations coming along to challenge them.

It is possible to improve in each generation. However, each generation takes at least 3 years. Gestation lasts an average of 343 days – well over 11 months, with the females being mated again 2-3 weeks after parturition. A female can be bred at the earliest at just over a year old, providing she is well grown. So her cria can in theory be on the ground about 3 years after the mother's own conception. A male matures between 2 and 3 years old. So, with a small amount of improvement in each generation it can take many years to upgrade the national herd quality significantly. Although there will still be many unimproved alpacas after this time, these animals are still of major benefit to the National herd, as they are producing, albeit probably less fibre, and not such fine fibre, nevertheless that fibre is useful to the industry as a whole. Alpaca fibre is an amazing commodity. I have learned that 28 micron alpaca fibre has the same 'handle' as 18 micron sheep's wool. In other words it feels like finest merino wool. So the 'unimproved' alpacas which are probably producing an average of 28 micron fleeces, are actually producing wonderful fibre which can be transformed into luxury garments. 18 micron alpaca fibre feels like clouds! If we can reliably produce less than 20 micron fibre, then the world is our oyster. The demand for this quality natural fibre from the top producers of luxury garments will know no bounds!

We look at far more than just fibre test results to determine our breeding strategy. We examine the style of fibre, and the conformation of the animal plays a large part in any decision. We need balanced animals, so that they work efficiently; with strong well-formed legs so that they can carry a cria without undue stress, or in the case of a male, mount the female and cause her to 'cush' for mating. The alpaca needs to have good dental formation, so that it can eat efficiently throughout its long lifetime – about 15 to 20 years. (Although minor dental problems such as slightly undershot teeth can be resolved efficiently by employing a horse dentist). The Stud males need to have even, well-formed testicles of good size and texture, to produce healthy sperm in sufficient quantities to fertilise the ova. Very small, poor textured or uneven testicles can result in sexual deformities in both male and female offspring, and therefore need to be avoided.

So, in addition to good conformation, we look at fibre test results – balancing the micron with the Standard deviation. Together these 2 measurements are computed to produce the Coefficient of Variation, and the remaining figure provided by the testing laboratory is the percentage of fibres over 30μ, known as the 'prickle factor', as these are generally the medullated fibres, similar to hemp in sheepswool, which can cause itching. (Some testing labs. state the 'comfort factor' instead of the prickle factor. This is simply 100% minus the prickle factor.) So, we need a low micron, a low SD, and a low percentage of fibre over 30μ.

Our criteria go on, and we look for alpacas producing a good weight of fibre, i.e.

high density fleeces with good staple length. Some of my original ex-zoo stock only produced half a kilo of fibre per year. Now we expect 2-3 kilos on average, with top Stud males producing more than 4.5 kilos per year. These very dense fleeces have tightly packed fibres, which form into crimpy locks, the locks themselves forming 'bundles'. This crimp and bundling should be even across the blanket area of the fleece, and continue over as much as possible of the entire fibre-producing area of the alpaca.

While the use of top quality Stud males in our breeding programmes is paramount, it follows that, if we are to actually improve the fibre quality in the next generation, then we also have to use equivalent top quality females in our breeding progammes. The male and female each contribute 50% to the genetic make-up of the cria (offspring). Hence the likelihood is that if a top quality male is put over a lower quality female, the resulting cria will be an improvement on its dam, but will probably not match its sire. However, if both the sire and dam are of similar quality, then there is a chance that an improvement over both parents can be achieved. Hence the fascination in breeding for genetic improvement.

The Peruvians had been selectively breeding alpacas for thousands of years before the Spanish invasion, shortly after which 90% of all the llamas, alpacas and indigenous peoples were dead from working in the mines, extracting silver for the insatiable Spanish coffers. The breeding knowledge died with the breeders, and the result was the many llama/alpaca crosses we now see in the Andes. But the Peruvians have been encouraged by their alpaca fibre industry to breed fineness and density back into their herds. We are able to build on their success by bringing some of their top alpacas to the UK, and continuing the selective breeding process. We are already producing some very high quality alpacas, and we need to continue improving for as long as we can.

25 Alpaca as a Commercial Business

Rachel Hebditch, UK Alpaca

At last… the four partners in UK Alpaca almost felt inclined to crack open the bubbly as their first worsted yarns in five natural colours, four dyed colours and a stunning baby alpaca silk yarn finally emerged from the spinners.

It had been a long road since a meeting in autumn 2003 when the four partners, John Arbon, a textile consultant, alpaca breeders Chas Brooke, Graham Scillitoe and myself decided after many cups of coffee to bite the bullet, put up the capital and set up a company to buy British alpaca fibre, process it and make yarns. Frustration at the slow progress of a viable fibre industry in the UK convinced us that the only way forward was to pay breeders for their fleeces upfront and to make our new company profitable.

Today there are at least 12,000 alpacas resident in the UK and the industry is growing fairly rapidly – as an alpaca has just one baby a year it can never be very rapid! Their fleece has been prized in South America for thousands of years and the rearing of alpacas and llamas played a crucial part in the structure of the Inca empire for clothing, food, transport and religious ceremonies. Cloth was the foundation of the stability of the empire and clothes were used to quell army mutinies, pacify defeated provinces, burnt as sacrifices to the gods and given to the general population as gifts.

Chas Brooke and myself run a herd of 160 alpacas in Devon under the banner of Classical MileEnd Alpacas after combining our two businesses. Classical MileEnd operates a successful alpaca breeding and stud business and has sold quality breeding stock, stud services and field companion or pet stock to new owners and existing breeders since 1996.

Our publishing business is centred around *Alpaca World* magazine, a full-colour independent quarterly, which goes out to subscribers mainly in the UK and Europe but also the rest of the world. It has proved to be very successful and is carried by agricultural traders such as Mole Valley Farmers, the SCATS chain and Carrs Billington in Cumbria. Like many other breeders we moved into the alpaca business after being successful in other careers – in my case television and in Chas's case the professional audio business.

Classical MileEnd Alpacas owns a stable of 15 stud males, imported from Australia and North America, that service our herd and females from other breeders on our farm or at their own. Our own ultrasound scanner is invaluable as you need to be convinced of a pregnancy in an animal whose gestation is eleven and a half months. In 2004 we pioneered the use of multiple ovulation embryo transfer (ET) in the UK, bringing over the Australian veterinarian Jane Vaughan, who has had great success with ET at home in Australia. This should rack up the rate of genetic gain in our herd and makes good use of females as recipients who are excellent mothers but lack the characteristics of the best alpacas.

The animals themselves, unlike sheep, have no urge to escape, are calm and biddable and very good 'doers' living on grass and hay and staying out all winter. The British climate's attempt at 'cold' must seem pretty puny to the alpaca as they have adapted to live thousands of metres up on the Peruvian and Chilean altiplano. Their fleece is exceptionally warm and light, second only to silk in strength and can be compared to cashmere. Alpacas come in four main colours, a pure black, white, fawn and brown so there is no need to dye the natural yarns.

Many breeders were desperate to find an outlet for their fleeces and when we asked for fleece in the winter and early spring of 2003/2004 three and a half tons arrived pretty quickly, two and a half tons were graded and sent to Halifax in the north of England to be processed into tops. A similar amount was collected in the autumn of 2004.

John Arbon, one of the partners, a textile graduate, is our technical brainbox and also runs his own company: John Arbon Textiles in North Devon that makes finished goods – hats, scarves, jumpers, home furnishings – from alpaca yarn and does a roaring trade in the warmest socks you could ever hope to find. He and I have now graded over six tons of fibre ourselves working with marker fleeces whenever we were unsure whether a fleece was baby or fine. We have three grades: baby, which is normally under 21 micron, fine, where the majority of animals sit at between 22 and 26 micron, and coarse. Costs are £7.50 a kilo for baby, £4.50 a kilo for fine and 0.75p for coarse. Although the micron counts are important, the fleece is graded according to its handle and thus is a 'hands on' job. At the moment we reject all the leg and belly fibre as we have no commercial use for it and only collect fibre from the blanket and neck. The coarse tops are in storage while a rug yarn which is 50 per cent alpaca and 50 per cent British wool is being trialled. If this is successful we should be able to pay growers substantially more for their coarse fibre. Grading was a steep learning curve, hard and dirty work. Our masks had to be changed several times a day and the colour of the water in the shower in the evening was not a pretty sight. Happily, at the end of the job, the company who processed our fibre into tops said our grading was spot on.

All UK Alpaca's yarns are processed and spun in the UK to the highest quality to provide a uniform, soft, lustrous worsted spun yarn. We produce double-knit yarns in natural undyed alpaca shades blended with fine British Blueface Leicester wool, to provide extra volume and spring to the alpaca. We also produce a coloured range of yarns, comprising natural alpaca blended with pre-dyed British wool. And for the ultimate in luxury knitwear we produce a natural coloured ultra soft alpaca yarn, made up of baby alpaca and unbleached Tussah silk.

Our natural range comes in parchment, fawn, brown, grey and is 70 per cent fine alpaca, 30 per cent Blueface Leicester wool. The black yarn is 100 per cent fine alpaca. The blended colours are fresh mint, moonlight blue, strawberry cream and sunset and are 70 per cent fine natural alpaca and 30 per cent British fine grade dyed wool. Our alpaca/silk blend is 70 per cent baby alpaca and 30 per cent unbleached Tussah silk. In addition to hand-knit yarns we are also producing a range of machine-knit yarns and rug yarns. We are using the worsted spinning system, which is best suited to alpaca fibre because of the fibre length. This produces a strong, lustrous, smooth and fine yarn, ideal for use in knitwear. The yarn is spun on a ring spinning system in either 100 per cent alpaca or as a blend with wool or nylon, depending on the performance requirement of the yarn. For general knitwear we are adding wool when possible to stop any migration and to produce a loftier, bouncier yarn. The wool enhances the qualities of the alpaca while producing good wear resistance. For rugs we are using a 50 per cent blend with coarse grade British wool to eliminate shedding of fibres and to provide good wearability without losing the soft feel of the alpaca. To maintain good yarn stability, the yarns are generally produced as two single strands folded together and then autoclaved (subjecting the yarn to high pressure) which sets the fibres in place in the yarn and stops distortion in the final product. This process also improves stability and the shape of the final product.

It took the best part of nine months to get a substantial quantity of yarn in stock as we had to endure the frustration of always seemingly being at the back of the queue at the scourers, topmakers, spinners and ballers in the north of England as the quantities we were sending up – around three tons each time – were very small beer to companies used to handling a hundred tons at a time. To get stock on the shelf earlier we also used Coldharbour Mill, a worsted spinning mill, in Devon, which is an industrial heritage site and uses a volunteer labour force. They were delighted to work with alpaca but can only deal in very small volumes.

Ideally we would like to create our own scouring, top-making and worsted/woollen spinning plant in the south-west of England. John Arbon is actively pursuing this idea as it would be a fantastic resource not only for alpaca fibre but also for small-scale wool producers.

UK Alpaca sold a substantial amount of yarn in 2004, is busy fulfilling a very large order for nearly half a ton of sock yarn in 2005, has launched a new website with online payment facilities to enable us to sell into the American,

European and Japanese markets and is placing our product into knitting shops all over Britain. The well-known knitting designer Sasha Kagan is creating patterns specifically for our yarn which will be printed in *Knitting* magazine this autumn.

The strap-line on our Classical MileEnd brochure is 'Completing the Circle' and this is what we are trying to do. The aim of the farm business is to breed alpacas with fine, dense fleeces that fulfil our needs as processors. UK Alpaca was founded to help create a viable fibre industry in the UK for the alpaca and provide returns for growers. *Alpaca World* magazine exists to deliver the latest research on all aspects of the alpaca and provide a reasonably priced advertising vehicle to attract new entrants and give existing breeders the knowledge to enhance their breeding programmes.

Introduction on
Welfare and keeping Alpacas

These guidelines are designed to promote health, happiness and a general well being amongst your herd, regardless of size.

The Alpacas

- Alpacas are naturally herd animals and only really feel safe with their own kind, they must not be kept singly.
- Generally they are hardy healthy animals and as with all livestock they must be checked once a day, preferably twice.
- By spending time with your animals you will get to know them, this often makes it easier to detect when they are out of sorts. The earlier problems are detected and help administered, the greater the chance of a speedy recovery.
- Alpacas usually give very little indication that they are feeling unwell until they are very sick. Early indications may include loss of appetite, spending more time lying around and not keeping up with the herd. Abnormal breathing and/or posture, lameness, discharge from eyes or nose and just generally looking depressed. Any unusual behaviour can usually be detected by a thorough check round.
- If there is ever any doubt pertaining to the health and welfare of your animals, veterinary assistance should always be sought.
- The British Alpaca Soviety maintains a list of veterinarians with practical knowledge of alpacas to whom reference can be made by your own vet.

You

- Never be afraid to ask if you have any problems. You could learn something new each day about alpacas and they would still appear to have an air of mystery about them.
- If you experience any problems with newly purchased alpacas your first point of call should be with the person you brought them from.
- Don't be afraid to question your vet, just mention how little a fully fleeced animal weighs before he approaches with the hypodermic. There are often many conflicting views and opinions regarding all aspects of these creatures.
- If selling animals make sure clients know and understand the minimum requirements involved in looking after alpacas.

- If possible visit the new homes and ensure paddocks are of an adequate size and that the animals will be safe and looked after.

Accommodation
- Adequate grazing should be provided for the number of animals kept.
- The stocking ratio for alpacas is four to five per acre, this should be reduced if necessary during winter or when grass is low.
- Four-foot sheep fencing using stock netting is suitable for alpacas as they rarely jump, however barbed wire should be removed. Post and rail and electric tape fencing can also be used, but avoid electric netting as animals can become entangled.
- It is advisable where possible to rotate grazing, allowing land to recover. Foot rot is not common in alpacas, however if conditions are extremely wet for prolonged periods, there should be an area of drier ground provided.
- Alpacas are hardy animals and can live outside all year round, providing they have some form of shelter, this includes good hedges and trees to tuck under as well as specifically designed field shelters. The above also provide a form of shade in hotter conditions.
- In larger fields it is advisable to have a small enclosure or catch pen. By feeding animals here they will become accustomed to the area and it will make catching them far easier for routine husbandry, training or veterinary care.
- Paddocks must be checked for any toxic plants and flowers and remember that the animals' long neck allows them to reach further than others.

Breeding
Alpacas are induced ovulators and as such can be mated at any time. On average gestation is eleven and a half months and it is recommended that mating be timed to ensure late spring or early summer birthings.

Young females are ready to be put to a stud male only when they have reached 60% of the weight of their mother or are 14 months old. Following a normal birthing and complete cleansing within 12 hours of birth, a female should be in a fit condition to return to a male from 10-14 days post partum.

It is known that some males are able to breed from about nine months of age however this is not normally possible until the male is between 2 to 3 years old.

During copulation the stud male intrudes through the cervix of the female and deposits sperm repeatedly into each uterine horn. This action can cause damage to the uterine lining and disrupt a developing pregnancy. Therefore frequent and indiscriminate mating should be avoided.

Cria should be weaned at around six months of age.

It is unwise for the safety of a newly born Cria to have expectant mothers birthing in a field with deep puddles, ponds or streams.

Hypothermia in cold or wet weather can be fatal to young and newborn Cria, adequate precautions should be taken to avoid this situation.

Feeding

- Different groups of animals depending on their status will have different nutritional requirements.
- Always ensure that there is enough grazing for all animals, if there is not and especially in winter months the animals should be offered ad lib hay or haylage.
- All animals require a constant supply of fresh clean drinking water.
- Heavily pregnant and lactating females and other animals during winter also require a supplement concentrate feed. When feeding concentrate ensure that the food is suitable and offered in the correct quantities to meet your animals nutritional requirements.
- Don't use haynets as the animals could get their heads caught and hang.

Handling

The majority of handling is easier to carry out in a small area, so a designated area to catch animals is a must!

- Always handle your animals with the respect they deserve, if you enter a pen in a mad rush with flailing arms and bullying tactics in mind you will never win! Calm, quiet and gentle, but with an authoritative manner is the way to go.
- Alpacas can be taught quite successfully to lead on a halter. This can be initiated with brief but frequent sessions, it takes time and patience and an understanding of your animals. A halter-trained animal can often make life easier when the vet comes to call.
- Some animals can become stressed, nervous or frightened when being handled and respond to this by simply lying down and refusing to move.

The more they are handled the more chance they have of becoming accustomed to it.

- As a rule alpacas will usually walk away from you therefore when moving your animals always walk behind them gently guiding them to where you want them to go.
- If no catch pen is available it is possible to catch an animal in a field with the aid of ropes poles or even a few friends or family walking around with outstretched arms.
- Always remember that stress is a killer, but not always clearly visible, please be aware of what you are doing to your animals.

Health

Alpacas are on the whole hardy and healthy animals that suffer from very few health problems, however a regular programme of daily inspection is essential.

A sick alpaca is likely to spend more time sitting or lying stretched out and is reluctant to get up. They will get left behind as the rest of the herd moves on and can often look hunched up and depressed.

Routine husbandry should include prophylactic worming, the frequency of this should be advised by your Veterinary Surgeon. Alpacas should be vaccinated with a seven in one clostridial vaccine such as Heptevac. Suitable wormers are those based on ivermectin or fenbendazole and all group animals should be treated at the same time. Ivermectin and Doramectin products will have the extra advantage of also treating some external parasites. Worming efficiency can be monitored by arranging for egg counts on fresh dung samples. The advice of your veterinarian should be sought at all times.

Nail trimming should be done as needed, but generally three times a year. Most alpacas will need shearing annually during which time attention can be given to the trimming of teeth, if required.

Cria should be vaccinated at four weeks and a booster given four to six weeks later. From then they should fall into the regular schedule of the adult herd. Worming of cria is normally commenced at weaning. Late born cria can be given A, D, and E vitamin boosters in the autumn as a precaution against rickets.

Diarrhea or excessive scouring, especially in young cria, can be fatal if not treated quickly and veterinary assistance should be sought immediately should this occur.

Alpaca can suffer fly strike. Be aware, that close inspection is needed if any alpaca is reluctant to move or showing behavior not normal to that particular alpaca, during the fly season. Heavily fleeced animals should have their fibre trimmed around the tail and down the rear legs to avoid faeces and urine contamination. Fly strike can also occur on other parts of the body, therefore a thorough inspection of the entire alpaca is recommended. Your Veterinary Surgeon can advise on products to help prevent fly strike.

Husbandry

Regularly catch and run your hands over your animals, a fully fleeced animal may not necessarily show outward signs of malnutrition. Body score them, check for burrs, brambles etc especially between the back legs as faeces and urine can collect and fly strike can occur.

- If possible weigh your animals regularly, weights are often indicative of health; sudden rapid weight loss should be investigated further.
- Males should be checked from approximately eighteen months old for the presence of fighting teeth and a professional person should remove these.
- Shearing should be carried out annually. Suris can be shorn every other year, but Huacayas need to be shorn every year.
- During the long winter months it may be an idea to give your herd a natural boost by giving them AD&E vitamins, this is especially important for cria as it helps to promote good bone growth and development. A deficiency of vitamin D can lead to rickets.
- In wet conditions liver fluke can cause problems in some animals, this is often determined by geographical location. Discuss with your vet and if necessary arrange for suitable precautions to be taken.
- Coccidiosis is a parasitic disease that affects alpacas, young animals seem to be more susceptible. A number of products are available which can be used to control this problem.

Transport

- Alpacas can be transported in a horsebox, livestock trailer or any other approved vehicle for the transportation of livestock providing there is enough room for the animal to stand.
- Animals should not be tied to the trailer in any way, as sitting is the norm.

- Flooring to the trailer should ideally be rubber, but failing that some straw or old carpet is sufficient to provide the animals with some form of grip.
- Entire males and females should travel separately and can be divided with a solid partition.
- Travelling time must be monitored and the animals only allowed a maximum of nine hours in twenty-four journey time, this complies with the animal transportation act.
- Depending on travelling time adequate stops should be made to provide the animals with clean drinking water and food. This especially applies to females with young cria at foot and also allows the cria time to suckle. This stopping time will also allow the animals to stand and defecate.
- It is advisable in case of accident or emergency to carry with you sufficient head collars and lead ropes for every animal being transported.
- Seek veterinary advice when deciding to transport heavily pregnant females, decisions should take into account travelling time and distance.

Weaning

Cria are usually weaned from their dam at six months of age. This ensures that there is enough time for the dam to dry up before the next birthing.

- The advised weight for weaning cria is twenty-five kg or more. Some cria will reach this weight before six months of age, seek veterinary advice before deciding to wean sooner.
- This time can be very distressing therefore it is important to put newly weaned cria out of eyesight and earshot from their dams.
- Males and females can be weaned together but it is advisable to separate the two at approximately ten months of age.
- Cria are usually administered their first dose of wormer at this time.
- Due to the structure of most peoples breeding regimes cria are usually weaned during the winter months, at this time a dose of AD&E would be beneficial to them, discuss this with your vet at the time.

Most importantly enjoy your animals!

26 Diversification into Renewable Energy

Carlshead Farms, Wetherby, Yorkshire

Gareth Gaunt's story is quite different from the other experiences related in this collection of case histories. Qualified as a veterinary surgeon and specializing as a horse vet in Yorkshire and further afield, Gareth was drawn back home to the 500-acre Carlshead Farms seven years ago, after his father underwent a kidney transplant operation. In order to generate a steady source of income, Gareth decided to put down 150 acres to short-rotation coppice willow which produced a three-year crop of tall timber which could be harvested and converted into biomass fuel for co-firing at Drax Power Station, Britain's largest coal-fired power station.

The British government has committed itself to satisfy 3 per cent of national fuel requirements from the output of renewables with a further target of 10 per cent by 2010. This will be achieved by encouraging co-firing in many of the coal-fired power stations in the UK, where wood is combusted at a 5 per cent mix with the coal. Renewable heating projects are also being encouraged as they help reduce greenhouse gases.

At the same time, Gareth Gaunt embarked on a more conventional project to convert two 300-year-old barns at Carlshead Farms into offices linked by a modern new build. The two projects were compatible but not interdependent.

RENEWABLE ENERGY FEEDSTOCK PRODUCTION

Willow coppice is harvested in the winter months when the sap is down using a converted sugar cane harvester. The harvester cuts the crop into 50–150 millimetre billets in one pass; the billets are then allowed to air dry for two to three months, reducing their moisture content from 55 per cent to below 30 per cent. The crop is now ready to use as a fuel feedstock.

The revenue parameters for this activity are a yield of (20 to) 30 oven-dried tons per hectare and a selling price of about £45 per oven-dry ton. Given the growing cycle and process time from harvest to delivery, there is a cash flow issue but this is addressed by DEFRA grants for planting, down payments from long-term contracts, farm Single Payments and staggered planting.

Other local farmers have taken the opportunity to follow Gareth Gaunt's example and have formed a syndicate, the Renewable Energy Growers, to satisfy the feedstock requirement of the local Selby plant. The syndicate plans to expand its collective growing area beyond 1,300 hectares, to raise commercial funding for the producer group and to engage in agronomy, farmer promotion, the provision of advice, government lobbying and group marketing.

THE OFFICE DEVELOPMENT

As other owner-developers in this group of case studies have indicated, the conversion of redundant farm buildings, particularly those that are centuries old, requires painstaking pre-work with the local planners, in Gareth Gaunt's case the Harrogate Planning Authority. Early discussion made it clear that this planning authority's prime objectives were to approve a development involving the new section connecting the two old barns, which would be both sustainable and environmentally friendly.

The tactic Gareth chose was to put in, as a stalking horse, an initial application based on a thoroughly boring design which he knew the planners would not like and then to change to an architect whom they recommended to enter a more sympathetic design for 7,500 square feet of accommodation with reception, boardroom and leisure area. The only point of contention related to the access, where the highways authority demanded an altered junction. However, the planners proved helpful in negotiations, the junction was left as it was, and the planning consent was granted. The single tenant for the completed office development is The Program Management Group, which was secured by marketing through Rural Business Centres.

The choice of architect was rewarding in an unexpected sense. Like other barn conversions featured in these case studies, the development received a CLA Farm and Country Buildings Award in the 2002 national architectural award scheme.

The rest of the farm has just been entered for an extensive Countryside Stewardship Scheme, which will dovetail nicely with a new Educational Trust set up this year.

THE OUTLOOK FOR RENEWABLE ENERGY

With fossil fuel prices climbing steadily and a government committed to reducing greenhouse gasses, the future for renewables looks bright. Wood-heating technology is commonplace in countries such as Austria and

Denmark; the boilers are highly efficient (typically 90 per cent), automated, and able to run on woodchips or wood pellets. Pellets have the advantage of fuel standardization and density, and will be suited to the domestic market. Larger woodchip systems such as the Talbott C3 range will be more suited to on-farm projects heating offices and houses. In the near future, small on-farm Biomass Generators, such as the Bioflame unit, will be able to produce heat and power, enhancing the value added for farmers. Small wonder, therefore, that Michael Meacher, the DEFRA minister, spent a day at Carlshead Farm recently and planned to chair a seminar there for Rural District Authorities and County Councils later in 2003. More recent visitors included Ben Bradshaw and Lord Whitty.

For Gareth Gaunt, what started as an opportunistic diversification from farming is fast becoming a new career with his appointment as Chairman of the Renewable Energy Growers, with the mandate to develop the undertaking into a major commercial enterprise. And, as a footnote, it comes as no surprise that the offices and houses at Carlshead Farm are heated by a 150 kilowatt biomass-fuelled boiler.

27 Market Gardening as a Family Business

Tim Copsey, Hillside, Seaton

The Copsey family have been market gardeners at Hillside near Seaton in Cumbria since 1860 with up to 160 acres under cultivation. As with all market gardens in the UK, the main selling season for produce is from the end of March to the end of June extending into July, according to weather conditions. The climate effects of global warming have induced noticeably warmer and wetter winters with more problems than benefits for growers. However, this is a stable business with sound prospects for the next generation of Copseys when the children grow up.

THE PRODUCT RANGE

The produce grown at Hillside consists of the classic vegetable and salad produce in general demand from wholesalers and UK retailers and ranges from brassicas, cabbages, courgettes, leeks and pumpkins to potatoes and lettuces. British growers today face strong competition from abroad, particularly for the more exotic vegetables, with wholesalers importing heavily year round, who are themselves in competition with supermarket chains that also source worldwide.

All produce is grown from seed supplied by Dutch seedsmen and 1.5 acres are maintained under glass and plastic for propagation and early growth. Including the family, all labour employed at Hillside is local.

CHANNELS TO MARKET

Supplying wholesalers of fruit and vegetables has become a bulk business. Potatoes are sold by the ton and green vegetables, such as leeks, in loads of 60 or 70 nets at a time. There are three or four wholesalers within 40 miles of

Seaton that Hillside supplies regularly and a delivery run to the more distant Gateshead market is made daily. Tim Copsey has experimented with other market channels but they have proved less successful. Produce is only sold to local fruit and vegetable retailers when the customer collects and the catering trade, which demands delivery in relatively low quantities, is unattractive.

One project in which Tim Copsey has taken part is the food cooperatives venture supported by the Rural Regeneration Unit (RRU) which has attracted both local and national media attention. The project involved Hillside in supplying vegetables in 2 lb bags to a Cumbrian cooperative for direct resale to the public, but the small size of bag and quality requirements make this type of trading uneconomic for a market garden normally selling in bulk.

OUTLOOK FOR THE FUTURE

Looking ahead, Tim is unsure whether the next generation of Copseys will wish to continue the business. DEFRA grants are available for expansion but the time-consuming paperwork involved in making an application and the cost, including the services of an adviser, are daunting – particularly when there is no certainty of achieving a successful result.

The farm Single Payment scheme (see Chapter 6) currently being phased in, which is related to acreage rather than production, could make it more profitable to grow less by 2012 when the full annual rate becomes payable – provided, of course, that the scheme remains in force and is not subjected to fresh direction from Brussels.

The Copseys also have one 'wild card' that they may choose to play. Hillside is on the edge of Seaton and has been designated for alternative use. A successful planning application for residential development would open up the prospect of cashing in. With a working day in marketing gardening that lasts from 5.00 am to 5.00 pm in winter and up to 10.00 pm in season, an alternative life of comfortable leisure certainly has its attractions.

28 | Fruit and Vegetable Retailing

Steve Hamilton and Jackie Johnston,
The Fruit Market, Cockermouth

Three years ago Steve Hamilton and his partner, Jackie Johnston, seized an opportunity in Cockermouth to take on the lease of a vacant shop in Market Place which had traded successfully as a greengrocer for more than 40 years and then passed into other hands on the retirement of the original owner of the business. The new owner's business had failed and the shop, No. 12A, had been vacant for two months.

THE START-UP

Steve had no previous experience in retailing, having worked as a driver for a local bakery firm, but Jackie had prior experience working for another fruit and vegetable retailer locally and in various food shops in Cockermouth. Both of them were motivated to run their own business rather than continue as employees.

Unlike many business start-ups, the owners did not require funding since they had sufficient savings to begin operations. Since takings are either in cash or by cheque, the partners operate a current account only with their bank from which payments to suppliers and for overhead costs are made. Initially, product suppliers demanded payment on collection, but once the business became established normal monthly credit terms were agreed.

LOCATION AND COMPETITION

The Market Place is not quite in the centre of Cockermouth being at the top end of the town. Nevertheless, although Market Place is quieter, car parking is easier than in the town centre which is an important plus-point for out-of-town shoppers. The somewhat off-centre location also carries the advantage of a more reasonable rate of council tax which is intended to attract new development to that end of Cockermouth.

So far, so good; but, on reflection, the partners' decision to set up shop seems quite brave. There are two greengrocer competitors within 200 yards of Jackie and Steve's shop, Fruit Market, one of them being a branch of the business in Workington for which Jackie had worked previously. Plainly, the new venture would stand or fall according to the product quality, good service and price competitiveness offered.

PRODUCT RANGE AND SUPPLY

The product range of Fruit Market is defined by the total range of fresh fruit and vegetables available from local growers and regional wholesalers, the latter also providing both fresh and chilled produce imported from continental Europe and further afield.

Local farmers' produce is confined mainly to root vegetables: carrots, turnips, cauliflowers and cabbage with potatoes, local free-range eggs and also some apples and soft fruits in season. Steve collects all local produce from farms within a radius of 8 to 18 miles of Cockermouth which helps to ensure continuity of supply. However, the bulk of the produce is sourced from three wholesalers, of which two are in Lancashire. The furthest afield is 150 miles away at Preston.

SALES AND CUSTOMERS

On re-opening the shop, it proved difficult to recover the lost business that the previous owner but one had maintained during his long tenure, although he provided good advice. However, the partners were helped by Jackie's product knowledge and familiarity to regular customers of the neighbouring fruit and vegetable retailers. Good, friendly service and a plentiful supply of fresh local produce priced competitively have built the business to a sustainable level in its first three years.

The catering trade was investigated as an alternative channel to market but found to be impractical.

The selection of Fruit Market by the RRU as a supplier to the local Heart Foundation provided welcome publicity, but personal recommendation rather than advertising is the most effective way of gaining new customers.

The customer base now extends from the town itself to a catchment area of about 13 miles around Cockermouth for which the town is its primary shopping centre. As the business has expanded, it is now supported by one part-time assistant in the shop to supplement Steve and Jackie's full-time involvement.

LOOKING AHEAD

The initial three-year lease has recently been replaced by a new five-year lease on favourable terms and the partners can look forward with some confidence. Steve cites Fruit Market's good location and the inclusion of as much locally grown produce as possible as key ingredients of its success.

29 Adventures in Diversification

Marie Stockdale and Alan Barrow,
Pow Heads Farm, Wigton

FARMING IN CUMBRIA – THE ORIGINAL BUSINESS

Pow Heads Farm is currently occupied by Alan Barrow and Marie Stockdale with their two sons Fred (14) and Eric (10). The farm was owned by Alan's grandmother and Alan's parents took up farming there when they married at the end of World War Two.

The farm lies at about 900 feet above sea level in an exposed position overlooking the Solway Firth. In the late 1990s the farm was used in a study designed to provide a frame of reference for forestry employees who needed to assess farms' shelter requirements. It was classified as 'very exposed' with little topographical shelter, which was subsequently addressed by means of the Woodland Grant Scheme and Countryside Stewardship. Overall, the land is designated 'severely disadvantaged'.

However, most of the grazing land is classified as 'improved' and, in the past, this and careful management allowed the farm to achieve a good stocking rate. Due to its size, it has never been possible to farm it extensively as a hill farm. Nevertheless, the position of the farm does mean that it has splendid views and a farm walk installed in 2000 allows the public to enjoy them and the conservation benefits of the Stewardship scheme.

BROILER CHICKEN PRODUCTION

In 1967 Alan's parents, Mr and Mrs John Barrow, decided to diversify into broiler chicken production. This venture proved successful and in 1984 they bought a large broiler site at Greenwood Farm, near Wigton, to ensure succession for both their sons.

The two farms were run together with one holding number. In 1999 Pow Heads suffered a severe financial blow, when the processing company withdrew its contract due to the small number of chickens produced and the remoteness and inaccessibility of the farm. By then, the chicken industry was suffering from cheap imports and there had been a widespread upheaval among the processing companies so that even the income from the large broiler site at Greenwood Farm, which had propped up Pow Heads for some years, was at risk. Indeed, there had already been some cutback in chicken placements.

These unwelcome developments signalled the end of intensive poultry production at Pow Heads.

CARRY ON FARMING

At this point in their efforts to make Pow Heads self-supporting, and in order to ensure the option of a future in farming for Fred and Eric, Alan and Marie recognized that the farm was overly dependent on subsidies and that the only profitable enterprise was their Christmas turkey and goose production. In 1999 their facilities were improved dramatically by converting the old broiler shed, but by 2000 pressure from Environmental Health Officers had caused the butchers that Pow Heads supplied to demand that their birds were dressed by the farm, where formerly the wholesale trade requirement was for plucking only. In order to supply this market and safeguard the Christmas poultry production, Alan and Marie had to invest in refrigerating the new facilities and the installation of shelving for dressed birds.

It was essential that the farm should develop some other enterprise. With the meat-handling facilities now at a high standard, it seemed sensible to build on the investment and to exploit the family's skills in its core enterprises of suckler beef and sheep rearing by retailing meat throughout the year. Of course, for this side of the business, refrigeration space was essential to hang the meat for the optimum amount of time and vacuum packing, which allows meat to be sold fresh for longer and actually improves the eating quality of some meat, was also required.

To that end Marie and Alan moved the farm more towards a 'smallholder' type of enterprise with lower stocking rates and a wider diversity of animals including pigs, ducks and chickens all year round. Quite quickly, they developed a customer base of people keen to source antibiotic-free, free-range meat. They also decided to address the strong demand for home-cured bacon and ham, in which Alan had the traditional skills and a considerable interest. The Environmental Health Officer required a door separating raw meat from the cured meat which added again to the investment.

Channels to market

They also considered carefully the possibility of joining a welfare-assurance scheme, such as Freedom Foods, in the hope that they could develop a year-round relationship with the member butchers, supplying meat under a Pow Heads Farm label offering quality assurance. However, in the end, they decided not to supply this market.

The activities on which they did focus were:

- [ ] selling at farmers' markets (initially);
- [ ] selling through Pow Heads Farm Shop (open two days a week);
- [ ] supplying packs for large families;
- [ ] supplying other farm shops.

Direct retailing will always be limited because of the remoteness of Pow Heads, although the advertised development of the adjoining small area of parish land (rare upland limestone grassland) developed for conservation and amenity use by Solway Rural Initiative has realized some 'tourist' potential for the farm shop and subsequent direct-mail sales.

Marie has deployed her computer skills in developing publicity material and a computer database which she pinpoints as the most important element in successful direct-mail marketing. Her background in small-hotel catering and basic hygiene qualifications has also stood the development of this enterprise in good stead.

PRESSURE WASHING – THE NEW INCOME SOURCE

Experience of poultry production for broiler processing alerted Alan and Marie to a quite different diversification opportunity. Poultry farmers are given such a short clearout time in today's broiler industry in which to clean out and sanitize their breeding sheds to rigorous hygiene standards (less than 14 days) that this activity has become a major problem for them to handle and they prefer to outsource.

Accordingly, the Pow Heads partners decided in 1999/2000 to become service providers specializing in the pressure washing of poultry breeding facilities from their own fully equipped trucks. The trucks can provide portable pressure washing for any farm building and the service is on call from Pow Heads. From small beginnings, servicing local poultry farmers, the business has branched out and now pressure washes as far afield as Preston, Darlington and even Beamish. Steady investment in additional equipment is required as the volume of business grows and the diesel-powered pressure washing now uses two vans, two trailers and a mini-tractor. Like all contracting, new contracts are gained by word of mouth from satisfied customers. However, this service business has the advantages of a heavy incidence of repeat business and an ability to schedule service calls in relation to identified eight-week poultry production cycles.

LOOKING AHEAD

The continuing progress of the pressure-washing business has put further development of direct retailing from the farm on hold, as Marie and Alan feel that they have taken it as far as they can without another injection of time and capital investment. Indeed, the farm could be relegated to 'hobby farm' status with very little stock, as a weekend and evening occupation. Further progress in both areas will be reviewed in two years' time when the future of farming may become clearer. The farm Single Payment scheme may have a bearing on the decision.

In the meantime, the pressure-washing service business is now the main source of income for Pow Heads. As Marie puts it: 'Prosperity depends on a network of fowl people!'

30 | Farm Shop Diversification

Julia Colegrave, Wykham Park Farm

Wykham Park Farm is situated about one mile south of Banbury in Oxfordshire. It is a traditional mixed farm of some 620 acres, sloping south towards the Sor brook. Built in the 1850s as an example of a model Victorian farm, the farmhouse and buildings are constructed of Banbury brick. It has been in the family since the end of the 19th century. About 200 acres of the land is permanent meadow land. The soils are classified Grades 2 and 3 and vary from clay loam to ironstone. Crops grown in the past have included cereals, oil seed rape, potatoes and onions. On the livestock side, the family has always fattened store cattle but from the end of the 1980s switched production systems and introduced an 80-head suckler herd.

Early forms of diversification on the farm included conversion of a stone barn, formerly housing cattle in the winter, to an agricultural engineering workshop. This took place in the mid-1980s. Later in 1999, we undertook conversion of a single-storey brick farmbuilding to provide just over 1,000 square feet of office space. This was then let to a graphic design company who have grown significantly in the last five years and are now requesting additional space.

THE ASPARAGUS ADVENTURE

It was in 1990 that the idea of growing asparagus first entered my head. Rather than a conscious desire to diversify, it was more a case of fulfilling my desire to grow a quintessentially English seasonal vegetable not widely available at the time, in order that a larger public could discover the pleasures of eating really fresh asparagus by buying direct from the farm gate. Other factors which came into consideration were that the cropping season fitted neatly into school term time and secondly, as potato growers, our specialist machinery could be used for establishing the asparagus beds.

Although aware of the dictum 'Identify your market first', it was difficult to interest local restaurants, pubs and wholesalers when we did not have product to show. Nonetheless, in the spring of 1991 we planted the first three acres of asparagus beds. So, when the first spears started appearing in May 1993, it was with some trepidation that we erected two temporary asparagus signs on the main road a quarter of a mile from the farm. Extraordinarily, it was like turning on a tap: the cars just kept pulling in and we suddenly realized that we had a niche product that the general public loved. It also highlighted to us the power of roadside advertising and the importance of recommendation by word of mouth.

I had also decided to offer asparagus by mail order with the marketing slogan 'Picked, packed and posted within 2 hours'. Sent by first-class post, we found that the asparagus could travel as far as the Scottish Highlands and Islands by lunchtime the next day and was very favourably received by members of the public unable to buy fresh asparagus in their home town or city. The small amount of advertising done in the early days just served to remind us that, unless targeted accurately, it is both costly and ineffective.

After the nightmare of grading all of the first asparagus harvest without a machine to help wash and trim the spears, we decided to invest in a Dutch stainless steel grader for the following year. This helped to ease the burden of grading and bundling although the labour requirement in the field was still very high as the crop was, and still is, harvested by hand. Every third year since our initial planting, we have added to our acreage with some asparagus planted for expansion and some for succession.

A number of years ago, together with several other asparagus growers in Worcestershire and Shropshire, we decided to form a cooperative to market our asparagus to the multiples. Under the name of Western Asparagus Growers we now supply most of the English asparagus sold by the Waitrose supermarket chain. Currently our acreage on the farm stands at 18 but without the availability of East European labour this growth could not have taken place. With unemployment at less than 1 per cent in Banbury, local labour has never been a serious option.

TOES IN THE WATER

It was not long before customers were saying to us 'What else do you grow?' We sensed that the public were becoming more concerned about the food they were eating and how and where it was produced. This sowed a seed in the back of our minds. Furthermore, since the demise of Banbury market in 1996, we were becoming increasingly disillusioned with the marketing of our fat cattle. A lot of them were destined for the multiples which meant long journeys for the finished animals to approved abattoirs, followed by a quick turn around to be on the supermarket shelves within the week. We knew that there had to be a better way forward for our meat.

Towards the end of the 1990s, the Farmers' Market movement was just beginning to take off in Oxfordshire, and so we decided to go along to the first of these markets in our area, at Bicester in December 1999. We took with us 25 lb boxes of our Angus X beef 'ready for the freezer'. Rather naively we assumed that people could cope with that quantity, but soon realized that we had misjudged people's buying habits as well as the capacity of their freezers! So it was back to the drawing board and the other idea we had been toying with: namely, selling our beef fresh and over the counter from the farm. It was the beginning of the farm shop.

We knew that we already had a loyal customer base with our asparagus customers. We also knew that we needed to upgrade the Victorian brick and slate shed, formerly housing the milking parlour, in which we had operated our seasonal shop selling asparagus, potatoes, onions and a limited amount of Christmas poultry. If we moved quickly, we felt we could use the forthcoming asparagus season to launch the shop officially. So we made the decision not to go down the more lengthy route of submitting grant applications and detailed business plans to various government agencies in the hope of securing some funding. We thought that the least risky alternative was to dip our toe in gradually and to buy all the equipment needed second hand. During the early months of 2000 we continued with farmers' markets taking beef in joint and cut form. This proved a very useful period for promoting ourselves and our beef, as well as gauging customers' reaction to what we were offering, ie fully traceable beef from our suckler herd of Angus X cattle, hung for a minimum of 3 weeks.

It was in this early stage that I was very fortunate to have found a mentor in a friend and neighbour. He had retired after a successful career in butchery in west London. Although his advice was 'Don't have a shop whatever you do', he was, nevertheless, always on hand to give practical advice, encouragement and help. I owe an awful lot to him and now realize that everyone needs a little luck somewhere along the line.

After building operations had been completed, John Craven kindly agreed to open the farm shop for us in May 2000. From the outset I wanted to try and run a shop selling local food for local people. Over the next few months I managed to expand the butchery side to include local lamb, pork and poultry, took on a full-time butcher and increased the range of goods for sale. Gradually the shop began to fill up and it was not long before a cheese counter and an additional member of staff arrived. On the farm we started growing more vegetables to sell.

CHANNELS TO MARKET – FROM PLOUGH TO PLATE

From the outset I wanted to make the shop attractive to all members of the public. I was particularly keen not to be seen as exclusive, especially as a lot of people knew us as the 'asparagus farm'. By continuing with farmers' markets we have been able to talk to customers, and, we hope, get our message across. Although the farm shop is nearing its fifth anniversary, one of the areas where we have not been successful is in winning over those customers who come every year just to buy asparagus. We would love to have them as year-round customers, but obviously shopping habits die hard. We haven't given up on them yet!

As the shop has grown and evolved, production on the farm has become more and more geared to what can be sold direct. Although we do attempt to grow a reasonable range of fruit and vegetables, it is not possible to produce everything but I do think that the general public is prepared to accept this. With the forthcoming mid-term review and farm Single Payment scheme in mind, we have entered into the Countryside Stewardship scheme and returned former parkland and other arable fields to grassland status. With the fairly recent introduction of a secondary Longhorn herd, our beef enterprise now produces just over 100 finished cattle per year. All these are sold direct at farmers' markets or through the shop. For a time we have wanted to produce our own lamb for the early spring trade, and so have started a small flock of 100 ewes to meet this demand.

I think that it is quite important to reinforce seasonality in people's lives. One way we can do this is by always offering something seasonal: whether it's wet walnuts from our own tree or haggis for Burns Night. Although only a small thing, it can mean an element of surprise for customers. All the experts point to this and periodic reinvention as being necessary if a business is to survive.

Although the newsletters that I produce regularly, but infrequently, seem somewhat anodyne to me, I am assured that the public are hungry for knowledge of what we are doing on the farm and want to make the link from plough to plate.

The situation we have arrived at now is a busy shop employing two full-time members of staff and three part-timers; this rises to about 20 staff during the asparagus season. Customer numbers average approximately 350 per week rising to about 600 per week during the asparagus season. Turnover is up 500 per cent in five years and shows promising signs of continuing to rise in the future.

About four years ago, we were delighted to be awarded the 'Les Routiers' accreditation for quality and service. Other benchmarks of quality we have gained are 'LEAF': linking food and environment, and FABBL: farm-assured British beef and lamb. I feel that paying attention to detail, controlling the books and doing a lot of the ordering myself are as important as being visible to the customers. That does mean long hours – particularly during the asparagus season, when work continues for seven days a week.

As turnover is increasing year on year, the question now has to be asked how much longer this can go on happening in the present sized shop. Last year we extended it by 150 square feet, but the increased space has been used up very quickly and we now find ourselves tight for space once more.

BUSINESS DEVELOPMENT PLANS

In the current premises we have expanded as much as we can; but the farm does have a number of traditional brick buildings, including a large granary, arranged around the former farmyard. These would lend themselves to extensive conversion plans. Before any redevelopment could take place, serious consideration would have to be given as to how it could be financed. Without the prospect of grant aid, it is difficult to see how such a large scheme could proceed. It would therefore be vital to seek professional advice early on to establish the likelihood of funding from the various government agencies. Ideas for redevelopment would involve demolishing rather outdated, asbestos-roofed potato/grain storage barns and reinstating some of the lost, traditional single-storey brick barns. The end result could be an attractive mix around a courtyard, consisting of:

- ☐ an enlarged farm shop with an in-house kitchen, preparing ready-made dishes for sale (recognized as a major growth area today);
- ☐ a coffee shop/restaurant enjoying a sunny south-facing position and attractive views of the farm and surrounding countryside beyond;
- ☐ an extension to the existing offices to give the extra space the current tenants have requested;
- ☐ remaining space let for some form of retailing, such as a wine warehouse or rural crafts;
- ☐ plenty of car parking in the central courtyard.

One very significant implication of any change in the size of the farm shop would concern staffing. At the moment we do not have to operate shift patterns, and we like to think that there is a degree of personal service. With a larger outfit and longer opening hours, this would inevitably change. Apart from this, there would be the problem of recruiting extra skilled workers such as butchers, bakers and cooks. As I see it, the solution would possibly lie in sourcing from Eastern Europe as indigenous labour in these skills areas is becoming increasingly difficult to find.

Talking to others in the trade is a helpful way of formulating ideas both for developing the business on a day-to-day basis, but more importantly, in the long term. Building up a business is one thing; maintaining it is quite another. The challenge facing us now is whether to stay the size we are, trying to improve what we do but frustrated by the lack of space, or to explore major expansion with all the added risk that would mean. The jury is still undecided and hoping for divine inspiration!

31 Livestock Markets – Dead or Alive? A Study of York Auction Centre

James Stephenson, Stephenson & Son, York

A GRAND OLD TRADITION

There was a time when every market town in England would have an actual trading market where farm products including animals were sold. With increasing pressure on town centres most of the markets have gradually vanished over the years, although a few steadfastly remain such as the ones at Malton and Darlington in North Yorkshire.

Selling by auction is a tradition that is almost unique to this country and one that has been put under near terminal pressure in recent years. This case study looks at the problems faced by the partners of York Livestock Centre and the ways in which they seek to resolve them.

HISTORY OF YORK MARKET

Ever since Roman times there has been a market in the City of York, which established itself just outside the walls where local farmers could gather their stock to sell them profitably to the Roman Garrison.

More or less in the same location, the market continued until 1971 selling cattle, sheep and pigs on two days each week, with the premises owned by the City Corporation. At one stage in the 1930s there would be eight auctioneers licensed to sell and all were vying for the farmers' trade.

In addition to the live auction, York was also a major centre for the sale of imported Irish cattle, which were shipped to Holyhead and transported by train to the Corporation farm on the outskirts of the city. Up to 2,000 cattle could turn up and they were walked along the road from the Corporation farm to the pens which ran round the outside of the Bar walls. The Irish cattle were actually shown to the farmers by turning them into the street for inspection and it wasn't long before the citizens and motorists raised more than eyebrows at the inconvenience.

In 1971 two of the old established auctioneering firms, English & Son of Pocklington and Stephenson & Son of York, got the opportunity to purchase a site on the new ring road and the old premises were quickly developed to boost the Civic coffers. The original site purchased by the auctioneers extended to 15 acres, to which a further 50 acres of adjoining lairage ground was added over the years. York was the first modern market to be built and set the tone for many that followed.

Reg Stephenson, the doyen of the firm, placed great emphasis on the flow of people, livestock and traffic. There are five acres of car park at the front for the public, two acres of lorry park at the back for the hauliers and two acres of covered accommodation in between for the animals.

The centre became hugely popular and expanded rapidly to a peak between 1980 and 1985. At this time there was a period in the spring of 1983 when they sold over 1,000 fat cattle for each of five consecutive weeks; and at the same time the fat pig market was accommodating up to 4,000 pigs a day, which were put through a sale ring with a revolutionary moving floor on the weighbridge.

The yearly turnover reached £40 million, but Isaac Newton's prophetic law would inevitably take its toll. This is Stephenson & Son's story.

THE CHANGING YEARS

An unwelcome wind of change was about to blow through the auction pens and there was little the market operators could do to halt it. There were three major factors that brought about the decline of the traditional auction market as we knew it.

Plagues and disease

The auctioneer's 'El Nino' carried with it a series of disease outbreaks that were all notifiable and highly contagious. We went from TB to swine fever, scrapie, SVD, blue-ear, and then through the spectre of BSE to the disastrous calamity of foot and mouth disease (FMD). Each outbreak was automatically punctuated by an immediate cessation of business for the auction market, which was perceived as a potential carrier of disease.

There was no compensation for losing business and we could be closed for as long as 12 months at a time. Inevitably each time controls were lifted, lost business had to be regained but some had found other marketing channels on a permanent basis.

There was and still is little excuse for all the epidemics that break out among our domestic animal kingdom. We are an island and like New Zealand we could quite easily keep out the trouble. Being British and having politicians with diminishing affinity to agriculture, we operate an almost open-door policy, although I do note that the current Minister of Agriculture is raising the number of sniffer dogs at ports from two to six!

Suffocating 'red tape'

Every industry complains about its paperwork but I think that agriculture has been hit harder than most and what makes matters worse is that farmers are not equipped to deal with it.

As markets, not only do we have to have a licence for the premises but we are also obliged to comply with all the regulation surrounding the identification and movement of animals. Currently every beast that comes through our gates has to carry an individual passport, which in turn has to correspond with its two ear tags and for which we have to send back notification of movement to DEFRA.

The same controls are about to be introduced for sheep, heaven help us, and so it goes on. The continuous imposition of red tape has for certain reduced any margin of profit and in many cases persuaded market operators to cease altogether.

Changing trade patterns

There has been a move for the bigger producers to sell their own stock. This has been stimulated and encouraged by the larger abattoirs, which in turn supply the major supermarkets. The supermarket domination has been a key factor in diverting stock away from the open auction market into a channel where the buyer has more control over price. Most believe this is not to the benefit of the industry but it is a fact of life and has brought about the demise of a lot of markets.

When the new York market was built in 1971 there would be round about 300 auctions still going in the country. Today there are 180 members of the Livestock Auctioneers Association. At its lowest point following the FMD crisis, York was reduced to trading around 200 fat cattle a week and its pig numbers had dropped from a peak of 4,000 down to 250.

It was time to change or die.

DIVERSIFICATION IN ALL DIRECTIONS

We have had a continuous development programme at York, which has been drip-fed into our operation as and when the core livestock business receded. Listed below is a range of activities that we have or hope to have established at the newly titled York Auction Centre.

Machinery sales

This was one of the first enterprises we introduced onto the site about 15 years ago and we now have one of the largest collective sales of agricultural machinery in the country, with our last catalogue comprising over 5,000 lots in eight simultaneous auctions. We draw in customers from both home and abroad and have even sold items over the internet. Our machinery sale website attracts an average 20,000 visits for catalogues each sale.

Horse sales

We have constructed a purpose-built equestrian sales complex with a heated ring, cage box stabling and a show paddock. We operate around 15 sales each year, selling up to 100 horses at each sale.

Motor auctions

We have struck out into the grey world of car auctions operating a weekly sale on a Wednesday evening and using the same facilities as for the horse sales. We now have specialist sales for 4 x 4 vehicles, light commercials and motor bikes.

Sunday car-boot and table-top sale

To take advantage of the national sport of retail therapy, we opened the gates on a Sunday for car-booters. This arrangement now operates all year round with over 100 stalls and the cafeteria serving 500 lunches of roast beef and Yorkshire pudding.

Farmers' market

York was one of the first and leading markets in the north of England, expanding last year to a twice-monthly operation with up to 70 stalls. This provides the opportunity for local producers to market their goods – predominantly food, but including some crafts. The market has recently undergone a full Soil Association inspection and achieved certified status under the National Association of Farmers' Markets rules.

City lorry park

The lorry park for the city had been in the centre where it was becoming increasingly inaccessible and unacceptable for local residents. With the financial support of the council we have recently opened a new floodlit lorry park for 30 vehicles to stop overnight, with catering facilities and security available. This dovetails with our daytime operations, providing extra income from the site during the dead hours of night.

Computer training

One project that appeals to current government thinking is computer education and with grant assistance we have set up a computer suite. We offer to farmers and others a tutored course at any level of computer literacy and at a Yorkshire price! Currently all seven computer stations are occupied on two evenings a week with our secretaries earning well-deserved extra money.

The food hall

We have carried out an analysis of covered space that is used and there is a serious under-utilization, which we are addressing. One project will be to create a purpose-built food hall that will incorporate the farmers' market, taking it onto its next stage of development.

The food hall would initially be open for the whole weekend from Friday night to Sunday lunchtime and provide a regular shopping venue for the discerning clientele who want to taste what they eat and know where it has come from.

The food hall would include a permanent cold room where food could be stored overnight rather than taking it backwards and forwards. The promotion of Yorkshire produce with strict rules of qualification could well attract a regional grant.

Auction store and chattel sales

We have built up a good programme of chattel auctions, which range from mundane household goods through to respectable antiques; and more recently we have introduced sales of electrical white goods and even carpets.

We try to hold these sales on the same days as a farmers' market in order to have as large a footfall as possible, and they have been remarkably successful. It is our intention to develop a permanent store and sales area for these auctions.

Country store

With the ever-increasing number of visitors to the York Auction Centre we are looking at the opportunity of establishing a country store to sell clothing and equipment. There is the possibility of a joint venture and we would hope that this could also market products manufactured in our Yorkshire region.

Business starter units

There is a strong demand for small offices, workshops and studio units for new businesses and we are planning a fully serviced and managed work-space that would be available on an easy in/easy out basis without formal long-lease commitments. The service provisions would include reception and central switchboard, computer network links, photocopying, boardroom and cafeteria facilities.

The way ahead

The sixth generation of the Stephenson family is now a partner in the business and we are hoping that all the changes will provide a platform for our family in the future. The core business of selling livestock remains but it will occupy only 20 per cent of our facilities.

32 | The Barn Brasserie

Michael Xenakis, Great Tey, Colchester

Unlike other rural entrepreneurs whose exploits are featured in these case histories, Michael Xenakis does not have a farming background himself, although his wife Elizabeth's family have been farming for some generations. Having worked in the City of London for 25 years, Michael's experience of rural development prior to the development of the Barn Brasserie was confined to a previous barn conversion 14 years ago for his family's weekend occupation.

However, in 1998 Michael Xenakis opted out of the luxury cruise liner group of which he had been a main board director for 15 years, and decided to move permanently out of the corporate world to develop a business venture in Essex in the area where he and his family now resided. The choice of business would be determined by his own knowledge and experience in the design, operation and business economics of catering for large numbers on cruise liners.

THE BARN BRASSERIE CONCEPT

In considering suitable venues for establishing a restaurant of consequence, Michael Xenakis was guided by the necessary conditions he had established for success. First, a building of striking design and quality development were essential. Relying on his personal eating-out experience rather than structured market research, Michael had concluded that people do not rate food and drink as the prime objective of going out for meals, although high-quality food, wines and service are an essential accompaniment. Eating out, he maintains, is one of the very few opportunities to communicate with family and friends in a relaxed environment away from the pressures of work and modern living in smaller spaces, cluttered with entertainment systems and IT. In the United States, for example, 65 per cent of food is consumed outside the home. The same need to 'escape' drives adults into garden centres and DIY stores at the weekend.

Following this logic, Michael Xenakis's concept of a relaxed ambience embraced the need for an open, airy restaurant space, unencumbered by the ancillary service facilities of kitchen and cloakrooms with a construction design and décor using natural materials: glass, timber and steel, and natural colours.

Introducing the Everhot

Nothing can match the appeal of the traditional kitchen range, with its hand-crafted good looks and quality cooking epitomising a relaxed, homely lifestyle in town or country. Nothing can match the unique appeal of the Everhot, which offers all the benefits of a classic solid fuel cooking range with none of the drawbacks. The Everhot is an electric heat storage cooking range that plugs into

a simple 13amp socket, and needs no flue or concrete base. Easily positioned alongside your standard kitchen units, it gives you all the control of modern cooking methods, together with the even baking and winter warmth of the traditional range. With its solid construction, large cast iron hotplates and two outstandingly spacious ovens, the Everhot is still around half the size and far less than the price of other leading brands. Fitting comfortably into the standard kitchen unit size, it has the further advantage of a full-width radiant grill in the upper oven. To top it all, the Everhot averages less than half the running costs of some other traditional ranges. Invented more than 20 years ago, and enjoyed by thousands of delighted owners across the country, Everhot is quite simply the best of both worlds.

Compact size – with its spacious top and bottom ovens and four saucepan hot and simmer plates, the Everhot still fits neatly into a standard 600mm wide kitchen unit.

Weight saving – built to last a lifetime, the Everhot is incredibly solid, but its 250kg weight means that the kitchen floor should not need reinforcing, and if you move, you can take it with you.

Flue free – because it runs on electricity, the Everhot needs no flue. Again, this makes installation easy, and also reduces energy consumption.

Energy saving – with its unique, energy saving design, the Everhot has extremely low electricity requirements, so you can simply plug it into a 13amp socket just like an electric kettle. Many owners have praised its 'miserly consumption'.

Total control – each oven and heating surface can be independently adjusted to the temperature you require. If a particular cooking area is not needed for long periods, you can switch it off or turn it down without affecting the other areas. So on hot summer days, you don't have to roast in the kitchen.

Grill – you'll have a 2.5Kw full-width radiant grill, which can also be used to rapidly boost oven temperature. Other comparable ranges just don't provide grills.

Maintenance-free – with a little care and affection, the Everhot will perform trouble-free year after year, with no annual servicing requirement (unlike other ranges).

The Everhot is ahead of its time – originally developed more than 20 years ago for those able to draw power from limited renewable resources. Innovatively designed to run at a constant temperature 24/7, and to plug into a simple 13amp power supply, it minimises power consumption and wastage, while maximising performance and versatility.

Made at Coaley Mill, a 13th century water-powered mill near Dursley in the old wool heartland of the south Cotswold valleys, the Everhot is the product of a long history of engineering innovation and quality manufacture. One of the reasons why an Everhot is available at such an affordable price is because all the energy used to produce it at Coaley Mill is generated using a state-of-the-art, environmentally friendly water turbine.

A carefully selected colour range offers you abundant choice for your kitchen.

Tel: 01453 890018   Fax: 01453 890958

Everhot Cookers
Coaley Mill, Coaley, Dursley
Gloucestershire, GL11 5DS
Email: sales@everhot.co.uk
Website: www.everhot.co.uk

The Grade II listed Brook barn, one of the largest thatched barns in England, was a clear but challenging choice, satisfying the main criteria for a restaurant of distinction and potentially providing a 'destination' and sense of experience which would draw eaters-out from a catchment area which Michael Xenakis characterizes as 20 minutes' driving distance. With four years' experience, the Barn Brasserie attracts diners from the Colchester, Witham, Chelmsford and Sudbury areas, as well as more local custom and 'ladies who lunch' from far and wide. But first, it was necessary to negotiate with the planners and to evaluate the development cost carefully in order to ensure that a restaurant could be created which satisfied fully the Xenakis concept.

A SUPPORTIVE PLANNING PROCESS

Up to 1999 Brook barn was a redundant agricultural building of historic interest that had fallen into disrepair. The building was largely in its original condition with the oak frame erected on bare soil ground. For this reason the approach for change of use and conversion by Michael Xenakis and his architect, Mark Perkins, was received positively by the local authority planning office. The main Xenakis requirements for ample windows and a vast open space, and a refusal to include kitchens in the existing building were accepted.

However, the planners were concerned that there should be sufficient car parking and insisted that disabled toilets should be accommodated within the building. The car-parking requirement was satisfied by establishing a car park in an adjacent green field and a compromise was reached on the second requirement by constructing a mezzanine floor within the building which provided sufficient space for all the washrooms. As with many planning applications the requirements of the county highways authority on access, exit and car parking were in many ways the most demanding.

The construction work involved jacking up the original oak frame with brick foundations and the use of reclaimed and original materials, in particular black weather-boarding, timber floors and interior oak beams. The completed development was recognized in the CLA national architectural award scheme, Farm and Country Buildings Awards. The judges praised the stylish, light modern feel of the magnificent restaurant within this historic building.

OPERATIONAL ASPECTS OF THE BRASSERIE

The Barn Brasserie has a seating capacity for 150 people and employs 50. All table staff are given a compulsory two days off each week to ensure that they remain bright and attentive. Typically, the restaurant serves 2,000 meals each week, all of which are cooked to order from fresh food ingredients. The menu includes fish, meat and vegetarian specialities with modern European and spiced Asian dishes. Prices range from full á la carte menu to £5.95 two-course lunchtime specials. There is a wine list of more than 100 wines.

Michael Xenakis acknowledges that there is a drink and drive factor, which has affected dining out habits. There is a greater use of taxis and a noticeable trend to drinking less but more discriminately. However, he doubts that there has been much impact on dining out frequency.

During the start-up phase, the Brasserie was marketed heavily in the local press and radio. Local radio was initially effective but it has become difficult to find fresh 'punch' messages that attract attention. The restaurant's overall performance has surpassed the original business plan reaching break-even point in the eighteenth month of operation. Michael Xenakis's own involvement in day-to-day management is now reduced from full-time to about one hour a day.

THE EVOLUTION PROCESS

With few years in operation and no consolidating period, planning the next stage required careful analysis of current demand and future trends. The decision was finally taken, with some imaginative input, to transform the next building in line into a meeting room. The Dealing Room now operates as a very modern event facility with local businessmen using it almost every day for a working meeting away from their own office environment. During the evenings the Dealing Room is often reserved for private dinner parties with guests in most instances celebrating birthdays and anniversaries. Wine tasting and small product launches and presentations are often held in this very versatile facility.

The final space within the Barn building complex to be put in full use is the Fish Colony. This 'seafood on the hoof' concept was inspired by the unique advantage of the Colchester oyster. With only eight tables and with the best oyster in the world on offer the Fish Colony opened the doors to the public last November to coincide with the opening of the oyster season. Other fish on the menu are smoked cod roe from Orford in Suffolk, smoked eel, salmon eggs and beluga caviar.

THE BARN AND FARMING

The culture in the Barn is to continuously present the client with something new and interesting. People consume more food away from their home kitchens and as a result the awareness on how food is grown and prepared is on the increase.

Food and farming is attracting unprecedented attention and the 'food integrity' is more than ever exposed and appreciated by the consumer.

The Barn is surrounded by farmland and we are fortunate to be able to grow food, which is to be consumed by our own clients. We are beginning the process in establishing a herb garden, a vegetable garden and a glasshouse. Our clients will have full access to the gardens and all growth will be totally organic.

A BROADER HORIZON

Michael Xenakis has proved that his restaurant concept is valid and is ready to apply the formula elsewhere. However, suitable buildings and locations are difficult to find. The formula relies on selecting a striking older building that can be restored and converted into a 'destination' of interest with a dining capacity of 150 which will attract eaters-out from a distance.

The location can be urban or rural, provided that it is 'within 20 minutes of the chimney pots'. Therefore, readers who have a disused warehouse or decommissioned chapel on their hands and are looking for an alternative use are welcome to contact Michael on michaelxenakis@aol.com.

33 | A Day in the Country and the Great Barn

Richard Stephenson, Upper Aynho Grounds, Oxfordshire

In 1985, when Richard and Di Stephenson bought Upper Aynho Grounds, a 270-acre farm with a fine 17th-century stone farmhouse, magnificent barns, cottages, a number of outbuildings, fish ponds and pheasant covers, they recognized that the amenity value of the estate probably exceeded its potential as a farming enterprise. Neither Richard nor Di had farmed previously, although there were farming interests in the family and their son Jeremy had trained at agricultural college. Richard's main occupation as senior partner in a busy North Oxfordshire medical practice was a major constraint on available time for development at Upper Aynho Grounds so that the successful ventures of the last 18 years reflect boundless energy, as well as business acumen in abundance.

EARLY ACTIVITY

The immediate priority on taking occupation was to make arrangements for the farming. From the outset all the arable land was contract farmed. A pair of farm buildings were set up for pig breeding, which Jeremy Stephenson managed. However, the industry's general move towards outdoor pig farming and the effect on prices helped to make the Aynho unit unviable and the activity was discontinued after five years.

A row of cottages – built originally for agricultural workers – linked by an arch to the house and forming one side of the original farmyard, was in poor condition but an obvious candidate for holiday lettings. They were duly repaired and improved. However, the Stephensons decided that due to their proximity to the main house and in view of their plans for the use of the adjoining barn, an imposing unused stone structure of 40 metres by 8 metres with a leaky roof but having potential as an entertainment location on a grand scale, it would be better to rent the cottages on short leases to more permanent or carefully selected tenants.

Before arriving at a strategy for the profitable use of the barn, the Stephensons focused on reorganizing the existing fishing arrangements. Richard decided to continue with game fishing, which was run on a seasonal subscription basis between April and October with re-stocking of the three trout lakes every three weeks. The game fishing runs as a club with 40 members and is a profitable sideline. Coarse fishing was considered as an alternative as this is more profitable, but, taking into consideration the position of the lakes and the possibility of using them for corporate entertainment, it was decided to continue with game fishing for trout. It should be emphasized that licences from the Environment Agency are required for stocking and fishermen require a rod licence to fish on private water.

By now the idea was forming of developing a corporate entertainment package, which would offer a combination of country activities with catering facilities as an attractive alternative to more conventional corporate events for clients and customers or staff meetings and celebrations. A key factor in Upper Aynho Grounds' market potential was its location and parking space for up to 200 cars. Situated 5 minutes from junction 10 of the M40 and 25 minutes from junction 15A of the M1, one hour from Heathrow and 45 minutes from Birmingham International airport and the NEC, the catchment area included then the major conurbations of Oxford, Northampton and Milton Keynes. Important population centres within reach now include Newbury, Aylesbury, Leamington Spa and Warwick, as well as nearby Banbury and Bicester.

In the late 1980s clay-pigeon shooting grew rapidly in popularity as a competitive hobby and as a leisure pastime for 'townies'. Country people had always shot clays in the late summer as a practice warm-up for the shooting season. Now in North Oxfordshire, licensed and unlicensed clay shoots in farmer's fields open to the public became commonplace in the winter months. Therefore, it was a natural extension from game fishing to introduce clay-pigeon shooting at Upper Aynho Grounds as a second country pursuit. It is important to remember that permission is required from the Firearms Licensing Department to approve the site, in order that a person may use a shotgun on the designated area of land without holding a shotgun certificate, in accordance with Section 11(6) of the Firearms Act 1968–1997.

A DAY IN THE COUNTRY CONCEPT

Most of 1986 was spent in planning and preparation. By the year's end the concept of 'A Day in the Country' as a new form of quality corporate entertainment had emerged. Richard and Di Stephenson were clear from the outset that the quality of the catering would be crucial to penetrating the corporate hospitality market. Three-course sit-down lunches in the ambience of a comfortable traditional building with fine wines served in cut glass goblets rather than instant coffee in plastic beakers were the necessary accompaniment to fly fishing for trout and clay-pigeon shooting, however good the sport or competent the expert instruction provided. To attract City bankers and multinational corporate managers and their clients and customers, oak-smoked Scottish salmon at lunch would be as important as the size of the morning's catch and marksmanship at the clays would count for less than the quality of the claret.

And so the A Day in the Country programme evolved. Over the years additional optional activities were added to the game fishing and clay shooting, including Land Rover 4-wheel driving on a 'jungle track', archery, pistol shooting and Pacer Pirates 'sand buggies'. Horse carriage or tractor driving, sheep dog trialling and cow milking – even falconry, skydiving and hot-air ballooning – are among the additional rural pursuits that can be provided on request. Clients can order in advance the combination of activities that appeals most to them and their guests, together with the menus for snacks on arrival, lunch, tea and dinner – for those wishing to continue the entertainment into the evening.

During 1986, the Stephensons realized that they needed some professional help with marketing and management expertise. Richard invited an old friend Nicholas Price to become a partner in the business. Nicholas had recently sold his hotel company and was an ex-chairman of the Best Western Hotel Group. He had considerable marketing experience with many contacts in the hospitality industry. Richard's own experience in the improvement and refurbishment of old buildings was more than sufficient for the initial task of making the first half of the barn inhabitable; primarily roof repair, draught proofing and the installation of fireplaces and chimneys. Management of the medical practice had given him the necessary business administration experience.

There were no kitchens attached to the barn and, to begin with, Di Stephenson and a small staff of part-time helpers recruited locally had their work cut out in serving freshly cooked meals for parties of 30 or more from the farmhouse kitchen across the yard in all seasons and weather conditions. As the business grew, kitchen facilities were installed in an outbuilding adjacent to the barn and the same part-time staff were employed.

EVOLUTION OF THE
CORPORATE HOSPITALITY MARKET

The business traded as a partnership until 1990, when on professional advice the business was incorporated into A Day in the Country Ltd. The heady days of lavish corporate entertainment peaked in the late 1980s towards the end of the Thatcher era but, as the megabuck market for high-profile hospitality events such as Ascot and Wimbledon faded, demand for comparatively modest and competitively priced, but still upmarket, A Day in the Country packages remained buoyant.

The market was changing in other respects too. The early 1990s saw a weeding out of many corporate hospitality organizers, as public interest dwindled and other outdoor activities in the countryside aimed at the fashionable 'corporate bonding' market, such as paintball war games, flourished for a year or two before the fad faded.

A Day in the Country was able to survive this tough trading period, as it was still able to offer its quality product at a competitive rate, owing to its low and controllable overheads. In the corporate field, two converging trends opened up new market opportunities for the company. On the one hand, cost-conscious corporates were moving towards 'away days' in which staff seminars could be combined with an element of relaxation among colleagues. On the other hand, the combination of corporate entertainment with conferences, presentations and product launches to major clients and customers was recognized as a cost-effective way of strengthening business relationships purposefully with a degree of informality. And so the concept of mixed days evolved from the original A Day in the Country. Corporate customers could bring their staff or clients to Upper Aynho Grounds for a half-day of meetings, first-class food and drink and a few hours of country sports.

Although this hybrid form of hospitality increased the company's ability to provide more days on which the activities could be offered as a half-day event combined with catering, the barn now had to be used both as a restaurant and a meeting room. There was also an emerging demand for a more formal meeting area with auditorium seating and audio-visual facilities. Fortunately, there was the opportunity to satisfy this demand by opening up the second half of the barn, an identical floor area to the original area which had served A Day in the Country so well.

THE GREAT BARN

By 1997 the annual turnover of A Day in the Country was such that Richard Stephenson was sufficiently confident of the market opportunities to apply for planning consent in two stages for the whole barn and extended, permanent change of use to conference centre and civil wedding venue – another developing market. The planning application included new draught-proof entrances to the whole barn, heating and insulation throughout and the addition of a luxury toilet and restroom facilities suite. After receiving planning consent, the work was carried out by local building contractors under Richard's close supervision. Car parking was also extended.

The new conference suite, named the Croughton Room after another local village, has a seating capacity of 120 (60 in classroom format) while the original Aynho Room maintains its seating capacity of 100. Receptions using both rooms can accommodate up to 300. With the expansion of activity to include large party events not involving country pursuits, such as conferences and wedding receptions, the original trading name was not always appropriate and the title 'The Great Barn' was adopted for those events, with hospitality occasions still focused on country pursuits offered under the original A Day in the Country trading name.

CONTINUING OPERATIONS AND OUTLOOK FOR THE FUTURE

As the business heads towards its 18th year of profitable operation, it is possible to begin assessing strengths and weaknesses. The flexibility of the hospitality events, meeting and catering facilities that are on offer at Upper Aynho Grounds is clearly a major factor in its continuing appeal to a wide range of profitable corporate and private function markets. At one extreme, The Great Barn can accommodate conferences plus catering of 120, at the other, small exclusive corporate days of 10 or more people.

This flexibility addresses business conditions where market prices have scarcely changed over the past 10 years and the Great Barn and A Day in the Country can continue to compete against mainline prestige events at about only one-third of their prices. Local large-party catering competition has increased, but few are able to offer the range and flexibility of the Upper Aynho Grounds product mix.

Wisely, Richard Stephenson has maintained a policy of maintaining overhead costs at a minimum. Richard and Di were joined by their son, Jeremy Stephenson, on a full-time basis after the Great Barn expansion in 1997 and Jeremy's primary function is now marketing and operations director for the business as Nick Price nears retirement. However, he also farms the 200 acres of arable land which have been taken back in hand. Aside from the three family members, the business employs a marketing assistant. The catering is now wholly subcontracted to a local firm set up by catering professionals that maintains Richard and Di's exacting standards.

A marketing budget of around 3 per cent of sales is allocated mainly to mail shots, advertising in the *Yellow Pages* and business magazines and a website that Richard and Jeremy regard as an essential promotional tool. Despite the focus on economy, rising establishment costs such as business rates and insurance premiums, which more than trebled in 2002 after 9/11, take their toll. Fortunately, whatever the economic climate the demand for wedding receptions is constantly increasing at such an attractive venue. Because of rising fixed costs the company has to operate for 12 months in the year as opposed to barely 6 months in the year prior to 1997. Many private functions also now take place throughout the year.

Nevertheless, the business at Upper Aynho Grounds continues to prosper and, barring an economic downturn, turnover looks set to increase yet again. In 2002 Richard Stephenson retired from medical practice and while keeping a watchful eye on the business does not wish to be involved in the long and unsociable hours associated with the catering industry. He can now devote his attentions to improving the amenities on this small estate.

The attention to detail and maintenance of the highest standards has resulted in the company winning five major awards in the last five years. For the third time the company won the coveted Venue of the Year Award in 2002.

In the last year, a ropes course has been constructed in a woodland area to expand the team-building and training facilities, meeting the increased demand from companies for this type of activity for their staff. Further expansion to provide smaller meeting rooms is planned and the New Rural Entreprise Scheme is being considered. This is run by DEFRA and has three bands of grant aid: 15–30 per cent, 30–50 per cent and 50–100 per cent.

Expert advice is needed to prepare the business plan. Accounts have to be produced for the past three years and planning permission obtained prior to the application being submitted. As DEFRA says 'You should expect to invest a considerable amount of time in collecting the necessary information and writing the Business Plan'.

Such bureaucracy can only serve to delay the project and it is to be hoped that the process could be simplified and accelerated. In the present climate this must be a forlorn hope. You are not, of course, guaranteed a grant at the end of this laborious process.

In conclusion, one must look at the advantages and disadvantages of opening up one's own home to the general public. All forms of diversification carry an element of intrusion and the proximity of the hospitality area to the main house has been a disadvantage, minimized by putting the entrance and car parks away from the private area. Weddings and evening parties can mean long hours and some noise but conference and corporate functions are more dependent on the economy and have a short lead-time whereas weddings can be booked up to two years in advance. The main advantage is that this is now a viable unit with a turnover that equates to a farm with many more acres than the 250 it has at present. This has enabled Richard and Di Stephenson to maintain and improve the property and provide a livelihood for the family. They may not spend large amounts on farm machinery but re-roofing the Great Barn, furnishing a conference centre or buying a generator are expensive alternatives. Above all they have derived great satisfaction from seeing clients return on many occasions to enjoy the hospitality. To do it, you have to enjoy it yourself.

Appendix 1: Contributors' Contact Details

The Barn Brasserie
Great Tey
Colchester
Essex CO6 1JE
Tel: 01206 212345
Fax: 01206 211522
Contact: Michael Xenakis
E-mail: michaelxenakis@aol.com

Carlshead Farms
Paddock House Lane
Wetherby
West Yorkshire LS22 4BL
Tel: 01937 582421
Contact: Gareth Gaunt
E-mail: gareth.gaunt@virgin.net

Tim Copsey
Market Gardeners
Hillside
Seaton
Cumbria
Tel: 01900 602115

The Countryside Alliance
The Old Town Hall
367 Kennington Road
London SE11 4PT
Tel: (020) 7840 9227
Contact: Nigel Henson
E-mail: Nigel-henson@countryside-alliance.org

A Day in the Country
Upper Aynho Grounds
Aynho
Near Banbury
Oxon OX17 3AY
Tel: 01869 810823
Fax: 01869 810892
E-mail: r.stephenson@accbsystems.co.uk

Dixon Wilson
Rotherwick House
3 Thomas More Street
London E1W 1YX
Tel: (020) 7680 8100
Fax: (020) 7680 8101
Contact: James Kidgell
E-mail: jameskidgell@dixonwilson.co.uk

Farming & Agricultural Finance Limited (FAF)
PO Box 4115
Hornchurch
Essex RM12 4DS
Tel: 01453 767644
Contact: Philip Coysh
E-mail: philip.coysh@rbs.co.uk

Steve Hamilton
Fruit Market
12A Market Place
Cockermouth
Cumbria CA13 9NQ
Tel: 01900 822027

haysmacintyre
Fairfax House
15 Fulwood Place
London WC1V 6AY
Tel: (020) 7969 5611
Fax: (020) 7969 5566
Contact: Phil Salmon
E-mail: psalmon@haysmacintyre.com

KSB Law
Elan House
5–11 Fetter Lane
London EC4A 1QD
Tel: (020) 7822 7532
Fax: (020) 7822 8906
Contact: Allison Grant
E-mail: agrant@ksblaw.co.uk

Larking Gowen
King Street House
15 Upper King Street
Norwich NR3 1 RB
Tel: 01603 624181
Fax: 01603 667800
Contact: Matt Howard
E-mail: matt.howard@larking-gowen.co.uk

The Natural Fibre Company Limited
Unit 12 Llambed Business Park
Tregarnon Road
Lampeter
Ceredigion
Wales SA48 8LT
Tel: 01570 493292
Fax: 01570 421432
www.thenaturalfibre.co.uk
Contact: Myra Mortlock
Tel: 01570 422956

Newfell Properties Limited
Tythe Barn
The Drive
Bourne End
Buckinghamshire SL8 5RE
Tel: 01628 533282
Contact: Geoffrey Fitchew
E-mail: gfitchew@btconnect.com

NFU Mutual Insurance Limited
Tiddington Road
Stratford-upon-Avon
Warwickshire CV37 7BG
Tel: 01789 204211
Contact: Tim Price
E-mail: Tim_Price@nfumutual.co.uk

Andrew Pym
The Elms
Everton
Sandy
Bedfordshire SG19 2JU
Tel: 01767 683545
Fax: 01767 683546
E-mail: PymAL@aol.com

Jonathan Reuvid
Little Manor
Wroxton
Banbury
Oxfordshire OX15 6QE
Tel: 01295 738 070
E-mail: jrwroxton@aol.com

Rural Regeneration Unit (RRU)
Unit 5C Lakeland Business Park
Cockermouth
Cumbria CA13 1QT
Tel: 01900 828870
Fax: 01900 828863
Contact: Dan Dempsey
E-mail: dan.dempsey@rru.org.uk

Smiths Gore
The King's Lodging
Minster Precincts
Peterborough PE1 1XT
Tel: 01733 894005
Contacts: Rupert Clark
E-mail: rupert.clark@smithsgore.co.uk
David Steel
E-mail: david.steel@smithsgore.co.uk

Stephenson & Son
York Auction Centre
Murton
York Y017 3AY
Contact: James Stephenson
e-mail: jfs@stephenson.co.uk

Marie Stockdale
Pow Heads Farm Meat
Sandale
Mealsgate
Wigtown
Cumbria CA13 9NQ
Tel: 016973 71325

Thring Townsend
Midland Bridge
Bath BA1 2HQ
Tel: 01225 340000
Fax: 01225 319735
Contact: Duncan Sigournay
E-mail: dsigournay@ttuk.com

UK Alpaca
Vulscombe Farm
Vulscombe Lane
Cruwys Marchand
Tiverton
Devon EX16 8NB
Tel: 01884 243579
Fax: 01884 243631
Contact: Rachel Hebditch
E-mail: Rachel@classicalalpacas.freeserve.co.uk

Whitley Stimpson
67 Hightown Road
Banbury
Oxfordshire OX16 9BE
Tel: 01295 270200
Fax: 01295 272784
Contact: John Skinner
E-mail: JohnS@whitleystimpson.co.uk

Wilsons
Steynings House
Summerlock Approach
Fisherton Street
Salisbury
Wiltshire SP2 7RJ
Tel: 01722 412412
Contact: Matthew Locke
E-mail: ml@wilsonslaw.com

Wykham Park Farm
Wykham Lane
Banbury
Oxfordshire
Tel: 01295 262235
Contact: Julia Colegrave

Appendix 2: Selected Information Sources

Agricultural Wages Board (England and Wales)
Nobel House
17 Smith Square
London SW1P 3JR
Tel: (020) 7238 6540

British Institute of Agricultural Consultants
The Estate Office
Torry Hill
Milstead
Sittingbourne
Kent ME9 0SP
Tel: 01795 830100

Countryside Agency
Head Office: John Dower House
Crescent Place
Cheltenham
Gloucestershire GL50 3RA
Tel: 01242 521381

DEFRA (Department for Environment, Food and Rural Affairs)
Nobel House
17 Smith Square
London SW1P 3JR
Tel: (020) 7238 6000

English Nature
Northminster House
Northminster Road
Peterborough PE1 1UA
Tel: 01733 455000

Environment Agency
Rio House
Waterside Drive
Aztec West
Almondsbury
Bristol BS32 4UD
Tel: 08708 506 506

Health and Safety Executive Information Services
Caerphilly Business Park
Caerphilly
Wales CF83 3GG
Tel: 08701 545500

Historic Houses Association
2 Chester Street
London SW1X 7BB
Tel: (020) 7259 5688

Lantra
Lantra House, NAC
Stoneleigh Park
Kenilworth
Warwickshire CV8 2LG
Tel. 024 7669 6996

The National Assembly for Wales Agriculture Department
Crown Buildings
Cathays Park
Cardiff CF10 3NQ
Tel: 02920 825111

The Planning Inspectorate
Temple Quay House
2 The Square
Temple Quay
Bristol BS1 6PN
Tel: 0117 372 6372

The Planning Inspectorate (Wales)
Crown Buildings, Cathays Park, Cardiff CF10 3NQ
Tel: 029 2082 3866

Planning Officers Society
Wycombe District Council
Queen Victoria Road
High Wycombe HP11 1BB
Tel: 01494 461000

Planning Officers Society (Wales)
Ceredigion County Council
Penmorfa
Aberaeron
Ceredigion SA46 0PA
Tel: 01545 570881

Royal Institution of Chartered Surveyors
12 Great George Street
London SW1P 3AD
Tel: (020) 7222 7000

Royal Town Planning Institute
41 Botolph Lane
London WC3R 8DL
Tel: (020) 7929 9494

Scottish Rural Property & Business Association
Stuart House
Eskmills Business Park
Station Road
Musselburgh
East Lothian EH21 7PB
Tel: 0131 653 5400

Town and Country Planning Association
17 Carlton House Terrace
London SW1Y 5AS
Tel: (020) 7930 8903

RELEVANT ORGANIZATIONS FOR WOOL PRODUCERS

These organizations have been supplied by the author of the case study featured in Chapter 24, on diversification into wool production.

British Angora Goat Society; www.allgoats.com
The British Coloured Sheep Breeders' Association; www.bcsba.org.uk
The British Llama and Alpaca Association; www.llama.co.uk
British Mohair Marketing; www.allgoats.com/breeds3.htm
The British Wool Marketing Board; www.britishwool.org.uk
Coleg Sir Gar: contact Lynne Abbott, tel: 01554 748399;
    e-mail lynne.abbott@colegsirgar.ac.uk
Cornwall Wool Initiative: contact Sue Blacker, tel: 01579 372100
DEFRA; www.defra.gov.uk
Glasu (ecological and sheep promotion and advice) in Powys, Wales:
    for a copy of *All Sheep Directory* contact Lee Price, tel: 01982 552224;
    email:leepr@Powys.gov.uk
Gwlan Teifi (cooperative of industrial spinners and weavers); Byron Williams
    (Secretary), tel: 02920 598886
The Natural Fibre Company Ltd; www.thenaturalfibre.co.uk
Natural Fibre News; tel: 01570 493292
NSA The UK Sheep Farmers Organisation; www.nationalsheep.org.uk
North Ronaldsay Sheep Fellowship; www.nrsf.co.uk
The Rare Breeds Survival Trust; www.rbst.co.uk
The Soil Association (regarding Organic Certification); www.soilassociation.org
The WoolClip and Woolfest, Cumbria; www.woolfest.co.uk

General business advice

The Federation of Small Businesses; www.fsb.org.uk
Business Link; www.businesslink.gov.uk

Retail and show

Please refer to the farming press for regional shows.
Country Living Fairs; www.countrylivingfair.com
National Association of Farmers Markets; www.farmersmarkets.net
The Royal Show; www.royalshow.org.uk
Three Counties Showground, Malvern; tel: 01684 584900

ADVERTISERS' CONTACT DETAILS

Alpacas of Wessex
Hingaston Gate
Marmhull
Surminster Newton
Dorset DT10 1NL
Tel: 01258 821499
Website: www.alpacasofwessex.co.uk

Bozedown Alpacas
Hardwick Road
Whitchurch on Thames
Reading RG8 7QY
Tel: 0118 984 3827
Website: www.bozedown-apacas.co.uk

Carter Jonas
127 Mount Street
London W1K 3NT
Tel: (020) 758 9693
Website: www.carterjonas.co.uk

Classical MileEnd Alpacas
Vulscombe Farm
Vulscombe Lane
Cruwys Marchand
Tiverton
Devon EX16 8NB
Tel: 01884 243579
Website: www.alpaca-uk.co.uk

Countryman
Dalesman Publishing Co Ltd
The Water Mill
Broughton Hall
Skipton BD23 3AG
Tel: 01756 701381
Website: www.dalesman.co.uk

The Countryside Alliance
The Old Town Hall
367 Kennington Road
London SE11 4PT
Tel: (020) 7840 9227
Website: www.countryside-alliance.org

Dixon Wilson
Rotherwick House
3 Thomas More Street
London E1W 1YX
Tel: (020) 7680 8100
Website: www.dixonwilson.com

Everhot
Coaley Mill
Coaley
Dursley
Gloucestershire GL11 5DS
Tel: 01453 890018
Website: www.everhot.co.uk

haysmacintyre
Fairfax House
15 Fulwood Place
London WC1V 6AY
Tel: (020) 7969 5500
Website: www.haysmacintyre.com

Lightfoot Alpacas
Lighfoot Cottage
Slip Mill Road
Hawkhurst
Kent TN18 5AB
Tel: 07802 263589
Website: www.alpacabreeder.co.uk

Naturals
The Old Vicarage
Llangybi
Lampeter SA48 8NB
Tel: 01570 422956
Website: www.thenaturalfibre.co.uk

Smiths Gore
The King's Lodging
Minster Precincts
Peterborough PE1 1XT
Tel: 01733 894005
Website: www.smithsgore.co.uk

Thring Townsend
Midland Bridge
Bath BA1 2HQ
Tel: 01225 340000
Website: www.ttuk.com

Tideline Books
49 Kinmel Street
Rhyl
North Wales LL18 1AG
Tel: 01745 354919
Website: www.tidelinebooks.co.uk

Westways Alpacas
Orchard Farm
East Chinnock
Yeovil
Somerset BA22 9EQ
Tel: 01935 863467
Website: www.westwaysalpacas.co.uk

Wood-Mizer
The Woodland Centre
Hever
Kent TN8 7LX
Tel: 01342 850999
Email: info@WMUK.net

Appendix 3: Further Reading

An Economic Evaluation of the Agricultural Tenancies Act 1995 (2002) The University of Plymouth Department of Land Use and Rural Management, Plymouth

Business Tenancies on Farms, CLA21 Handbook (June 2001)

Code of Good Practice for Agri-Environmental Scheme and Diversification Projects within Agricultural Tenancies, available from the DEFRA website: www.defra.gov.uk

Code of Practice for Commercial Leases, 2nd edn, DTLR (2002)

Model Storage Licence Agreement, CLA22 Handbook (June 2001)

Report of the Policy Commission on the Future of Food and Farming (January 2002), available from the Cabinet Office website: www.cabinet-office.gov.uk/farming

Reuvid, J (ed) (2002) *Going Public: The essential guide to flotation*, London, Kogan Page

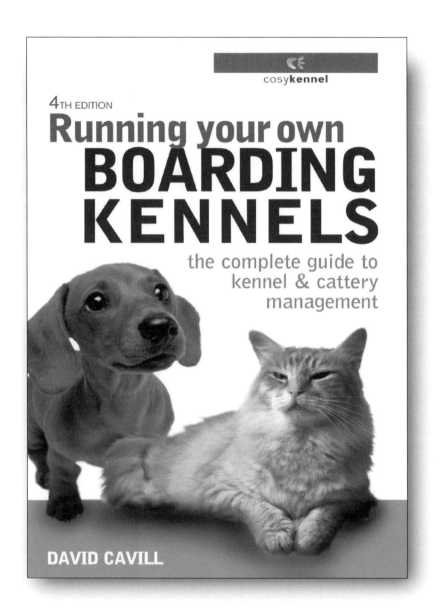

cosy**kennel**

4TH EDITION

Running your own
BOARDING
KENNELS

the complete guide to
kennel & cattery
management

DAVID CAVILL

0 7494 4422 3 Paperback 176 pages

For further information on how to order, please visit

www.kogan-page.co.uk

KOGAN
PAGE

Index

INDEX OF ADVERTISERS

Further Reading from Kogan Page

The First-Time Manager: The First Steps to a Brilliant Management Career, 3rd edn, Michael Morris, 2005

How to Be an Even Better Manager: A Complete A to Z of Proven Techniques and Essential Skills, 6th edn, Michael Armstrong, 2004

Start Up and Run Your Own Business, 3rd edn, Jonathan Reuvid, 2004

A Guide to Working for Yourself, revised 22nd edn, Godfrey Golzen and Jonathan Reuvid, 2004

The Business Plan Workbook, 5th edn, Colin Barrow, Paul Barrow and Robert Brown, 2005

Do Your Own Market Research, 3rd edn, Paul Hague, 1998

Financial Management for the Small Business, 5th edn, Colin Barrow, 2001

Forming a Limited Company, 8th edn, Patricia Clayton, 2004

How to Prepare a Business Plan, revised 4th edn, Edward Blackwell, 2004

Law for the Small Business: An Essential Guide to all the Legal and Financial Requirements, 11th edn, Patricia Clayton, 2004

Marketing Plan Workbook, John Westwood, 2005

Raising Finance: A Practical Guide for Business Start Up and Expansion, Paul Barrow, 2004

Starting a Successful Business, 5th edn, Michael Morris, 2005

Successful Marketing for the Small Business, 5th edn, Dave Patten, 2001

The above titles are available from all good bookshops or direct from the publishers. To obtain more information, please contact the publisher at the address below:

Kogan Page
120 Pentonville Road
London N1 9JN
Tel: 020 7278 0433
Fax: 020 7837 6348
www.kogan-page.co.uk